Close
Encounters

A Media Memoir

By the same author:

The Arnhem Report
The Man with No Name
Dustin Hoffman
Cannes: The Novel
Wimbledon 2000 (also a novel)
The World Is Not Enough: A Companion
Tom Cruise: All the World's a Stage.
Richard by Kathy (Richard Whiteley)
Pirates of the Mediterranean
Fierce Creatures (novelisation)
Streep: A Life in Film

CLOSE
ENCOUNTERS

A Media Memoir

WITHDRAWN

IAIN JOHNSTONE

SB

SPELLBINDING
MEDIA

LONDON

Published by Spellbinding Media 2014

First published in Great Britain in 2014 by
Spellbinding Media
Third Floor, 111 Charterhouse Street
London, EC1M 6AW
www.spellbindingmedia.co.uk

Spellbinding Media Ltd Reg. No. 08482364
A CIP catalogue record for this book is available
from the British Library

ISBN 978 1 909964 07 5

Typeset in Photina by ForDesign, London
Printed and bound by TJ International Ltd, Padstow, Cornwall

For Ralph and Theo and Arthur

'Live all you can; it's a mistake not to. It doesn't so much matter what you do in particular, so long as you have your life. If you haven't had that, what have you had?'

Henry James, *The Ambassadors*

Contents

CONTENTS

Preface

A memoir has a certain amount in common with a detective story. The writer of the latter begins at the end and will know the concluding crime and why it was committed. With a memoir you start at a point, usually late in life, and then go back down the paths that took you to this point.

The danger is that you will make it look as if you were in charge and took firm, purposeful steps to reach the conclusion. But, of course, you didn't. Luck – good and bad – happenstance, mistakes, moods – misery and joy – serendipity, timing, external events and, above all, other people will have played an overwhelming part in how things turned out.

Maybe a more predictable career path – a dentist, an accountant or a fishmonger – will temper some of the risks. My dad joined the Post Office when he was twenty and worked for it for forty-two years until his retirement.

I was ten years old when I first saw television in 1953 – the coronation. Five years later I began to watch the evening programme *Tonight* with Cliff Michelmore, Kenneth Allsop and Alan Whicker. That was where I wanted to be – even as a tea boy or a runner – it was stylish, intelligent and took risks. When things went wrong there was a wonderfully World War II attitude – 'Seems the film hasn't arrived after all, someone should take a shufti, but let's press on with a topical calypso.'

I did manage to work for the BBC in consecutive two-year contracts, ending up on a programme called *Tonight*. And I hated it. I discovered I was a bit more comfortable sailing my own ship.

In the media people like to tag you and maybe this is no bad thing. After my bicentennial films about John Wayne and Clint Eastwood I became regarded as 'the profile man'. This had a dual advantage: it opened a few doors in Hollywood and it helped get the stuff on the air. Sometimes, as with Robert Redford and J.K.Rowling, I was even *invited* to interview them.

I respected and admired the people I profiled; otherwise, why bother? There were hiccups. The loudest occurred on a snow-covered hill just outside Telluride, Colorado. It was 1978 and Richard Lester was directing *Butch and Sundance: The Early Days*. I was making a profile of Richard and needed short interviews with the leads: Tom Berenger, who was playing the young Paul Newman, and William Katt, as Redford. Tom was fine – he went on to make *The Big Chill* and *Someone to Watch Over Me*. But Katt was a prickly character. The second question into our interview he yelled at me: 'Are you suggesting I only got this part because I look like Redford?' Without waiting for my reply he yanked off his mike and stomped off into the snow never to speak to me again. His acting career has continued and he was last heard of, if at all, in *The Secret Lives of Dorks*.

John Wayne's undoubted patriotism brought about a public view of him as a right-wing hawk. This was true of him in conversation in private but what he also was was an extraordinarily gracious and thoughtful man. When I first met him in the mountains of Mexico, he sent a car for me to come to dinner at his ranch that night. And when he realised I hadn't enough material for my bicentennial profile, he asked me to come on a Pacific cruise with him and his family. Better than a chat in a hotel room with the attendant PR saying: 'You have five minutes left.'

Clint was more mild mannered. When he directed he would start the shot by saying something like 'any time you're ready, compadre' to the actor. I asked him why he did that and he said he hated the way directors would shout 'Action!' in his face and then expect a natural performance. When you spent time with him, you learned he was happy to sip beer and say very little – a bit like they do in cowboy films.

Paul Newman was a reserved man and let his wife, Joanne, a warm, friendly woman, do most of the talking. Paul had a considerable social conscience. Since his son, Scott (by his first wife), died of an overdose he channelled much of his earnings into charity, many millions more when his salad dressing became such a hit. He insisted I came to dinner with them after the show and later asked me to do some interviews for him (including him, again).

Robert Redford is a loner and possibly a bit lonely. There was a period of nearly twenty-five years between his marriages. He told me he fancied Barbra Streisand a lot on *The Way We Were* but was afraid to ask her out on a date.

Nothing shy about Barbra. She speaks her mind continuously and what she wants she usually gets – microphone levels, rearranged scenery, props, men. So petite and so powerful. And generous in inviting me into her house and, later, on to her set.

Yul Brynner was the nastiest man I ever interviewed. He actually thought he *was* the King of Siam whom he had played all his life in *The King and I*, although he does earn a Brownie point for rounding up *The Magnificent Seven*. Jimmy Stewart was the nicest. Jack Nicholson once said to me: 'It is possible to be the nicest person in the world,' and I cannot think of anyone nicer that Stewart. A great actor and a great war hero, although he would undoubtedly deny it.

The old school of stars – Wayne, Stewart, Chuck Heston and Gregory Peck – were united by a common courtesy. Was it because they came to fame before the paparazzi and ubiquitous 'celebrity' magazines turned the media into an enemy? It seemed almost matter-of-fact for Marlon Brando to take me and the crew out to dinner after our interview. They had filmed him at work for three weeks and evidently gained his respect.

Warren Beatty is an engaging lunch companion but, once on camera, weighs his words with caution, making sure he doesn't give a hostage to fortune. Woody Allen is endemically funny – his stand-up skills have not deserted him – but has little time for small talk, at least with me!

Peter Sellers, too, could not stop himself being amusing and, if there was any danger of this, would lapse into a series of impersonations. Never seen in public was his impression of George VI giving his first Christmas Day broadcast before his stutter was cured. 'I'm speaking to you today from B ... Ber ... B... ingham Palace.' It was Princess Margaret's favourite.

Laurence Olivier told me how he liked to prepare his film parts from the outside in. To play a Dutch doctor in *A Bridge Too Far* he asked for his costume – a rough-hewn wartime suit with itchy trousers – a few days early. 'I walked around my garden in it, got a bit of soil in the turn-ups, that sort of thing.' He seemed happy to chat during breaks and when I asked him what his favourite role had been, he had no doubt. 'Archie Rice in *The Entertainer*. I had seen *Look Back in Anger* about an angry young man and I asked John Osborne to write an angry old man for me. It gave me the chance to do a seedy music hall act – badly. Critics said it was about the decline of Britain but for me it was about the decline of Archie, a performer whose time has passed.' Olivier knew I had aspirations as a film maker and advised: 'If you want people to think your film is *significant*, it's a good idea to cut away to a shot of a cat rubbing itself against a lamp-post. They'll read something into that.'

4

It's interesting to note the shift in influence among the Pythons over the past forty-five years. Initially John Cleese was head boy. Something he wasn't at Clifton College, nor even a prefect. The staff could sense the rebel in him. Once, when parents were present, he had a loud brawl in the school yard with a fellow pupil in a blue track suit. He dragged the fellow up some stairs and then reappeared on a balcony, picked the chap up and flung him thirty feet down to the stone surface below. People were aghast but it was, of course, a blue-track-suited dummy he had prepared earlier. Not good preparation, however, for leading the school.

But John put together the Python team. Graham Chapman was his writing partner from Cambridge so he was a must. They used to watch the children's show *Do Not Adjust Your Set* on Thursday afternoons and John felt it was 'much the funniest thing on television'. So Cleese hired Michael Palin, Terry Jones, Eric Idle and the animator, Terry Gilliam, from the show to make up the Python team. They were determined men: Idle and Jones had been head boys at school and Gilliam class president and prom king. But Cleese started the series and left it three years later when he thought it had run its course.

The five surviving Pythons were reunited in 1998 at the US Comedy Arts Festival in Aspen, pretending to have Graham's ashes in an urn which they spilt all over the stage. Barclaycard made an offer to reunite the team at some vast venue in Vegas but this time it was Michael Palin who said no: for one thing he had no wish to meet corporate executives after the show.

In 2003 the finance for a film Eric was due to make fell through but, undaunted, he put together a body of actors, bought the rights to some old Python sketches and went from town to town in the *Greedy Bastard Tour*. He realised that the material had stood the test of time and, in an inspired move, he and composer John Du Prez turned *Monty Python and the Holy Grail* into a musical, *Spamalot*. It was a walloping Broadway hit winning the Tony for Best Musical in 2005. Soon there were productions from Sweden to South Korea, from the Czech Republic to Japan.

Why should other people reap the benefit of Python's brilliant material, Eric argued and this time there were no dissenters among the other four. All now in their seventies, the famous five will play the 20,000-seater O2 Arena in London and who knows what the future will hold?

Fun company didn't come any funnier than Peter Cook. We were having a nightcap in his suite in New York – it was about 2am. Peter was flicking through the television channels as usual. We caught sight of a young woman, momentarily topless as she changed to go out. Peter established the film was on CBS, picked up the phone and managed to get through to their complaints woman. 'I am sitting here with my lady wife, our son Logan who is seven, and little Brandi who is only four,' he said in an American voice. 'We have been watching your television channel and have just seen what I can only describe as a mammary gland. I find this outrageous.' The woman was instantly apologetic, promising to report the matter in her log, never wondering why such a family should be gathered round a TV in the early hours of the morning. Cookie loved making such calls, even for his own amusement.

The ten days I spent with Muhammad Ali were among the most memorable in my life, but possibly not in his. Some years later he was sparring in London with John Coker, an Olympic heavyweight who worked in the BBC. 'I'd like to see that BBC fella who made that film about me,' Ali said to him. 'What was his name?' Coker asked. 'John Smith,' the Champ replied.

This book is about my professional work and encounters. But, in any life, the professional crosses over into the personal. I went to North Africa for *Life of Brian* and met my future wife, Mo. And after a somewhat frosty start at ITN, Richard Whiteley became, for forty years as close a friend as it was possible to have. When he died I felt as if I had lost a brother. I still do.

In his play *Huis Clos* Sartre has a character, Garcin, from beyond the grave say: 'Hell is other people.' That's fiction and obviously speculation. What has been true so far for me is that life is fundamentally enriched by other people.

PS The snaps from my scrapbook which decorate this book have been variously taken over the decades with cameras ranging from the Box Brownie to the Nokia cell phone. The quality doesn't seem to have improved much.

Rejected by the BBC ... Saved by ITN

It was 12 June 1983 and I was eating dinner at the White House with Christopher Reeve, Gene Hackman, director Richard Lester and father and son producers, Alexander and Ilya Salkind. Two tables away, Ronald and Nancy Reagan were with some suits from Warner Bros and executives from the Special Olympics for which *Superman III* had held a charity premiere. Four not-so-Secret Servicemen stood round their table, easily identifiable by their white short-sleeved shirts and prominent earpieces.

It had been a busy day. Earlier, Ambassador Sargent Shriver, the founder of the US Peace Corps, and his wife, Eunice Kennedy Shriver, had given us a brunch in their garden. Eunice, younger sister of JFK, had founded the Special Olympics for people with intellectual disabilities. Her elder sister, Rosemary, had had a lobotomy, causing her to be permanently incapacitated. Eunice's daughter, Maria, and her boyfriend, Arnold Schwarzenegger, acted as waiters. Arnie had yet to find fame as 'The Terminator' or, indeed, 'The Gubernator'.

Chris had had drinks with the Reagans before dinner. The President told him he had lived in Galesburg, Illinois at the same time as George Reeves, the first Superman. They'd started in Hollywood at the same time and appeared in a couple of films together. Politics were only fleetingly touched on; Chris had been publicly critical of Reagan's policies. (The President remembered the occasion, writing later in his diaries: 'I'm just optimistic enough to think Reeve might have changed his mind.')

9

But it was a cheerful and informal evening. 'President Reagan will not be wearing a tie tonight,' advised a letter left in my hotel room. 'So male guests are advised that they need not wear one, either.' The Beach Boys provided the after-dinner entertainment. At the end of their set, Nancy went across to the podium where she was enveloped in a swaying bear hug by an unsteady Brian Wilson. The Secret Servicemen exchanged worried glances but the President roared with laughter.

What was I doing there? It so happened that I had worked on the television side of a trio of Superman films thanks to some Close Encounters with the Salkinds.

Eighteen years earlier I was sitting opposite a gloomy careers officer at Bristol University who was going through my file. My projected degree was a Third. That ruled out any chance of a career in the Civil Service, let alone the Foreign Office. No top bank would be interested in me – nor any major company. She suggested my best hope would be to become a primary school teacher. She had contacts.

I politely declined and said I wanted a career in the BBC.

She shook her head. 'Not a chance. We've never had a General Trainee there. The BBC has the pick of people with Firsts from Oxford and Cambridge.'

But during my final summer at Bristol I had fluked a part-time job on the local BBC programme *Points West*. I read out the local news twice a week which, I discovered, was probably the easiest legal way to make a living, especially at five guineas a bulletin. I was also allowed to make little film items and a veteran reporter told me you should stop the camera car on the way to the location and take a shot of the signpost to cover your introduction. So if it was 'In Weston-super-Mare today, the beach donkeys have gone on strike due to the heat' you had something to illustrate it with. The regional television experience probably got me through the preliminary interviews to the 1965 Final Board for the BBC Traineeship. There, I was pretty sure I was ahead of the field. What Oxbridge type would know about shooting signposts?

Unfortunately, I was unable to manoeuvre the five severe intellectuals who grilled me on to the subject of donkey strikes. Rather the reverse. Konrad Syrop, Head of External Service Productions and translator, from the Polish, of *The Ugupu Bird* by S. Mrozek, asked me what I was reading. And for some perverse, career-suicidal reason, I lied. A copy of Anthony Eden's memoirs lay by my father's bed. I cannot recall ever having opened it but, in that moment of insanity, I told him that this was my current reading material. Syrop asked me what I knew about Eden's position on Chamberlain's Appeasement. I told him the truth: nothing. He then began to draw an elaborate doodle on his pad which he finished while the others, unnecessarily, continued to question me. I should have asked him for it afterwards.

It wasn't so much the letter of rejection that upset me but its final sentence: 'I wish you well in whatever other career you choose to pursue.' The condescending bastard. There was no other career. I immediately wrote to every independent television company I could find. The few that replied were not exactly encouraging.

My parents had relocated to West Kirby, a Deeside town on the Wirral Peninsula. I was driving my dad's car along Meols Drive one day during the summer holidays and some boys gestured to me for a lift. I stopped and, almost instantly, became part of the gang. One of them, Miles Meredith Jones, worked for his father as a trainee cotton broker in Liverpool. He would spend his lunch hour at the Cavern Club. A few of us drove up to join him one Friday when Joe Brown and The Bruvvers were playing. I was mightily impressed when Joe squeezed past us as we queued in the dank corridor and asked: 'Do you have to pay to get in here?'

The support group was the Beatles, who had yet to release a record. During their pulsating delivery of 'Twist and Shout' we had to leave. John Lennon stopped singing and shouted from the stage, 'Where do you think you're going, Miles?' 'We have to get Debbie's father's car back,' Miles shouted back. 'Well, time it better next time,' John retorted.

There was a next time. It transpired that Miles's father employed Jim McCartney, Paul's father, as a humble runner, taking samples of cotton to other brokers. When we went backstage the yet-to-be Fab Four treated Miles with mock reverence. They were a friendly bunch, almost indistinguishable from each other. Years later, when I worked with Richard Lester on *Superman II*, he told me that when he started out with them on *A Hard Day's Night* he was faced with the problem of four stars who were pretty well all the same person. So he shaped the script making John the cynical one, Paul the vain one, George the philosopher and Ringo the loner. And, amazingly, those personalities stuck with them from then on.

I had agreed with my parents that, if I failed at the Beeb, I would study for solicitors' finals. This was an intensive nine-month course open, after graduating, to those who got Firsts and Seconds. John and Mary Conkerton, both gifted lecturers, had left the College of Law and set up shop in Liverpool College of Commerce. On my first day John told us, quite simply: 'If you work, morning, afternoon and evening for six days a week you will pass; if you do not, you will not.' And he was right. The Conkertons taught me how it was possible to study really hard, something which had eluded me for three years at university.

The College of Commerce largely consisted of sixteen years olds who had failed nearly everything. Our most famous old girl, whose picture adorned the canteen wall, was Cilla Black, once a cloakroom attendant at the Cavern. It was somewhat incongruous to see us graduates queuing up for lunch under it with assorted teeny-boppers. Although my head was crammed with legal facts, my heart still belonged to television. The gods smiled on me in the unexpected shape of the Prime Minister, Harold Wilson. He was finding it hard to govern with a majority of only five seats so, with the opinion polls in his favour, he called an election for the spring of 1966.

I got a phone call from David Nicholas, the deputy editor of ITN, who had my begging letter and who asked me to come down to London. There he explained that Sheridan Morley (son of film star Robert), their late-night newscaster, was leaving for the BBC and with an election coming ITN needed a replacement. Rosamond and Evelyn, the twin daughters of the ITN editor, Sir Geoffrey Cox, who were a year below me at Bristol, had seen me on *Points West* and had told their dad, so Mr Nicholas hoped my audition would be as competent as they said.

It must have been: I was hired.

On 1 March 1966 I walked through the doors of Admiralty House in Kingsway to start work at ITN. Peter Snow thoughtfully showed me round the newsroom. He, Andrew Gardner and Gordon Honeycombe were on duty, all of them over six foot three. Geoffrey Cox was said to favour tall men as when he, five foot five, was a scrum-half in New Zealand, it was the big second-row forwards who protected him in the line-out. Reggie Bosanquet was a little shorter but irreplaceable because of his overflowing mailbag.

Sheridan Morley was still there for a month. (Sherry became a friend and, later, as Arts Editor of *Punch*, promised me the job of film critic when Dilys Powell retired but, unfortunately, the magazine died before she did.) There were two trainees who had joined as subs/scriptwriters the previous September: Geoffrey had merely hired the editors of *Cherwell* (Oxford), Mike Morris, and *Varsity* (Cambridge), Richard Whiteley. Mike was very friendly and offered me a temporary bed in his Putney house, but Richard wasn't and didn't speak to me for six months.

I learned how to sub-edit for the main bulletins at 6 and 9pm. My items were mainly 'extras' to be used only if the film broke down. The output editors were wary of us youngsters ever since Richard had put the weight of the jockey instead of the odds in the Cheltenham Gold Cup result and hundreds of furious punters phoned in.

Learning to write scripts was less easy. In the speed to get film inserts on air, the telecine machines were fed them in black-and-white negative, which they then converted to positive on transmission. So you never saw a proper positive image in the cutting rooms and sometimes had to guess who was who from the cameraman's dope sheet. This was especially hard at Commonwealth Prime Ministers' conferences as most of the PMs were black and all you saw going into Number 10 were a series of white blobs.

As a newscaster, the bane of my life was the inquest into the assassination of the Nigerian PM, Sir Abubakar Tafawa Balewa. I usually got past his name OK but it took such an effort that you usually tripped up on a word in the rest of the sentence, like 'coroner'. I alternated the short 11pm bulletin with Sherry. It was only watched by insomniacs – and cat burglars. No, not true. Then, as now, magazines liked to do short pieces on new faces on the telly, but I had very little to tell them, not having been a Butlins Red Coat or lingerie model, as some TV presenters are today.

I answered an ad in *The Times* for a room by Regent's Park. Two flatmates interviewed me and, yes, I could have Michael's room – he had gone to Cape Town for a year. The curious thing was that he had left all his clothes and belongings behind. After a while, since I was a bit short on wardrobe, I began to wear his ties on the telly. Then, one night, I came home a little sozzled after some drinks in the Green Room and spotted an opened letter on the kitchen table. It was written on thin blue paper. I picked it up and saw that it was from Michael. It was dated the previous day and, on the top, was stamped: HM Prison, Wormwood Scrubs. Evidently, Michael had been a little free with his credit card. 'There are people in here from Marlborough, Clifton and Stowe,' he wrote, 'and we usually share a table at lunch.'

At 9.15am on Friday 21 October 1966, after several days of heavy rain, thousands of tons of slurry (excavated mining debris) slid down a man-created mountain and on to the village school at Aberfan in Wales. Eventually, the bodies of 116 dead children and 28 adults were found.

The rescue effort was vast and unceasing: 24/7, as they say today. ITN had live landlines to the cameras and reporters on the scene within hours and the pictures came back to Admiralty House pretty well non-stop over the next ten days. I still had to read out my bulletins, but, more importantly, it was all hands to the video-editing machines, day and night. Beneficiaries of the microchip technology would be amazed to see 2-inch-wide brown video tape, with the sound running unseen 28 frames behind, being physically cut by editors with razor blades. It was the job of us scriptwriters to see what was fit for public consumption. What was unsuitable can best be described in Conrad's words: 'The horror! The horror!' The cruel irony was that I learned more about making television during that week than I have before or since.

15

After about a year and a half at ITN, I had a meeting with Geoffrey Cox to find out where I was going: the main bulletin or maybe a foreign reporter? The answer was neither. He felt my talents were best suited to being a chief sub-editor. This held minimal appeal. Being young and impetuous I didn't factor in the thought that things can change – people, too. Geoffrey left for the newly founded Yorkshire Television within the year. But I had seen the future of older chief subs and they were underpaid and frustrated at the repetitive work. At my parents' urging, I wrote around to a few City law firms and one of them, Freshfields, asked to see me.

Hugh Peppiatt, the Senior Partner, was a gentle, kindly man. He wrote to me later in the week offering two years' articles at £700 a year. This was generous: several of my Bristol contemporaries had been offered no money. 'Get some out of the family trust, old boy' was a not uncommon refrain. My parents were delighted. If I went on to make Partner at one of the top four City firms, my mother, who had grown up in comparative poverty, told me my path to wealth and comfort was assured. But I had the nagging feeling that it was a path going in the wrong direction – for me. Nevertheless I accepted. Konrad Syrop had won.

I gave my notice to ITN and, on a Monday morning four weeks later, entered Freshfields, under the lee of the Bank of England where Peppiatt's father, as Chief Cashier, had his signature on the bank notes. The office was thickly carpeted and fairly modern, polished and threatening. It's your stomach, not your brain, that tells you when you've made a big mistake. Very uneasily, I took my place at a desk but can remember nothing whatsoever of what happened that day and the next. Except what was happening in my mind. I had read once how Nicholas Monsarrat, a law graduate from Trinity, Cambridge, had just walked away from his intended law firm, to a life of writing freelance articles and, later, *The Cruel Sea*. So I followed in his footsteps, writing a long letter to Peppiatt on the Wednesday thanking him but explaining that I just didn't have the mental make-up to be a solicitor.

He wrote back with such sympathy and courtesy that it brought tears to my eyes, a state that I was in when I called my father. I knew he had made sacrifices to pay for my schooling and university maintenance but there are cardinal turning points in one's life and I had turned down the law. He was stunned and a bit silent. My mother was angry.

2

Epiphany in India ... *Straw Dogs* with Dustin Hoffman

I sat self-pityingly in my room in a rented flat on Campden Hill in Kensington, consoled by my flatmates, Alan Riding, who had a job at Reuters, and Nigel Miller, who was at ABC television. More application letters. My bible was the BBC Handbook and I bombarded all the television departments like a turret gunner. One responded. The BBC's Presentation Department was holding a Board. It was more gentle and more jocular than the General Trainee one and I suspect a shared sense of humour got me the job. A guy called Roger was leaving to go to Granada. He gave me only one piece of advice: 'When you drive up to the barrier at Television Centre on your first day, the commissionaire will say: "Do you work for the BBC?" and you will proudly reply: "Yes" and he will say: "Well, then you can't come in."' True. The coveted spaces were reserved for bosses and stars. A one-armed war veteran called Vic was the commissionaire *Obergruppenführer*. Eric Morecambe said that he always asked for tickets for their shows, 'but there's no point, he can't clap'.

Presentation was divided into two parts. Primarily, it ran the network transmission and did trailers for forthcoming attractions. The other part was Programmes, notably *Late Night Line-Up* with 'the thinking man's crumpet', Joan Bakewell, and also Sherry Morley.

I was a production assistant to a producer, Tony Staveacre. He loved the music hall and so when Richard Attenborough started shooting *Oh! What a Lovely War* in Brighton, Tony directed a documentary called *The Ragtime Infantry.*

Ralph Richardson (playing Sir Edward Grey, Foreign Secretary at the time) told me he had grown up in Brighton and on 4 August 1914, when he was twelve, he stayed out until after dark, playing on the beach. When he got home his father reproved him with the words: 'You're late, and war has been declared.' 'And for many years I thought that it must have been me who started it,' Ralph confessed.

I had discovered, slightly to my surprise, on *Points West* that the producers were often in awe of the senior presenters, even though they may have hired them in the first place. The balance of power tends to shift as the front man acquires a bit of fame. So when the Controller of BBC1 wanted to bring back *Points of View* with Robert Robinson, my bosses were a bit apprehensive about asking a major television personality at that time to do a ten-minute complaints programme. Robert chaired *Ask the Family* and *Call My Bluff* and had replaced David Frost on Saturday-night satire where Kenneth Tynan had made television history by saying 'fuck' to him. So I was deputed to be the messenger.

I didn't feel any easier when a polite but formal Robinson opened the door of his Cheyne Row house. Mick Jagger was his neighbour. (But I did feel more relaxed when, forty-four years later, his widow greeted me and my wife at the same door for her memorial drinks for Bob and I was flattered to discover we were the only people from BBC TV there.)

Actually, I always felt a tad uncomfortable calling him Bob, having watched him from afar as Robert. He knew why I had come and pressed a Scotch into my hand. It was pretty clear he was interviewing me. Our conversation strayed on to Tynan's famous outburst and he told me that the following Sunday morning he had been window-shopping on the King's Road in Chelsea when an elderly lady introduced herself to him as Lady Normanbrook, wife of the Chairman of the BBC. 'My husband and I were watching your programme last night,' she said. Jesus Christ, thought Bob, I'm for the chop. But she went on: 'And, do you know, I've been saying that word to myself ever since.'

After a couple more Scotches, Robinson said to me: 'Right. I'll do *Points of View* and you will produce it.' I'm not sure that had been the intention of my boss, but I was made an acting producer and off we went. Robert was the master of the television essay and his influence on me, with his precise use of words, was considerable.

As it was on Will Wyatt, a trainee from radio, who was seconded to be my assistant. The three of us formed a team and went on to make *The Fifties*, using Pathé newsreel from the period. Like all good presenters, Robert was instinctively a producer. When we looked for material in the viewing theatre, Robert jumped up with glee as an Italian footballer skilfully scored by kicking the ball over his own shoulder in an international against England and the commentator then referred to their team as 'the acrobats from spaghetti-land'. It has to be said that *The Fifties* owed not a little to Brian Inglis's *All Our Yesterdays* on ITV which was coming to the end of the forties, so we cut them off at the pass.

A couple of years later Will showed me his application form for a new job to get my comments. I advised him that he shouldn't use adjectives like 'excellent' to praise his own programmes. I may have been wrong, as he went on to become Managing Director of BBC Television and I didn't.

Robert and I managed to get out and about a bit more with a couple of documentaries. The first, *Robinson Cruising*, was a two-week trip around the Med on the *SS Canberra*. P&O gave me freedom to film but were pretty angry about the final programme which was not the fifty-minute advertisement they hoped for. Instead of Bob rolling off a Whickerish list of statistics, '2,238 passengers, 960 crew, 14 tons of beef, 20,000 bottles of wine,' you know the sort of thing, there was an undertone of asperity in his commentary as he observed that cruises were for people who didn't really want to go abroad and be poisoned by filthy foreign food. The formality of a black-tie code for dinner at sea and the string of ribbons on the captain's chest, none of them for combat action, were gently ribbed.

It was a rare time to be at the BBC: you came up with a good enough idea and sensible budget and off you went. But the old bureaucracy still lingered. Without even informing me, my head of department drafted a craven reply for the BBC's Managing Director's response to the Chairman of P&O's stinging letter. I managed to get hold of it some months later. Quite a lot was factually inaccurate, not least the grovelling apology for 'staging' a passenger being seasick over the side. I didn't stage it. My cameraman spotted a young man about to heave, and quickly caught his vomit on film. The chap sportingly agreed to let me use it.

The second documentary, in two parts. caused less controversy. We spent ten weeks in India shooting *From Shepherd's Bush to Simla*, following in the tracks of Emily Eden (sister of the Governor General, Lord Auckland) who kept a diary of the 1838 summer move from the heat of Calcutta to the Himalayas. Auckland had an entourage of 12,000 people; I had only twelve, but that was quite a sizeable crew by today's minimalist standards.

Of course, we tried to be a bit controversial, not least by starting with a shot of Bob's bum as he got his gamma globulin injections.

And when we contrasted the fearful poverty of people living on the teeming streets of Calcutta with the rich members of the verdant Tollygunge Club, I later persuaded a vicar in Richmond to have his congregation sing the forbidden verse of 'All Things Bright and Beautiful' as an accompaniment:

> The rich man in his castle,
> The poor man at his gate,
> He made them, high or lowly,
> And ordered their estate.

We had to have stamps in our passports saying that we were 'certified alcoholics'. This was because the Indian Prime Minister, Morarji Desai (a man who preferred his own urine to alcohol), had instituted 140 'dry days' a year. When Bob interviewed Mr Desai, the PM appeared to fall asleep. 'Suffers from narcolepsy,' Robinson whispered to me, never for a moment thinking that his questions might be somewhat prolix.

At Benares, the oldest holy city in the world, we rose at 4am to film the faithful undergoing total immersion in the Ganga. We hired a couple of boats: one for me and the camera crew, the other for Robert to talk to a Hindu historian.

As the dawn rose over the sacred river that morning I had, well, not quite an epiphany, but a sensation of certainty that this was exactly where I wanted to be and what I wanted to do. In India, with a BBC crew, learning about a vastly different culture, being paid for it, bringing our experiences to the nation, spending the evenings with Robert, the perfect dinner companion, and Adam Low, a brilliant Cambridge graduate who knew more about India than anyone I'd ever met (his father had been born there and it was his academic subject). It was nirvana. I had beaten Konrad who was probably sitting in his shabby office in Bush House pushing paper. Hooray! I needed to keep up the film-industry side of the department. In 1969 Dustin Hoffman won the BAFTA for Most Promising Newcomer for *The Graduate*. At thirty-two, he was considerably older than the usual recipients of this prize and already well established on Broadway. And probably one of the world's most bankable stars, demonstrating his versatility with the tramp-like con man, Ratso Rizzo, in *Midnight Cowboy* the same year.

So when I learned he was coming to Britain to make *Straw Dogs*, I pulled every string to get on to the Cornwall location and make a profile of him. The set was closed for the first two weeks so that Dustin could get to know Susan George, his young and beautiful female lead, who had learned that she got the part when the star dropped his trousers in front of her.

Very Dustin. He had a wicked sense of humour and he was a perfect and articulate subject for a documentary. He told me that when Mike Nichols asked him to do a screen test for *The Graduate*, Dustin phoned him to say he wasn't right for the role. 'Why?' asked Nichols. 'Well, he's a kind of Anglo-Saxon, tall, slender, good-looking chap,' replied the actor. 'And you're Jewish,' said Nichols. 'That's right.' Nichols paused and then he said: 'Inside, Benjamin Braddock is short and Jewish.' I asked him: 'What did you do in the screen test?' Dustin replied: 'I tried to play tall and Jewish.'

The story of the siege of Trencher's Farm is well enough known now. For *Straw Dogs* the director, Sam Peckinpah, cast T.P. McKenna and Jim Norton, whom he had seen in David Storey's *The Contractor* at the Royal Court, adding Del Henney and Ken Hutchison with Colin 'The British Are Coming' Welland as the local vicar – Dustin referred to him as 'old frilly teeth'. Off set, Ken became Dustin's partner in crime. At dinner one evening in the staid Tregenna Castle Hotel where we were all staying, Ken surprised fellow diners by shouting out: 'Ever seen an Eskimo pee?' The room fell silent as Dustin jumped on to a table, unzipped his flies and a cascade of ice cubes tumbled out.

He was more serious about his work. His agent had advised him not to play the second lead in *Midnight Cowboy* – the ostensible star was Jon Voight whom he had understudied in *A View from the Bridge* on Broadway. But Dustin knew he could come up with something original. 'I wanted to be bold with it. I didn't want to portray a documentary-type character. I wanted him to be a little distorted, almost in the way Daumier draws. I think I felt like Ratso for many years in New York.'

On the Cornwall location, there was incessant input from Dustin at every turn, improvising dialogue, making suggestions to the English actors, doing unscripted things like trying to get into the driver's seat of his car from the wrong side because his character was American. Peckinpah tolerated him. He knew that when it came to the edit he was king. The prolonged siege was his moment, just as he had created the deaths in slow motion for *The Wild Bunch*. His theory about the previously timid Hoffman character was: 'Maybe he incited this violence. Maybe he's waiting for them. These things have a way of happening.'

Especially if Sam, an ex-marine, was around. He spent his time throwing knives at anything made of wood. At the end of shooting he got furiously drunk, beat up his girlfriend and wrecked the cottage they were living in.

I saw a little of Dustin over the years, not least on *Agatha* where he had taken a small part to complete a two-picture contract with Warners for whom I was working. 'I just want to get the fuck out of here,' he confided to me on the Harrogate location. He was off to rewrite and star in *Kramer vs Kramer* with Meryl Streep. It was not a marriage made in heaven, on or off the screen. When their characters were arguing about custody in a restaurant, he unexpectedly swiped a glass of wine with the back of his hand against the wall. It has to be admitted that her shocked reaction was palpable. But Meryl wasn't pleased. She knew how to act, without tricks, and informed him: 'Next time you do that, I'd appreciate you letting me know.'

I kept in touch with Sue George. She invited me to her thirtieth birthday in her house by the Thames and, much later, I helped her a little with her memoirs (although her agent told me they wouldn't sell as she wasn't prepared to write about her relationship with Prince Charles). She did tell me an amazing thing, though. When they had wrapped *Straw Dogs* interiors at Twickenham Studios after the notorious rape scene which the British censor managed to turn into a buggery scene with his cuts, Sam continued to shoot. She managed to find out what he was up to. Various nubile girls were drafted in to be 'raped', ostensibly for body close-ups. But these were wholly unnecessary. Unknown to them, they were just doing it for the director's delectation.

3

Starting *Film '71* ...
Marilyn Monroe ... and Marriage

Presentation Programmes was a small and maverick department, not burdened with a label such as current affairs, science features or religion, which would define its remit. We also had a fast track to the Controllers because we could get programmes on the air quickly, having our own small studios. I knew the gentle charm of Michael Aspel could go further than newsreading so I persuaded him to introduce my children's programme, *Ask Aspel*, a request show which was a sort of forerunner of one later introduced by Jimmy Savile – but without that man's posthumous scandal. We knew it had an audience when schoolchildren would address Mike in the street as 'Ask'. He and I would eat dinner after the programme. He gave up newsreading and would later regale me with the attempts of some Miss World contestants to curry favour with him.

In late summer 1971 I was asked to get a regular film programme going on BBC1. ITV's *Cinema* seemed to have stuttered out, so I invited Michael Parkinson, its former presenter, to lunch, ostensibly to pick his brain but secretly hoping he might come over to the BBC to do my show. He told me he was, in fact, coming to the BBC anyway but to host another show. It was to be called *Parkinson*.

I knew I wanted a superior television essay with criticism laced with wit that would not go amiss in a quality Sunday paper. At ITN I had been impressed by the foreign reporter, Jacky Gillott, and I was further impressed when she brought out a cracking novel, *War Baby*, a panorama of the post-war years following the story of a young evacuee. Jacky could present, she could write and she loved cinema, so the job was hers. The Controller gave it the green light and I came up with the formidably clever name of *Film '71*. (It's still running, forty-three years later, with lovely Claudia, who has hair that could grace a shampoo commercial, and a young man sitting beside her.) Television film programmes up until then had been craven in the face of Wardour Street: they needed free film clips and didn't want to bite the hand that fed them. I told Jacky we would need to pull the sharp sword of criticism out of its scabbard ... or words to that effect. She did. The first film to be stabbed was *Corky*, an unwatchable mess about a stock-car racer. Following her review, it didn't take long for MGM to refuse to give us any more clips, followed by Paramount and then Columbia after they opened films which she reviewed adversely. I got word that the Film Distributors Association (FDA) was meeting to make the ban blanket. If so, we would have a very pure television essay, rather like the historian A. J. P. Taylor who used to give TV lectures without illustrations or notes. But the chances of the Controller letting that continue on his channel were somewhere between nil and minus a million.

A lovely man, Donald Murrey, who ran Columbia's marketing in the UK, took me out to lunch. I could see that the FDA needed us as a shop window as much as we needed their clips. So we reached a Great British Compromise. I would start the programme with films that were going to be well reviewed and put the stinkers in the back end.

That seemed to work OK. But in the middle of the run, Jacky and her husband, John, decided on a life change and moved to Somerset to live off a self-sufficient farm. For a while she used to come up to London for a couple of days a week and stay in my flat but, by

Christmas, she told me it was incompatible with raising her young family. (I visited Jacky in Somerset the following year but, sadly, the other people who promised to join her commune had let her down. I believe she became increasingly depressed and, in a letter to a mutual friend, wrote that she hoped to leave it and live with the writer, Michael Holroyd. He, too, let her down and in 1980 she took her own life. She was only forty; a beautiful and talented woman.)

I needed a new presenter. There were no obvious names so in 1972 I engaged a series of guest presenters who would do a couple of programmes each. First up was Philip Oakes who had been film critic of the *Sunday Telegraph* and even written the movie, *The Punch and Judy Man*, for Tony Hancock. His scripts were good but he lacked that vital chromosome which just makes some people telegenic.

Ever since I read a review by Oscar-winning writer Frederic Raphael which contained the line 'Nabokov's anal imagery falls between two stools', I knew I wanted him to have a go and he didn't let me down script-wise, but .... that chromosome. Irma Kurtz was a lovely American writer living in London but she ran into a bit of bad luck. I had gone skiing during her stint and my cuddly assistant producer, Don Bennetts, produced her programmes. (Don was an Australian who lived in Chelsea with a monkey called Hash and its owner, Althea, who had a box in the Albert Hall where we would go for a drink and smoke cigarettes (you could then!) during the Proms.)

Don decided to start Irma's first show with that year's winner of the Golden Bear at the Berlin Film Festival. Unfortunately there was, as yet, no print in Britain so he shipped one in. Thus that evening's programme began with a two-minute clip of a black-and-white Greek movie with German subtitles. This did not endear that edition of *Film '72* to the public – or the Controller.

Irma, determined to make amends in her second show, delivered a very harsh review of *One Day in the Life of Ivan Denisovich*, a film which was at least in English. She then turned to the fim's star, Tom Courtenay, who was sitting beside her in the studio and he, to put it mildly, EXPLODED for the next five minutes.

I had a hunch that whoever followed Irma might look quite good. A showbiz writer at the *Daily Mail* – the Baz Bamigboye of his day – Barry Norman had been made redundant after the paper's merger with the *Daily Sketch*. Undaunted, he freelanced, writing amusing Wednesday columns in the *Guardian*. I saw him on *Line-Up* one night and he was equally entertaining. So I invited him to Television Centre, where I had put one of his columns on autocue. After a cheery lunch, we went to the studio and he read it out. It looked as if he might possess that elusive chromosome so we used him several times. He went on to become a permanent fixture.

The BBC had bought the rights to the Academy Awards and it was agreed it would show ninety minutes of the ceremony in the *Omnibus* slot the following night. Since it tended to go on for an eternity, I flew to New York to discuss with the BBC producer there, Peter Pagnamenta, how best to edit it. Satellite time cost a fortune then, so we came up with a plan. Peter would watch the show live on TV; I would listen to it on the BBC phone line in London. When it finished, we would discuss what to leave out and he would do a rapid rough edit of it before putting it on the satellite, giving me a few hours to refine things before transmission.

The high point of the ceremony that year was an honorary award to the silent-screen actress, Lillian Gish. She had done the rounds of British television at the end of the previous year plugging her book, *The Movies, Mr Griffith and Me*. She told the same stories whenever I happened to tune in, her favourite being how her director, D.W.

Griffith, had left her floating down the river on an ice floe while the crew went off to lunch. These stories were related again at the Oscars so I suggested to Peter that this would make a good twelve-minute cut.

Three days later the Director General of the BBC received an enraged letter from the President of the Academy demanding the heads of whoever had committed this *lèse-majesté* to Miss Gish and vowing the BBC would never have the Oscars again. Like most of these quarrels, it blew over. But Pagnamenta and I became friends in adversity and when he returned to Britain he asked me to come and be one of his assistant editors on the renewed late-night current affairs show *24 Hours*. Flattered to be asked and by the promotion and reasoning that this was largely why I had wanted to go into TV in the first place, I went. It proved to be a resounding mistake.

As a fond farewell to my film life, I suggested to the Controller a documentary on Marilyn Monroe. On 5 August 1972, it would be exactly ten years since she died. I flew to Los Angeles and tried to round up the usual suspects but, of her three husbands, only Jim Dougherty agreed to appear. He was a cop in the LAPD and suggested we meet at Burro Canyon Shooting Range where he was doing a day's course. It made for a good start to the documentary, Jim blasting off his .44 Magnum (always wake the viewers up!).

Theirs had been a marriage made not in heaven but by Norma Jeane's foster mother who was moving east, so for her ward it was either the orphanage or the altar. Jim did manual work at a defence plant (along with Robert Mitchum) and Marilyn went to school; she was only fifteen when they met. Later he went to war and she got a job inspecting parachutes, where a chance photograph led to her being signed up with a modelling agency and the rest is much-repeated history.

By chance the novelist Alistair MacLean, whom I had made a documentary about, had bought her Beverly Hills house, where she allegedly entertained various Kennedys, and he allowed me to be the first person to film there. In New York, alumni from Lee Strasberg's Actors' Studio recalled how she was truly talented and, in Galway, John Huston recounted the nightmare of *The Misfits* which ended her marriage to Arthur Miller and led to the early demise of Clark Gable followed, a few months later, by Marilyn herself.

The person with the most insightful take on Marilyn was George Axelrod who had written *The Seven Year Itch* and *Bus Stop* – both films in which she starred. He was taken with how bright she was and insisted, quite sincerely, that her marriage to Arthur Miller was a combination of her brains and his beauty. Rich since *Breakfast at Tiffany's*, George now lived in London and we became friendly. One evening, when he invited my first wife, Renate, and me to dinner at his Chester Square house, the other guests were Gregory and Veronique Peck. Renate put on her glasses to make absolutely sure it was him. Greg told her that although he was born Eldred Peck in California he had started out in New York where he dropped the Eldred and used his second name, Gregory. He worked as a tour guide at Radio City Music Hall and as a model for the catalogue of Montgomery Ward, the mail-order retailer. Stars love to talk about their humble beginnings.

Renate and I had had an on-again-off-again relationship since university and she suggested that getting married might stabilise it. So we did, with Richard Whiteley as best man. To have a honeymoon partly on the cheap, I managed to become a delegate to the Venice Film Festival and a marvellous fixer called Bunty got us a room at the posh Hotel des Bains (where Dirk Bogarde passed his final days in *Death in Venice*). Dinner on the first night was so horrendously expensive that we ate future meals in small cafés down where the Lido ferry landed.

After a week, we checked out. I went to pay the bill but the receptionist said there would be no charge. Bunty had evidently fixed it so that our room, meals and wines would be paid for by the Festival. All those thrifty pizzas! We travelled down to Rome and picked up a London *Sunday Times* at the station which said my Monroe programme had been quite good. In fact, it had been the sixth most popular programme of the week. This went some way to stop me being annoyed with myself over those many delicious missed meals.

4

Watergate ... a Professor at Boston ...
Pete 'n' Dud

The main mistake in becoming a deputy editor on *24 Hours* was that being a deputy anything is a pretty thankless job – at least it was for me. Too many bosses in the Current Affairs department; too little freedom. I had a brief to look after cultural matters on the show but they were inevitably dropped to make way for the situation in Vietnam or the Middle East. I should have smelled that one coming.

The redeeming factor during the long wait for our 10.30pm transmission was a friendship with the main presenter, Ludovic Kennedy. During the Second World War, he had served in the navy and so had his father who came out of retirement only to go down with his ship. An Old Etonian, Ludo told me he had taken elocution lessons to soften his voice for broadcasting. Years later, I helped him a bit on a book about his wife, Moira Shearer, star of *The Red Shoes*. His final posthumous act was for his family to be given unprecedented permission for a secular service in Christ Church, Oxford's cathedral.

Pagnamenta left for *Panorama* and was replaced by a curious cove called Bunce who managed to make the late nights in dingy Lime Grove even less interesting. I resolved to leave but, as a parting shot, to prove that we could get ratings of more than a million, I made a profile of John Cleese whom I vaguely knew through the broadcasting guru, (Sir) Anthony Jay. That evening, 5.25 million viewers watched the programme.

If Lillian Gish had got me into this mess, Richard Nixon got me out of it. In the summer of 1973 it was decided to throw over the entire programme to coverage of the Watergate hearings. Initially I looked after the London end but in early July the head of our Washington team, (Sir) Richard Francis, had booked a holiday in the Caribbean with his mistress – expecting the hearings to be over. But Americans are hard-working folk and the hearings continued throughout the summer. So I flew to Washington to do his job – and loved it.

I remember coming down to breakfast at the Georgetown Inn and finding Clive Sydall, one of our producers, eating lamb chops for breakfast. I asked him how he had acquired this habit and he said he had been there so long and eaten through the breakfast menu so many times, he just thought he'd try something new.

Washington was so alive that summer; the eyes of the world were focussed on it and to be a tiny part of this momentous event was exciting. I went to the Caucus Room on Capitol Hill each day to make notes about what we would choose for the edit. The hearings were halted several times each session so the panel could go off and vote in the Senate. Jeremy Campbell, the *Evening Standard* correspondent and a Washington fixture, knew everyone involved and introduced me. So I talked to H.R. Haldeman (laughing and friendly) and John Ehrlichman (pretty guarded), known as the 'Berlin Wall' so protective had they been of their President and, later, to White House Counsel, John Dean (slippery), whose evidence stitched up the other two. All three eventually went to jail.

I was amazed how helpful the Senators were. One day I needed a clarifying interview with the chairman, Sam Irvin. His office called back saying that he'd come down to the Caucus Room at 7am the next morning to tape it. British politicians didn't do things like that at the time. Due to the time difference we would have to finish editing at 5pm each day, and could then enjoy Georgetown nightlife, a heady mix of bars populated by students and stewardesses. I was sad when it was over; we held a wrap party round the pool at, appropriately, the Watergate complex where the break-in had taken place.

Renate had wanted to spend a year in America so I contacted Russell Harty, then a chat-show host. We met in reception at Television Centre. 'I'm going through my fan mail and sucking a Fisherman's Friend,' were his first words to me. Russell had taught Richard Whiteley at Giggleswick School in Yorkshire, and was subsequently a Visiting Professor at Columbia University in New York. He told me to apply through the American Embassy in London and Boston University showed interest in a BBC type. So I nipped up to BU after Watergate, there to be interviewed by Dean Gerhard D. Wiebe who anointed me a Visiting Professor of Broadcasting for the next academic year.

I must have done something right in Washington. On my return to the BBC, I was summoned to see my personnel officer. He asked me to reconsider my resignation and even handed me a prepared contract which contained the wonderful sentence: 'Your appointment will be effected by S.Pers.O.P.Tel.111 in conjunction with S.Pers.O.P.Tel.11.' Even though the outward face of the BBC might have changed with shows like *That Was The Week That Was*, the back room remained as it was in the era before WWII. The document was a thirty-year contract, bringing me up to my sixtieth birthday. I asked S.Pers.O.P.Tel.11 why they didn't just put me on the staff and he replied, a little bashfully, that they didn't think I was the sort to move up the administrative rungs but I should regard programme producing as a secure job, 'like a dentist'. What I didn't say was thirty more years at Lime Grove would seem like thirty years at the dentist.

If there were a competition for the ugliest campus in America, Boston University would win by a light year. Two rivers of square concrete buildings were bisected by a six-lane highway with a tram running up the middle. Nevertheless, the place attracted a fair degree of talent such as Joan Baez, Saul Bellow and Martin King Jr – he added the Luther later for good measure. The last two became Nobel Laureates so the teaching cannot have been too bad – until I came along. There was a sprinkling of attractive Jewish girls in my classes who had remarkably similar backgrounds. In their forties, their rich fathers had divorced their mothers to go off with their secretaries so, to punish them, mother would send the daughter to the ludicrously expensive BU instead of four free years at their state university. Some would arrive at lectures in open-topped Mercs or with dogs, or both.

Renate and I rented an apartment at the foot of the more salubrious Beacon Hill populated by 'Boston Brahmins'. As the poem goes:

And this is good old Boston,
The home of the bean and the cod.
 Where the Lowells talk only to Cabots
And the Cabots talk only to God.

Renate wrote freelance articles and I studied books about sound and how to direct and light a studio: something Dean Wiebe never warned me about and something other people had done for me at the BBC. I learned what a 'kicker' (backlight) was but failed to co-ordinate my lighting in exercises where there were both white and black faces in frame.

We spent some jolly weekends skiing in Vermont or driving further on to eat snails with friends in Montreal, but it was fairly clear that the marriage was dilapidating and we spent Christmas apart. She went to a funeral in Berlin where, I believe, she met someone and I went to Mexico to stay with Alan Riding, who was now the *New York Times* correspondent there. We spent Christmas Day eating sandwiches in the foothills of Popocatépetl, made famous by Malcolm Lowry's *Under the Volcano*. I loved the book and, in 1977, went back to make a documentary to commemorate the twentieth anniversary of Lowry's death. He had grown up on Merseyside so I enlisted my dad to help with the early research. Jack discovered that not only had Lowry won the junior championship at the golf club he went to every day in his retirement, The Royal Liverpool at Hoylake, but that his nephew's garden backed on to ours in West Kirby. Alan and I returned to Cuernavaca and found the cantina where Malcolm would go for his daily dose of mescal. I filmed myself in the bar sipping one and asked the aged barman if he had ever met Lowry. He nodded and spoke something in Spanish. 'What did he say?' I asked Alan. 'He said that Lowry was in last Thursday,' Alan replied. Some people will do anything to please.

None of my students at BU, as far as I know, went on to win Nobel Prizes but my teaching must have been adequate enough for Dean Wiebe to ask me to stay on. That was kind of him, but the student jibe 'those that can, do; those that can't, teach' rang in my ears. My brightest student, Bruce Feirstein, wanted to be a newscaster but I told him he wasn't right (didn't have that chromosome) and urged him to write. He subsequently made a name for himself with *Real Men Don't Eat Quiche*. He later would arrive in London in 1994 to write the first three Pierce Brosnan Bond films, which completely reinvigorated the series, spoilt me a bit with his expense account and came for dinner every Sunday. Marcia Lewis, my outstanding female student, asked me to a party at her house where the recently formed Boston band, Aerosmith, were also guests – although I hadn't a clue who Steven Tyler was. Marcia worked with me on nearly all the programmes I subsequently made in the States and was taken on by David Frost and then Bob Hope. We never had an affair but she remains, to this day, my closest female friend. (In my Boston days I did come a little bit too close to a couple of post-grad students ... or did they come a little too close to me?)

To keep my telly hand in, I went on the local WGBH news, initially to talk about Ted Heath's three-day week in England in 1974. I would ring Will Wyatt in London for the latest news and then pontificate knowledgeably. Thereafter they gave me a weekly slot.

I read that Peter Cook and Dudley Moore were coming to Boston and called John Higgins, a friend and Arts Editor of *The Times*. Would he like a piece on them and the American reaction to their revue *Good Evening?* He said he would.

The pair had nothing to do on Sunday so the three of us ended up in my clapped-out Camaro en route to Harvard Square for lunch. The car radio was tuned to the local 'All Oldies' station. Commercial radio was about to arrive in Britain and Peter resolved to start such a station. His innovations such as The Establishment Club and backing *Private Eye* tended to work wonderfully but the wind off the River Charles blew away this passing thought.

In those days, few restaurants in Cambridge, Mass. were open on Sundays but Peter spotted one called 'Acropolis'. 'I have a sneaking suspicion it may be Greek,' he observed. It was, but this didn't matter to Dudley as he didn't want to eat. It was part of his diet never to eat on Sundays. He informed the (Greek) waitress that he just wanted a glass of water. She pointed out that there was a cover charge of two dollars which he would still have to pay. He said he was happy to do so. She insisted that he could have a bowl of lemon soup that cost less than two dollars. He still declined. She persisted. I feared we might get into a *Five Easy Pieces* situation when Jack Nicholson wanted some toast in a diner and the waitress said she couldn't do that. So he ordered a chicken mayo sandwich, asking her to hold the butter, the mayo, the lettuce and the chicken – the last between her knees. She ordered him and his friends to leave the restaurant which they did, not before he swept four full glasses of water, cutlery and plates off the table with one gesture.

Dudley, being a scholar of Magdalen College, Oxford, did not resort to such boorish behaviour but just charmed the bemused girl away.

Peter turned to me: 'It's part of Mr Moon's weight-reconciling regime. He intends to write a diet book about it but has got somewhat stuck after the first line which, if I correctly recall, goes: "Don't eat on Sundays."'

'Mr Moon?' I asked.

'He always calls me that when he's being nice to me,' Dudley explained. The term of endearment originated on a flight that Dudley had taken to Genoa and found himself sitting next to Sir John Gielgud in first class – this was many years before the latter was to play his butler in *Arthur*. They fell into conversation and Dudley mentioned he was going to meet his girlfriend at the Hotel Splendido in Portofino.

'Ah, Portofino!' Sir John exclaimed. 'You must meet the estimable Rex Harrison. He has a villa of some luxury there. I shall write you a letter of introduction.' He called for some BEA notepaper, took out his pen and began to compose it. Carefully sealing the envelope he handed it to Dudley, who thanked him.

'Don't forget to see Rex,' Gielgud reminded him when they parted at Genoa Airport. Dudley assured him that he would do so.

Dud, or the man better known to Sir John Gielgud as 'Mr Stanley Moon'.

He had no intention of doing so and, the moment Sir John was out of sight, tore open the envelope. The letter began: 'Dear Rex, This is to introduce my good friend, Mr Stanley Moon.'

Peter, a fount of information (some of it useful) told me: 'Rex built the villa just after the war with his first Teutonic wife, Lilli Palmer. It was on the site of a German bunker, so she got preferential rates.'

At the time I was only passingly acquainted with Peter and Dudley. I knew Alan Bennett better; Russell Harty was Alan's closest friend. But Alan was not, it transpired, Dudley's. 'At one stage during *Beyond the Fringe* in New York he just stopped talking to me ... except when we were performing,' Dud recalled. 'I don't know why. I must have annoyed him in some way.'

'I think he fell out with himself,' Peter interjected. 'I'm not sure Alan enjoyed doing the same material night after night.'

Cook on the other hand had no such aversion. Indeed his 'One Leg Too Few' sketch had progressed from a 1960 Pembroke College, Cambridge, revue to the same year's Footlights show to *One Over the Eight* with Kenneth Williams in the West End to *Beyond the Fringe* on Broadway to the previous night's Boston performance of *Good Evening*. I suppose for Cook (and, later, Dudley as Mr Spiggot, the 'unidexter' applicant for the role of Tarzan) to do a show without the sketch would be the equivalent of Frank Sinatra doing a concert without singing 'My Way'.

Cook's widow, Lin, told me he improvised the sketch straight off in front of friends in his room at Pembroke. The word 'unidexter' just spilled out of him – it has no meaning, other than that 'dexter' is the Latin for 'clever'. The routine originally ended with a two-legged man coming in and Cook saying: 'Good Morning, Mr Stanger, I believe you are auditioning for the role of Long John Silver,' but had to be dropped for the two-man show.

Peter claimed to have been inspired by a school butler at Radley, Mr Boylett, who once pointed out a stone beside the school drive and claimed he had sometimes seen it move. Thus, at Cambridge, Cook once extemporised for two hours on the subject of gravel and the sketch that persuaded Adrian Slade to admit him to Footlights was entitled 'Arctic Bores – monotonous reminiscences of Polar explorers'.

As I got to know Peter better over the years, I could see that boredom was fundamental to much of his humour. His park-bench character, E.L. Wisty, would provide detailed information on newts, tadpoles and ants. Towards the end of his life Cook attended a *Private Eye* celebration dinner in a West End hotel. He hadn't realised he was expected to speak. But he rose unsteadily to his feet, grabbed the menu and just read it out in the most boring way imaginable. It was the funniest speech of the evening.

And this boredom characterised his daily life. With a mind as acute and alert and inspired as his, he sought entertainment in information. He bought stacks of newspapers and magazines every day and surfed the television and radio well into the night. I rarely heard him referring to classic books or theatre, but he knew more about Watergate than I did. That didn't make him a seer. He told me he had placed a bet that Nixon would survive his full term in office until January 1977. He even sent the President a telegram advising him not to resign and received a polite reply thanking him for his support. In the event Nixon resigned in August 1974.

Peter invited me down to New York to watch *Good Evening* from backstage at the Plymouth Theatre. It was probably the only place I could get. The show was a sell-out thanks to reviews such as 'two of the funniest and most inventive men in the world'. They had been graced by celebrities from Cary Grant to Groucho Marx, Charlton Heston to Henry Kissinger and his posse of bodyguards (he was then Nixon's Secretary of State).

Word had it that Peter had been drinking but his timing seemed fine to me. I recalled the time Richard Burton had been challenged to drink a bottle of vodka between the matinee and evening performance of *Camelot* and had actually managed to down two. When asked how he had been, his co-star, Julie Andrews, had replied: 'A little better than usual.'

Cook joked with me a bit between sketches and while being interviewed by Dud as Sir Arthur Streeb-Greebling, proprietor of 'The Frog and Peach', and even managed to squeeze my name in as a waiter whom he had to fire for leaving frogspawn on a plate. 'What will he serve next? Tadpoles?' But it was clear in the wings there was now little love lost between him and Dud.

He didn't join Peter and me when we went to eat at Rosie O'Grady's afterwards. That didn't matter to some fellow diners who congratulated us on the show. Admittedly I had longish hair at the time, but they must have been sitting very far back in the theatre.

Peter himself brought up the subject of Dudley's discontent. 'He gets pretty pissed off when I've been drinking, but the real reason is Tuesday.'

'What happened on Tuesday?' I asked.

He drew on his cigarette. 'Tuesday Weld. Once known as Susan Ker Weld, daughter of Lathrop Motley Weld. Slightly mad child actress and drinker, star of *The Cincinnati Kid* and other lesser films. I had, what you might term, a very fleeting affair with her. It lasted for a whole night. She woke me up rather thoughtlessly in the morning and told me I had to leave as her ex-husband, Claude, was coming to take their daughter to school. I told her it was before my getting-up time. So when he arrived, I sat up in bed and said: 'Bonjour, Claude'. He didn't reply. I suspect he didn't understand me as he was more Jewish than French. But Tuesday was, in a word, displeased and that rather precluded any further romantic activity.'

I asked him why Dudley should be upset about that.

'Well, not for the first time, he followed in my romantic footsteps. I think they may have been more suited to each other being of a similar height and her fondness for musicians. I believe she once dated Elvis Presley – whatever that entailed.'

It transpired that Dudley was not only 'dating' Tuesday but was very much besotted with her. They were to marry and have a son, Patch. It is commonly thought that the rift between Pete and Dud was because of the former's envy at the latter's Hollywood success, but the Tuesday issue was a greater fissure. This was exacerbated by the fact that Peter was living in London with Judy

Huxtable, a former model, and he had told her of his fling with Tuesday whom she now cordially hated. When they married the following year in Sardi's Restaurant, Dudley was not there, Arthur Cohen, their producer, being best man instead.

With the imminent arrival of Judy in New York, Peter was fearful of contracting a transmittable sex disease. Thus, after dinner each evening, he would go for a massage 'with relief'. He carried with him a copy of *Screw* magazine which helpfully listed such places, rating them not with stars but erect penises. Peter had no compunction about going through the listings in the crowded restaurant and, settling on one he had not visited before, invited me to accompany him. But I chickened out.

Before I left Boston, I read that a movie was shooting just down the coast. I knew the book and thought that if I did a location report I might be able to sell it to *Film '74*. I could make it cheaply by hiring a couple of graduates to be my crew. So I found the name of the unit publicist and called him, pointing out that this could be held until the film's release and would be good for UK marketing. 'You may as well come down,' he replied laconically, 'nobody else seems much interested.'

Later they would be. The film was *Jaws*.

5

Jaws ... Steven Spielberg ... David Frost ... Arianna

Martha's Vineyard is a small island off the coast of Cape Cod where the well-heeled inhabitants of Beacon Hill have their holiday homes. It came to international notice in July 1969 when Senator Edward Kennedy drove his Oldsmobile off a wooden bridge and into a tidal pond. This drowned his passenger, Mary Jo Kopechne, and ruined Kennedy's chance of ever being elected President. Thirty years later, almost to the day, his nephew, JFK's son John, crashed the plane he was piloting into the sea, killing himself, his wife and her sister. Ten years after that I was eating there with my wife on the terrace of Nancy's restaurant when President Obama, his wife and two daughters turned up for lunch. It was only them, although six black SUVs filled with security men waited below to escort them home. That night it was announced on the news that Ted Kennedy had died.

On 5 May 1974, Steven Spielberg started shooting *Jaws* on the island. He was scheduled to be there for 52 days, but it turned out to be 155. He thought at the end he would never be employed again. But when we arrived on the second day of filming, spirits were high. I had admired Steven ever since he made *Duel* – the frightening ordeal of a man hunted by a 'driverless' truck – when he was only twenty-four. Now it was a great white shark that was doing the hunting.

His stars were Robert Shaw, who mostly had to fly in from Canada for tax reasons, Roy Scheider and Richard Dreyfuss. 'I don't like low-key actors,' he told me. 'I like actors who give me too much on the first take, so I can bring their performance down to life levels.'

He was extremely film-literate, using the famous track-forward-zoom-out shot when Scheider, on the beach, realises a boy has been attacked, from Hitchcock's lift shaft in *Vertigo*, only reversing the technique. Twenty-five per cent of the film was shot from the shark's point of view at sea level. This added to the menace. The mechanical sharks, who were all called Bruce and had been constructed in California, promptly sank when they were launched into the Atlantic. This caused part of the huge overrun; the other factor, as Steven had realised early on, was that when you shoot from boat to boat it is nigh on impossible to line up a shot as both of them move continually with the wind and the tide.

Although he had artistic control, the young director was very much under orders from the Unit Manager, Jim Fargo, who urged him to get more and more shots. 'But these won't match,' Steven complained to him. 'We began the sequence in sunshine yesterday and now it's cloud.' 'Well, get some umbrellas,' Jim ordered, 'and we'll do the close-ups.'

Spielberg and Dreyfuss, both bachelors, had some fun in the evenings with the sun-kissed girls who were holidaying on the island. Richard told me Steven lost his virginity that summer. Steven maintains that this was untrue and that Richard was just pissed off because he stole his girlfriend. The debate remains unresolved. I kept in touch with Steven and, although I obviously didn't know it then, was to work with him on eight future occasions.

Despite its problems, *Jaws* was the first major summer blockbuster: 67 million Americans went to see it, the first film to earn more than $100 million dollars at the box office. It transpired that I was the only person to film on its location and my ten-minute report

Steven Spielberg all at sea on *Jaws*.

proudly sits in Universal's twenty-fifth anniversary DVD and Blue Ray set.

On returning to Campden Hill, Renate told me there was someone else and she left to live with, and later marry, him – a magazine journalist like herself. We had no children, nor very much of anything else, so there were no assets to split; it was a reasonably amicable parting.

So there I was in the summer of 1974: thirty-one, no wife, no job. Fortunately, in Boston I had done some reviews and interviews for the nightly Radio 4 arts programme *Kaleidoscope*, and I contacted the Head of the Department, a Hungarian called George Fischer, to see if I could do some more. He asked me to come to Broadcasting House. As luck would have it – looking back, I think I relied a little too much on luck in my undulating career path – one of the presenters was leaving and he said he was prepared to try me out for a month. George gave me a long lecture on the importance of the correct use of the English language in such a job, ending with the words: 'We will with you a contract make.' I muddled along for a year, despite my wholesale ignorance of music, ballet, literature and the fine arts. After all, at Bristol I had only studied law ... and not a lot of that.

Towards the end of the summer I got a call from David Frost who asked me what I was doing. 'Very little,' I confessed. 'Good.' he said, 'Lunch at the White Tower next Tuesday at 12.47.'

I had known Frostie from my Presentation days when I was assigned to a short series called *Frost Over America*. It was a luxuriously untaxing job. He was becoming as famous in the States as he was in Britain with his nightly *The David Frost Show* which went up against Dick Cavett and Merv Griffin in prime time. The idea was to take ten of his best programmes, remove the commercial breaks, edit them down for the BBC and tape a short intro from Frost.

He had a permanent theatre on West 44th Street in New York and an office in the star dressing room. As I was shown in, he was coming to the end of a highly romantic phone call. 'Diahann Carroll,' were his first words to me, 'I think I may be in love.' (Diahann was a black chanteuse who had been married to a Las Vegas tycoon and later became engaged to David. They never married; I think his mother, Mona, might have disapproved.)

I was somewhat in awe of Frost. He had been in the Cambridge Footlights with Peter Cook. David was the first pure member of the television generation. Other TV presenters had come from journalism or the theatre but David came pretty well straight from Cambridge to present *That Was The Week That Was* when he was twenty-four and never did a job outside of television, save that of being an entrepreneur. In 1963 the *Observer* showed photographs to people to determine who was the most famous person in the UK. Harold Wilson was third, the Queen second, and Frostie first.

I was further impressed back then when a waiter came over from Sardi's with David's lunch on a tray. We went through the list of celebrity interviews I should look at, agreeing to meet again at the end of the week. Tennessee Williams, Orson Welles, etc, were naturals, but Barbra Streisand and Julie Andrews presented problems. When we lunched at Sardi's that Friday, David said CBS had refused to clear the songs Streisand had sung on *The David Frost Show*, but maybe I could change their minds for the UK (I failed). Julie Andrews had primarily come on the show to promote the plight of Vietnamese orphans. She showed a long home movie of them. 'Oh, just cut all that out,' he suggested, somewhat ruthlessly. 'She'll never see it.'

Now here we were again, four years later, at the White Tower restaurant in Soho. He said that after his transatlantic commuting to do weekend shows for ITV, the BBC had made him an offer to come back to them. He still had his finger in myriad pies, but by doing a series of one-on-one interviews he could fit them in and I could produce them.

Aubrey Singer, controller of BBC2, took me to see Alasdair Milne, once a producer on *That Was The Week* and now the Head of BBC TV, for his approval. 'He'll kill you, boy,' was pretty well all he said. As the series progressed, I could see what he was getting at. What David wanted, he got, regardless of my programme budget. (Alasdair was to be killed, professionally, a little earlier than me when the BBC Chairman, Marmaduke Hussey, fired him as Director General. He went to work for Noddy Enterprises, his friend, Donald Baverstock, having providentially married Enid Blyton's daughter.)

I put together a production team including Helen Jay, semi-famous in the papers for being a leggy 'Jaybird', (she and her twin sister, Catherine were the glamorous daughters of a Cabinet minister) who came to work in tears one November morning since a Clermont Club chum of her boyfriend, Dominick Elwes, had murdered his children's nanny and scarpered. Helen knew him well: he was 'Lucky' Lucan.

The BBC kindly allowed me to fly first class to America so that David and I could have serious programme discussions on the plane. These did not always last long as he would swallow a couple of barbiturates after dinner and be out to the world. On one occasion, due to strong head winds, the plane had to land in the Azores to refuel. We were allowed off and the economy passengers filed past the sleeping Frost. He was still asleep an hour later when we reboarded. On awakening for landing, he didn't believe me when I told him, even when I showed him a postcard I had bought of the islands. He asked the stewardesses if it was true and they assured him it was.

When awake, David was good company. He related a TWA joke. Stewardess: 'Sir, would you like some TWA coffee?' DF: 'No, but I'd like some TWA-T.' He kept at his feet a book of jokes he had heard and scribbled down and he memorised them on the flight for future use. Peter Cook had once, unkindly, labelled him, the 'bubonic plagiarist'.

I had chosen the television station WTTG in Washington, where I had done my Watergate editing, for David to tape an interview with Senator Edward Kennedy. He was at the forefront in the Democratic campaign for healthcare at the time, although this was not of great

Ted Kennedy whets David Frost's appetite with the size of Clyde's cheeseburgers.

concern to British viewers. The main interest was whether he would follow his brothers in standing for President. He ruled out any chance of doing so in the 1976 election. (He was to succumb to temptation and family persuasion in 1980, but the incumbent, President Carter, beat him soundly in the Democratic Primary. Post Chappaquidick, Ted was not a man the country could entirely trust.)

He had suggested we go to Clyde's, a popular Washington hamburger restaurant, for lunch. I called for a reservation. 'We don't take reservations,' snapped the woman on the phone. So I said to her: 'It's for Senator Edward Kennedy and David Frost.' 'I don't care who it's for,' she retorted, 'first come, first served.' I'm always amused by the way people on TV frequently say the main benefit of their fame is to get tables in restaurants. I told Ted, who was sanguine. 'I'll call Ethel,' he said. And when we got there, sure enough, there was the widow of Bobby Kennedy robustly holding on to a table for four. Part of the attraction of the place was that the waitresses were in shorts and on roller skates. Our conversation was less than lofty. Ted said he had just bought his six-year-old son, Patrick, a turtle. He thought turtles didn't move much but this one did, all over his house. And it liked to eat hamburgers. Ethel was feisty and perpetually called Frostie 'Dave'. 'She's the only person in the world who does that,' he told me afterwards.

Alasdair Milne was right: on occasion I lost my casting vote as producer. I didn't think Evel Knievel's attempt to jump the Snake River Canyon in Idaho was in any way relevant to *The Frost Interview*. But David phoned Aubrey Singer and countermanded me. As a protest, I didn't go. David stood beside Evel and his jet bike as a pastor pronounced a blessing on the daredevil. David then wished Evel 'Happy landings' and Knievel took off into the sky where his parachute opened, landing him on the same side of the canyon from which he had taken off. ABC Sports had been unwilling to pay the price Knievel wanted for the jump so it was broadcast closed-circuit by Top Rank Productions to movie theatres. I asked David: 'Why the pastor?' and he said Evel had told him the man had sold a lot of tickets in the south and west. What David didn't tell me was that he had been hired by Top Rank to commentate on the event.

We further fell out when he told me he had persuaded Martha Mitchell, the loony wife of John Mitchell, Nixon's jailed Attorney General, to do a studio interview back in London when the series began. She had agreed to do it for two first-class air tickets, for her and her friend, and three nights in two suites in Claridge's. I calculated this would come to more than three times my programme budget, so I called David at The Plaza, New York, and left a message that he should not book her. I was staying at the St Moritz Hotel and asked the switchboard to hold my calls when I went to sleep. But that didn't stop Frost. He talked his way past the operator and woke me at 2am to say he was furious and had called Aubrey who approved the overspend. (Martha became extremely drunk on the plane when she later came over for the show and, seizing a tray of champagne, began serving drinks to other passengers while claiming she had once been an air hostess.)

I was less than happy as I flew back to London. Why bother to be a producer who had no power? But when I eventually introduced David to the production team, he was his usual effervescent self. I was to learn that he was a man who didn't hold grudges. Indeed I rarely heard him speak ill of anyone. Life had been remarkably kind to him and he was the same to others. He wasn't impervious to criticism – his name had hardly been out of the papers for more than a decade – but he had so many rings in the air that he was on to the next project before the current one was reviewed. Naturally, Evel Knievel was ridiculed in the press. David read the critics but they had as much effect on him as a child throwing snowballs at an express train. Work spilled into leisure. At dinner at his house in Egerton Crescent, he fondly brought out a book of cuttings from his days on *Varsity* at Cambridge to show Eamonn Andrews his weekly column: 'An Old Codger Writes'. The Irishman and his wife were bemused.

Maybe the arguments made us a little closer, with him having a bit more respect for me. (He was to hire me to produce him in shows for his company, Paradine, although not, sadly, the interviews he did with Richard Nixon, preferring a London Weekend TV producer, John Birt.) But that was three years away as we ate a nervous Sunday lunch before going in his chauffeur-driven Bentley, to visit Cicely Saunders, who had founded the world's first purpose-built hospice, St Christopher's. I had met Cicely for an item on *Midweek* but it was, inevitably, not used – probably replaced by Arthur Scargill or some more 'worthwhile' cause.

The patients, many close to death's door, put us wonderfully at our ease as we talked to them. Neither David nor I had ever visited such a place before but the atmosphere in St Christopher's was truly humbling. Courage, optimism, peace, friendship. Cicely had managed miraculously to quell fear and self-pity. She was a Mother Teresa without the nonsense. David agreed she merited a programme to herself and we drove away more than a little wiser about the end of life's journey.

It was a motley series: from Cicely to Martha, from Brian Clough, who took Derby County from the Second Division to English Champions in three years, to Matthew Manning, whose automatic writing could stop the frequent poltergeist activity he attracted. David said we should get some 'sex in by the back door', so he interviewed the racy and outspoken Anna Raeburn who had just been made *Woman*'s agony aunt.

A general election had been called for October 1974 and the BBC wanted David to interview the party leaders. Jeremy Thorpe was the most fun, entertaining the dinner table afterwards with imitations of his rivals. Heath didn't stay for dinner and refused to answer David's much-repeated question as to whether he privately liked Harold Wilson. Harold, as PM, used the advantage of being interviewed at 10 Downing Street. I went along there for a recce and was met by a political secretary who asked me: 'Which room do you want to do it in?' I wasn't exactly prepared for this, never having set foot in the place before. But I hope I put on a confident face as we took a tour, settling on the White Drawing Room. 'Yes, the PM will be pleased with that,' my escort said.

David and Harold knew each other well and we retired to the PM's study for brandies after the interview. Harold replaced his familiar pipe with a large cigar, and David joined him. The enigmatic Marcia Falkender was there – Harold treated her as a secretary-cum-nurse-cum-political wife. Joe Haines, his press officer, poured the drinks. I didn't like to say anything but my brandy tasted ... well, not like brandy. Eventually Harold mentioned the same thing and asked Joe to bring him the decanter. It was labelled 'Sherry'. There was that sort of sense of confusion in the Wilson inner circle.

The Frost Interview brought an unexpected bonus. David had been invited to a celebration of Arianna Stassinopoulos's book *The Female Woman* in the famed Greek tavern 'Apollonia'. He couldn't go and passed the invitation to me. It came attached to a tsoureki (a sweet Greek roll). Arianna, the first foreign President of the Cambridge Union, had written the book as a riposte to Germaine Greer's *The Female Eunuch*: a feminist polemic. I didn't know many people there, but the author was warm and welcoming, not betraying any upset that her fellow Cambridge star hadn't come. She had become prominent through appearances on television's *Face the Music* and due to her relationship with *The Times* columnist, Bernard Levin, whom she had met on the show. Bernard had made national news when on *That Was The Week* he was punched on the nose by the irate husband of an actress to whom he'd given a bad review.

I was slightly surprised to be invited to a couple of dinners at Arianna's flat. There tended to be about twenty-four people at these meals, many of them recognisable faces. I was unable to entertain in such style (or at all) so I invited her to lunch. We exchanged life stories, as you do. She told me she was no longer with Bernie; it was not a relationship that was going the way she wanted as he was a confirmed bachelor, in the true sense of the phrase, and couldn't contemplate having children.

When she rang to thank me, she asked if I was free on New Year's Eve, which I was. So she invited me to her flat. I went, expecting another dinner party, but it was only me. She had been invited to three parties that night and asked if I would escort her. We went to all three; the first was an opulent dinner at Claridge's, hosted by a Greek friend. I cannot recall the other two but I am unlikely to forget that in the early hours of 1975 we fell into bed.

What followed was – for me – as much a musical education as an affair. She taught me about classical music, we went frequently to the opera and concerts. She suggested we write together, which we did. But I didn't have her stamina. Quite often she would stay up all night writing. She was in demand as an after-dinner speaker and I went with her. She usually began by studying the faces of those present and then announced: 'I see before me the most intellectual gathering since George Bernard Shaw dined alone.' This always got a laugh.

I met her friends, most notably Frank Johnson and John O'Sullivan, parliamentary sketch writers for *The Times* and *Telegraph* respectively. After a couple of months, I asked Frank: 'Why me?' He replied: 'After Bernie, she just wanted somebody normal' – which, I suppose, I was. When the Frost series ended, I was unemployed but Arianna kept the faith, taking me to places such as Lady Sonia Melchett's regular Monday evening drinks in Chelsea. Like Madame Verdurin in Proust, Sonia didn't invite you to these gatherings; you just knew if you would be welcome. After Ari and I split up, Sonia encouraged me to still come which I often did. I spent part of one evening talking to the serving prime minister, Jim Callaghan. He was drinking orange juice. He told me he had decided to abstain from alcohol while he was in Number 10.

Arianna constantly infused me with confidence, but our romance was too good to last. Towards the end of the summer, I was aware she was seeing Bernard again. I had to go to the States to make a profile of Telly Savalas, then wildly popular as the star in *Kojak*, and she suggested I stay with her sister, Agapi, who lived just off Sunset Boulevard. That softened the blow.

In 1980, realising that things with Bernie had no future, Arianna left to make her mark in New York – which didn't take her long. It was said that she was the highest flying Greek since Icarus, but she flew much higher than that. In 1986 she married her millionaire, Michael Huffington. I had to work in Hong Kong at the time of the wedding but I encouraged my wife, Mo (more later), to go anyway. She took an old boyfriend, Andrew Neil, then editor of *The Sunday Times*, who happened to be in town. Le tout New York was there. The reception was in the Manhattan Club. When they went in, they bumped into Rupert Murdoch, who was waiting for his wife, Anna, to return from the loo. 'What are you doing here, Andrew?' demanded his boss. Andrew introduced Mo and explained her connection to Ari. A familiar growl greeted Rupert. It was Henry Kissinger, also waiting for his wife. The conversation turned to the possible Reagan attack on Libya. 'Surely he won't do that?' Mo asked the former Security Advisor. 'He's moved the Sixth Fleet into the southern Mediterranean,' Kissinger replied. 'He has to – if only to save face.'

Mo had to fly back to London the next day to her job as a PA in the BBC. The conversation at the morning meeting was all about Libya; there was fear of an outright war. 'Reagan won't do it,' pronounced the Head of Department. 'Yes, he will,' blurted out a jet-lagged Mo. Her boss glared at her. 'Who says so?' he enquired patronisingly. 'Henry Kissinger,' she found herself replying.

The subsequent history of Arianna has been publicly chronicled. Two lovely daughters, a gay husband, her political swing from right to left, a campaign against Arnold Schwarzenegger for Governor of California, her sale of *The Huffington Post* for $315 million dollars. I sometimes stay with her and Agapi when I'm in LA. But she still doesn't pay me for my articles. Maybe she will, if she serialises this book.

6

Ten Days in the Life of Muhammad Ali

Easily my most exhilarating experience as a documentary film maker was the ten days I spent with Muhammad Ali. He has an aura and a presence as powerful as his punch.

The BBC had dealings with the boxer when they covered his fights and I knew the person to contact was Howard Bingham, his 'main man'. Ali was not averse to a little loose change when it came to interviews but no-one in the UK had made a fully fledged TV programme about him. I spoke to Howard on the phone and we made a deal: I would film intermittently over a three-week period and each day I did so I would pay $300 in cash. 'Into Howard's hand?' I asked. 'No,' Howard replied, 'into Ali's.'

Marcia Lewis, who had worked on the US Frost shows, met me at JFK and we set off into the Pocono mountains of Pennsylvania in search of Ali's training camp, Deer Lake. Unfortunately, like the Presidential retreat at Camp David, it was not marked on any map. When night fell we got hopelessly lost, finally making for a blue light in the hills. Beneath it was the run-down Dusselfink Motel with, no doubt, Norman Bates jibbering at reception.

In the morning, not having risked getting knifed in the shower, I asked Norman if he knew the way to Ali's camp. He pointed to a nearby hill. 'Top of that. You won't have no problem. The Champ likes people to come and watch him train at ten.'

We found Howard, a short black guy with ragged teeth and a pronounced stutter. He was Ali's photographer, and also his best friend. My film crew were already there and we managed to catch the Champ emerging from his log cabin with two women who, it transpired, were Belinda, his wife, and Veronica, who was to be his next wife. He paid no attention to us as they progressed to the gym. He was training for a world-title fight against Britain's Joe Bugner in Kuala Lumpur. (Bugner, to his credit, was to go the distance.)

A couple of hundred people had come to watch Ali train with his sparring partners. His favourite was Jimmy Ellis, who had become WBA heavyweight champion in 1976 while Ali was suspended for refusing to join the military and fight in Vietnam. After the serious business was over, Ali entertained the assembled crowd, showing us the now legendary 'Ali Shuffle' and how he had used the 'Rope-a-Dope' to beat George Foreman in the Rumble in the Jungle in Kinshasa the previous year (1974). The art was to lie back against the ropes and let them take the pressure out of the punch.

Finally he caught my eye. 'Are you BBC?'

I said we were.

'Did Joe Bugner send you here to spy on me?' he asked, getting a good laugh from the crowd.

I promised he hadn't and asked the Champ if he had a message for Joe.

Without pausing, he came across and addressed my camera. 'Joe, I told you when you was sparring with me in England and Ireland and Switzerland that one day you'd be a contender for my crown. I'm eight years older but I'm still the greatest. I'm still the best boxer of all time. I'm still the dancing master. I still float like a butterfly, sting like a bee, his hands only hit what his eyes can't see. And now he sees me and now he don't. He thinks he will, but I know he won't. Bugner, they tell me you're good, but I'm twice as nice and I'll stick to your button like wine on rice.'

To laughter and applause he pulled on his dressing gown and stepped out of the ring. I went over to him and, slightly embarrassed, slipped the $300 into his hand. Without embarrassment he transferred it to the pocket of his robe and said: 'Come tomorrow. I'll show you around.'

He was as good as his word. 'This is the first and only unique fight camp for boxers, the only one in the world.' He had started it four years previously with an 'Abraham Lincoln-type log cabin' and expanded it. Now there was the gym, a large kitchen where twenty people could eat, two bunkhouses for the fighters, guest cottages, a stable and corral for horses, all built, cowboy fashion, from logs.

Ali proudly took me over to a large bell, high up on a wooden tower. He pulled the rope. 'This here looks like the Liberty Bell. I ring it every morning at 5am and the fellas who are still in bed come out and we go for a three-mile run.' I rather hoped he wasn't going to ask me to stay. 'Then I do three rounds on the heavy bag, three rounds on the speed bag and three rounds on the jump rope. Then when I'm paining I start my sparring. I'll be tired and exhausted but if I have to go fifteen rounds against Joe Bugner, I'll be ready.'

He had ringed the camp with huge rocks that carried the names of his heroes: Joe Louis, Sugar Ray Robinson, Rocky Marciano and many others including his favourite, on a twenty-ton lump of coal, the first black world heavyweight champion, Jack Johnson.

'My dad's called Jack Johnstone,' I mentioned.

The Champ stared at me: 'But you a white boy.'

Belinda joined us and showed off the campfire, where they and the children ate on summer nights, and their Shetland ponies, Heckle and Jekyll. The tender side of Ali came out as he spoke of his hopes for his son, Muhammad Ali Jr. 'I just want him to get educated. I regret that I should have studied harder in school. I'd like him to take up a trade, be a doctor or go to law school.' (In the event Jr. went to work in a funfair saying he wanted to be 'his own man'. It was Ali's daughter, Laila, who followed her father into the ring.)

On our final day's filming at Deer Lake, the Champ and his team arrived back from Philadelphia in their minibus. He was wearing a loud pink suit. 'Just bought this in "Big Man,"' he told me, adding with a grin, 'with your money.'

Ali's lack of education, I was to learn, was a continuing worry to him. 'One day I'd like to take up some courses, mainly on reading and writing. So I can study more.'

'What's wrong with your reading and writing at the moment?' I asked.

'I don't read too good and I can't spell, hardly at all. I can write my name but I'm well able to employ lawyers to deal with my contracts.'

Later, when we went to Harvard, where he was to address potential lawyers and scientists and, maybe, Presidents, he told them: 'I'm very flattered to come here because when I left high school you could never make me believe that one day I would be lecturing to people like you. I got out of high school with a D minus average and I only got that because I had won the Olympic gold medal.'

But, before that, we were to return to his home town of Louisville, Kentucky where his parents still lived. He hadn't been back for several years, although his parents had helped him create his Pennsylvania camp. His father, Cassius Clay Sr, a sign writer, had painted a 'Rules of the Kitchen' plaque on the wall and his mother, Odessa, advised on furnishings. 'They don't get along too well,' he warned me before we met them. 'They're getting a divorce.' (They never did.)

I flew early to Louisville because my researcher, Veronica, had tracked down the chairman of the group of Southern millionaires who had owned Cassius Clay from 1960 to 1966. William D. Faversham, now in his eighties, was as patrician as his name sounds; he would not have been out of place in *Gone with the Wind*.

'I'd seen him a lot as a kid,' he recalled. 'Gangling youngster, no punch, but able to flit around. But after he won the Olympic Gold I got hold of a black man – I suppose that's the word you have to use now – who worked for me and knew Cassius. He invited him and his parents and his lady attorney – she was murdered three years later, they never found out why – to my home and I had a programme worked out which they liked. I told them the type of people who were in my group were not the type of people who needed to make money.'

So the Louisville Sponsorship Group was born. They gave Cassius $10,000, ten men at $1,000 each (Faversham got in for free) and agreed to split his winnings 50–50 with him for six years. Whether they needed money or not, they made a great deal of it out of the boxer, not least when he knocked out Sonny Liston in 1964 to take the world title.

The 'Louisville Lip', as he became known, was always a supreme self-publicist, frequently predicting in which round he would knock his opponent out. In the early days there were rumours that Faversham would slip some cash to the opponent to make sure this happened. But, naturally, he denied that. And after the six years were up, Ali's predictions continued and they were just as accurate.

Ali had returned home for a show fight to raised money for the Muhammad Ali School of Boxing. It used to be called the Columbia Gym and he was eager to introduce me to Joe Martin, the policeman who used to run it.

The Louisville Lip returns home.

'He was twelve years old,' Joe recalled, 'and he came to me to report that someone had stolen his bike. He was real hostile and he wanted to whip whoever had done it. I said: "You'll never beat anybody if you don't know how to. Did anybody ever teach you to fight?" He said no and I said "Well, you should come here and learn before you start picking fights."'

So he took the boy to the Columbia Gym. That was how it all began. But, unknown to Joe, Cass would sneak away for additional training at the Presbyterian Community Center in the poorer east end of town. His first coach, Joe Martin, was waiting at the gym for him and they tearfully embraced. Joe was black, and still training poor kids. 'I put him in what was called the "Peanut" division,' he told me. 'There were fights every Saturday afternoon. He was twelve years old and weighed eighty-seven pounds when I put him in his first one. He lost that, pretty bad. But he trained harder than anyone else, and he got a little better.'

Clay had grown up in a segregated Louisville. When he returned in 1960 from the Olympics, blacks were still not allowed to book hotel rooms. A waitress refused to serve him in a diner so, disgusted, he threw his Gold Medal into the Ohio River.

A substantial number of people had gathered by Ali's old house the next day – word had travelled fast that the Champ was back in town. 'I get a feeling here that I don't get anywhere else in the world. They used to call me CC. I can avoid this if I want to by staying on my own property,' he whispered to me, 'but I read somewhere that service to others is the price we pay for our time here on Earth.' He picked on one man, a cheerful chap of his own age. 'Hey, Samson, you used to beat me up every day.' He threw a playful punch to the delight of the crowd. 'I told you I'd come back one day and take my revenge.'

His father, a mere spectator looking slightly down-at-heel, stood and watched his son. When he assured me that he had always known Cass would be world champion, from the age of twelve, his words were somewhat slurred. Cassius Sr had had his battles with alcohol and more than once fell foul of the law for drunken assault.

No such fate was likely to befall his son. The Mayor of Louisville had invited a group of people to his home (us included: Southern hospitality) to celebrate the return of the prodigal. When Ali rose to his feet to toast him, he spat out the contents of his glass. It was Chablis: not a Muslim drink.

Ali was always aware of my camera. 'This guy is from London. I got more fame in London than anywhere in the world. This is our mayor. He's a young, hippie mayor – not old and fat and bald-headed like the previous mayor. And this here's my wife, Belinda.

Now you girls in London, when I come back there, don't give me no trouble.'

The following day we flew up to Cambridge, Massachusetts, where Harvard Yard was so thronged when he (wearing 'my' pink suit, I was pleased to see) was driven through it in an open-topped jeep, that one might have thought that the university had closed down for the day. Ali had somewhat stunned the President of the Class of '75 by actually accepting his invitation to speak. It had, the President told me, become the hottest ticket the university had ever known. He introduced Ali with the words 'the best-known face on the planet'.

After some initial joshing, Ali looked at the primarily young faces in front of him and warned them: 'One day you're going to be wealthy and powerful, and when you make it we have a tendency to forget what we were yesterday and the worth of the people around us.' He then delivered what was tantamount to a sermon on the virtue of friendship – 'you're tested on many subjects here at school before you get out, but the examination on friendship is the most difficult thing in the world.'

I had been slightly surprised at Ali breaking off training to give the speech but his reason became more apparent when he told the students: 'The person who taught me all I'm talking to you now, all my spiritual wisdom, is the Honourable Elijah Muhammad.'

In 1975 the cities of both Boston and Louisville were involved in bussing protests. This was when black children from inner-city schools were bussed to schools in the suburbs to obtain racial balance. Ali was asked what he thought about it. He was vigorously opposed. 'God made us into nations by putting Chinese in China, Mexicans in Mexico, Hawaiians in Hawaii, Englishmen in England, Zairians in Zaire. I don't hate nobody. I just like my own. Ain't nothing to me like a pretty brown soul sister. And this nice handsome blond fellow down there, ain't nothing to him like a big, pretty blonde lady. And a Pling-tang-tong [Ali-speak for Oriental] ain't nothing to him like another Pling-tang-tong.'

His lack of prejudice only slipped a little when a voice from the back requested him to do the Rope-a-Dope. 'Someone's asking me to do the Rope-a-Dope. He paid a dollar to get in and he wants to see the Rope-a-Dope. He must be Jewish.' This, like all his wit, was greeted with rapture by the audience.

Later I went round to the Ritz-Carlton Hotel to congratulate Ali on his speech and say goodbye to him and Belinda. His last words to me were that he knew his life in boxing would be short 'probably four or five more years. Then, without the training, I can do all the things I've wanted to do, cut the grass, go out with the family, go to the beach. Like normal people.'

But it wasn't to be. True, he retired in 1979. But he returned to face the reigning champion. Larry Holmes, and not only lost but, for the first time in his life, was so hurt that Angelo Dundee refused to let him come out of his corner for the eleventh round.

Boxing had taken more of a toll on him than he realised and in 1984, when he was only forty-two, he was diagnosed with Parkinson's disease and his mind and body began to degenerate. But not his will. He was the USA's Honorary Flagbearer at the 2012 London Olympics and, although he was unable to carry the Stars and Stripes around the stadium, rose from his wheelchair to stand beside it.

Was he The Greatest? BBC sports viewers thought so; in December 1999 they voted him Man of the Millennium, giving him more votes than the three other finalists added together.

Personally, the ten days I spent with Ali were ten of the best.

7

The Cowboys: Clint Eastwood
and John Wayne

In 1976 the BBC went to town with numerous political and historical programmes for the American Bicentennial. They also wanted to celebrate Hollywood and I was asked to make profiles of two major stars. I had done an interview with John Wayne at the time of *True Grit* and had sent him an Aztec chess set as a thank you. So I called his son, Michael, who came back to me saying that his father, though not very well, would be honoured to represent his country.

If Wayne stood for the traditional Western, the man who had revived it in a very different style was Clint Eastwood. I knew from Merv Griffin, a friend and neighbour of his, that Clint wouldn't even appear on his chat show. He claimed he was not a wordsmith and it wasn't really his style. Nothing ventured, I asked Alistair MacLean if he could help me get to him. Eastwood had starred in MacLean's *Where Eagles Dare*. Alistair said he would see what he could do.

He must have done a good selling job as the following week I got a call from Clint's PR man, Dick Guttman, giving me a confidential number to phone the next Sunday. Eastwood answered. He had been well briefed, had actually seen my Ali documentary and asked what sort of programme I had in mind. Not particularly prepared for this, I blurted out that I would interview him, obviously, and hopefully Sergio Leone, who directed the Spaghetti Westerns, and Don Siegel, who did the *Dirty Harry* films, and critics such as Dilys Powell, of *The*

Sunday Times, who greatly liked him, and Pauline Kael, of the *New Yorker,* who didn't.

There was a pause and then he said: 'OK, we can do it in Carmel. I'm cutting a new film, *Josey Wales,* up there – well away from Hollywood. Get in touch with Joe Hyams at Warners to sort out the details.'

I arranged to meet Hyams in LA. He was a veteran fighter pilot with a crew cut whose job at Warners appeared to be to keep their biggest star sweet. Joe said he was surprised that Eastwood was prepared to give the BBC a day.

So Marcia and I caught up with Clint in his back garden, if several thousand acres of the Californian coast can be called that. He was soft-spoken and unfailingly polite, introducing me to his wife, Maggie, who was off to play tennis, little Alison, who had just turned three, and his bassett hound, Sydney. He also introduced me to two tiny deer whom someone had rescued from a storm and brought to Eastwood's home for sanctuary.

A gentle Clint feeds the foundling foals.

We just settled on a couple of rocks, rolled two cameras and started to talk. Clint had been well known on American television in the early sixties as Rowdy Yates in *Rawhide*. His film break famously came in *A Fistful of Dollars*. I had previously talked to the director, Sergio Leone, in EUR (Esposizione Universale Roma), Mussolini's purpose-built district south of Rome. He told me he had not heard of Eastwood but wanted to cast James Coburn in his film. This made sense as Coburn was one of *The Magnificent Seven*, a Western version of Kurosawa's *Seven Samurai* and *Fistful* was a remake of the same director's *Yojimbo*. But Coburn wanted too much money, as had Steve *Hercules Unchained* Reeves. A friend had told Leone to take a look at *Rawhide*. He ran an episode and liked what he saw. 'Clint said very little in the show I saw, but what struck me was his indolent way of moving, like a cat.'

'I got a call from my agent,' Eastwood recalled, 'asking me if I'd like to go to Europe and make an Italian-German-Spanish co-production of a remake of a Japanese film in the plains of Spain and I said: "Not particularly."'

And the rest is history and would have been so three years earlier in the States if Leone hadn't failed to clear the American rights. It had been apparent that Leone was pretty annoyed that Clint hadn't made more films with him and asked me, somewhat patronisingly: 'What's he doing now?' I didn't tell him that *Life* magazine had carried a cover photograph of him with the strapline 'The World's Most Popular Film Star'. But he probably knew that, anyway.

It was a combination of the Spaghettis and *Dirty Harry* that had propelled Eastwood into this position. Dirty Harry, a cop who takes the law into his own hands, had also propelled him into controversy. I told him Pauline Kael's view of Harry as bordering on being a psychopath: 'His affectlessness when he kills is the beginning of a new nihilism,' she had said. 'The scripts are shaped in terms of what these stars believe.'

Clint was not going to take this sitting down. 'I'd say she's crazy. It's not about a man who stands for violence. It's about a man who can't understand society tolerating violence, who stands for the rights of the victim. We convicted Nazis at Nuremberg for not adhering to a higher morality. Well, that's what Harry does.' Nevertheless, the film was used to train police in the Philippines, not a country where you would want to fall foul of the law.

We cantered through Clint's early life. Before *Rawhide* he was part of the Universal Talent School – and we talked about his directing debut in *Play Misty for Me*. 'Who wants to see Clint Eastwood play a disc jockey?' asked the Universal executives. 'Who wants to see him play anything?' he replied.

We broke for lunch at The Hog's Breath Inn, the restaurant he owned in Carmel. 'I kinda liked the names they gave to British pubs. We just tried to be a little more outrageous.' The menu offered a 'Dirty Harryburger' and a 'Fistful of T-Bone'. Clint kept his office and cutting rooms in the complex. He was generous to his employees: his editor, Ferris Webster, who cut *The Magnificent Seven*, worked for him in to his seventies. But less so to any producers in his company, Malpaso, who rose to profit participation in their films. They didn't stay too long, neither did his civil partner after his divorce, the actress Sondra Locke, (who was to expose his wealth in a court case he stupidly brought, and walked away with a chunk of it. Like so many actors he was not easily parted from his cash). The lunch bill for us all, including Marcia and the crew, came to $36. I was unsure whether to pick it up, this being his restaurant, but Clint pre-empted me by handing it to Hyams. 'Can we get this on Warners, Joe?'

Having finished the afternoon inquisition, I asked him if he would jog along the sandy beach at Carmel for my opening shot. We got there to find it still quite crowded. 'Do you think you'll be able to do it without people staring?' I asked him. 'We can get away with it once,' he replied in an experienced manner. Luckily I had two cameras and the sequence came out exactly as I had envisaged it on the first take.

My film, *The Man with No Name*, proved popular with more than eleven million viewers. The bulletin posted on the BBC's weekly notice board which noted the ratings, adding 'this is a remarkable figure for a documentary'.

Clint invited me to keep in touch and, over the years, made me lunch a few times in Malpaso's small bungalow on the Warner lot at Burbank. It was always avocado salad washed down with a couple of beers drunk from the bottle. I learned that he was quite content to sit and talk very little, like buddies do in cowboy films. When he came to Europe to direct *Firefox* on location in Vienna he asked me if I would be interested in making a film for the studio of him directing and I jumped at the chance. As a director he worked very quickly, a legacy of directing some episodes of *Rawhide*; very few second takes and on to the next set-up as soon as possible. Meryl Streep noted the same when they were making *The Bridges of Madison County* on location in Ohio. 'Sometimes he'd begin to shoot before the lights were fully set up but he'd say: "That was pretty good, let's move on." I think he had a date on the golf course at 4pm most days!'

He loved going to the Cannes Festival ever since, as a Warner executive unkindly confided to me, 'the French began to refer to his films as his oeuvre.' He didn't stay in the Hotel du Cap with the other stars but on a yacht in the Old Port. However, he indulged himself by eating in a different three-star Michelin restaurant every night.

Clint later came to London to open Warners new multiplex in Leicester Square. There was dinner afterwards at the Arts Club in Mayfair. I was delayed, being involved in the television coverage, so my wife was introduced to him on her own. 'You're much thinner than my husband,' she remarked. 'Yes,' Clint agreed. 'But Iain's got more hair than me.' The evening ended with everybody, stars – like Walter Matthau and Faye Dunaway – and mere mortals alike, gathered round the piano with Clint and Dudley Moore tinkling out old favourites and singing some of them. They were quite well oiled when they staggered off down Dover Street, little and large, arm in arm. I wondered what passers-by made of the sight.

Unexpectedly, the Wayne programme created rather more problems. Michael Wayne, film producer and John's son, had suggested we film a weekend when John Wayne was being honoured in Chicago and then maybe do some more in Burbank. As it turned out, the Chicago events were, well, uneventful. Wayne was lauded at the University of Notre Dame as 'the most popular and respected movie actor of all time' and when he received the Freedom of the City, Mayor Daley told him: 'Your name is synonymous with the enthusiasm that built this great nation over the past two hundred years.' Certainly, wherever he went people would call out things like 'You're a real American and what could be better.' But his speeches were polite and short and self-effacing – not the sort of stuff documentary profiles are made of.

I flew to Burbank to cover Wayne on *The Shootist*. I was not to know then that this was the last day John Wayne would ever work on a movie. The film, with not a little irony, was about a gunfighter dying of cancer who finally dies by the bullet, in the manner in which he lived. I knew the director, Don Siegel, from my Clint profile film. 'Duke's in a pretty filthy mood today,' he confided. Indeed he was, countermanding much of Siegel's direction, even in his death scene when, after a glance through the camera at his stand-in, he warned Don: 'I'm going to make goddamn sure you don't shoot up my nose.' When he had to deliver the line to his prospective undertaker: 'You're going to fill me up with that goddam juice', Wayne announced to the crew, 'I can't say it without it sounding like "goddam Jews".' This failed to produce much laughter among some of the crew, nor my assistant, Marcia, who is Jewish.

And that was it. Wayne had been courteous but was not well enough to make the wrap party, which we filmed. *Hamlet* without the Prince. I had barely enough material to make a fifteen-minute item for a magazine programme. John Wayne's reputation will never die but I could see that mine was going to take a substantial knock when I returned to the BBC virtually empty-handed. I composed my apology to the Controller in my head as I drove back to my hotel, the Sunset Marquis. The receptionists there were attractively impudent. Jonathan Miller, when he was working in LA, said he used to get the greeting on returning to the Marquis in the evening: 'Nobody called. Nobody loves you.' But somebody had called. Pat Casey, John Wayne's assistant and girlfriend. I rushed to my room and called her back.

'Duke wants to speak to you,' was all she said. The familiar growl came on the line. 'Haven't been feeling too good and I know you haven't got a lot of material for your show,' Wayne said. 'Why don't you and your girl get down to Acapulco by April 8th. Pat and me and the kids are going to take a trip on *The Wild Goose* (his converted minesweeper). You can bring your camera on board for a day and we'll do a few things. Stay at the Hilton and I'll call you.'

Wayne had once said to me that your luck can turn around on a dime and mine just had. I had come to learn that the bellicose Wayne was a courteous and thoughtful man.

By coincidence, my old friend and *New York Times* correspondent, Alan Riding, was already there. Howard Hughes, the reclusive billionaire, had rented the top two floors of the Princess Hotel, where it was rumoured he lived in some squalor. It was now thought that he had died and that his body had been secretly flown out of Acapulco to Houston, Texas. His aides certainly didn't want the Mexican government to extract death duties.

Among the camera crews camped outside was Domingo Rex, filming for ABC, but who would join me on Wayne's boat so we were able to plan some shots. It was he who coined the Mexican joke 'Howar Hugh?' 'Very well, thank you', which seemed funnier at the time.

On the morning of my thirty-third birthday, 8 April 1976, Alan and Marcia clubbed together to give me a greatly unwanted parachute ride. You ran down the beach and a speedboat whisked you a few hundred feet into the air, ending up looking into the thirty-fourth-floor bedrooms of the skyscraper hotels that fringe Acapulco Bay. Actually, it was unexpectedly exhilarating.

But when we got back to the hotel, an excited receptionist informed me that John Wayne had been calling me all morning. I telephoned him back. 'Where've you been?' he demanded. 'We're all about to sit down to lunch. Get yourselves over to the Club de Yates.'

I didn't recognise Wayne when Marcia and I stumbled into the saloon where he and his family had already begun to demolish their lobsters. 'What kept you?' demanded the familiar voice coming from the bald man in the middle. I had never seen him without his wig before but I had seen the classic encounter at Harvard when a student had yelled at him: 'Mr Wayne, is that real hair?' And he had shouted back: 'Yes, it is. It's not my hair, but it's real hair.'

'Where were you?' he asked. 'We were down on the beach with a friend of mine from *The New York Times*,' I explained. 'I'm surprised anybody has friends on *The New York Times*,' he growled back. 'Left-wing intellectuals'. And then, as if to mollify me, added: 'Although Bosley Crowther used to give me pretty fair reviews.' (Crowther had been the paper's film critic for nearly thirty years until 1967.)

With Duke at the table were his three youngest children by his wife, Pilar: Aissa (twenty), Marisa (ten) and Ethan (fourteen) who had been named after Wayne's favourite character, Ethan Edwards, whom he played in John Ford's *The Searchers*. Also at the table was a short, chubby guy who, I was to learn, was one of Duke's best friends. Danko Gurovich, a former motorcycle cop, had built up a string of motels in Arizona where Wayne had property investments. He and Danko had discovered a mutual love of cards, practical jokes and tequila.

Wayne showed Marcia and me down to our cabin which had only one double bed. As I've said, we were friends but not lovers, not that I told Duke that. He knew that all real men slept with their assistants, as he did with Pat.

The Wild Goose was a 135-foot converted US Navy minesweeper. Wayne had let certain military trappings remain and added to them with innumerable regimental plaques and flags from troops serving in Vietnam. They appreciated his continuing support, against the wave of public sentiment. Wayne himself had always felt more than a little guilty for not fighting for the country he loved. In 1943, when he should have been called up, he was thirty-six and the father of three children so got an indefinite deferment. Instead he volunteered for the United Services Organization Camp Show tours in the South Pacific to entertain the troops.

The Wild Goose meant the world to him. 'When I step on board, I yawn,' he told me. 'I can escape everything.' Indeed it was a perfect place for a film star to find privacy and play with his children but there wasn't too much of that on this trip as he was still unwell, so he read and rested and played cards with Danko.

The children, on the other hand, knew how to enjoy themselves. They, together with Marcia and myself, swam and water-skied and fished and sunbathed. Ethan showed me his father's cache of weapons. He had a .22 rifle for shooting sharks, shotguns for hunting when they went onshore, a spring-loaded catapult for trap-shooting and an automatic-16 carbine for good measure. Ethan also advised me the most comfortable place to sleep was to bring a mattress and sheet up to the deck.

I did this to give Marcia some privacy. But the Pacific night was so stiflingly hot that it wasn't long before she and Aissa and Melissa joined us under the moon. In the morning we were awakened by a Mexican police launch as six heavily armed policemen climbed on board and settled themselves at the outdoor table.

'What are they looking for?' I asked the ship's captain, Peter Stein.

'Drugs,' he replied.

'Surely John Wayne is the last person likely to be smuggling drugs into America.'

'I know,' he said. 'What they really want is Duke's autograph.'

That evening we put in at the port of Zihuatanejo, where we adults had been invited to dinner at the home of Wayne's friend, Pedro, the Eastern Airlines representative. As Wayne walked among the local Mexicans from the tender to the car, they treated him with polite respect and he treated them almost as children. In the drive up to the hillside home, I realised he might have had a little too much tequila early on as he began to sing:

Duke Wayne at home on the Sierra Madre Range in Durango, Mexico.

I'm mad about the boy,
On the silverscreen
He melts my foolish heart in every single scene,
Although I'm quite aware that here and there
are traces of the cad
About the boy.

'That's your fellow countryman, Cary Grant,' he said, poking me in the ribs.

'Surely it's Noël Coward,' I countered.

'Nope. It's that English faggot Mr Archie Leach Grant.'

This was not an argument that I wished to pursue so I changed the subject, certain I was right. (But I wasn't, not completely. I looked it up when I got home. Noël had written the song about Cary after seeing him in a movie in 1932 – probably *Blonde Venus* with Marlene Dietrich.)

Duke got pretty drunk that night – too much of what he termed 'the who-hit-John' – and must have woken in a foul mood as the first thing I saw the next day was him throwing Aissa's pyjamas into the Pacific. 'That's what happens to girls who don't keep their rooms tidy,' he warned her. This did not augur well as it was the day Domingo was due to come and film.

As I might have surmised from what he did to Don Siegel, Wayne pretty well took over the direction of my documentary, staging scenes as in a movie rather than permitting the family to be observed.

At lunch, Ethan was commanded to say grace – 'Lord, we thank you for this food and letting us come down here and having so much fun, which most other peoples can't do–' until Wayne interrupted him with the words: 'Amen. Dig in!'

Duke staged a fairly stilted scene where he discussed the route in Captain Peter's cabin and a more tender one on the bridge with little Melissa where he pointed to the white rocks of Ixtapa saying that 'Beneath them, in this Bicentennial year, we capture the Red Coats, although these red coats are really lobsters.'

By the time he had staged the firing of the sunset gun and the folding of the Stars and Stripes, shouting at the sailors: 'You don't have to finish it, we'll be back on me' – something I left in the finished film to exculpate myself from some of the direction, Wayne closed the show with a salute to camera and the words: 'Well, another day and, let's hope, another dollar.'

I could see I would be hung out to dry by peers and critics alike if this was all there was, so, with a slightly hesitant heart, I persuaded him to do a bit more interview and led him on to the subject of women's lib and minorities. A red rag and a blue touchpaper combined, this caused Duke to erupt. 'You, and your liberal colleagues,' he jabbed with his finger, 'probably don't believe in opening doors and tipping your hat to ladies. And if some of those minorities would drop their hyphenated-American status and realise they're better off here than anywhere else in the world, they'd stop their whining and bellyaching.'

I felt a bit guilty about this, but hoped I had avoided the *The Waltons* feel the documentary was beginning to acquire. I knew that Duke's outbursts were short-lived, and when we sat having a drink before dinner he told me a story of how a new actor on a 'Pappy' Ford film had asked the legendary director for another take of his scene which he thought wasn't quite right. This was unheard-of but Ford agreed. After the retake he asked the guy if he was now happy with it. The actor said he was. So Ford strode to the camera, opened the magazine and tore out the exposed strip of negative – at this point Wayne handed me a strip of Domingo's discarded film which he had been hiding – and gave it to the actor saying: 'If you like it, you can have it.' How I wish my crew was there to capture that but they were long gone. In the years to come, producing audience shows, I was to realise that the gems frequently came not during the taping, but in the Green Room afterwards.

Most people can remember where they were when they heard President Kennedy had died. But I can remember as vividly where I was when I heard about John Wayne's death. It was only three years after our trip: 12 June 1979. I was staying in the Atlantic Tower Hotel, Liverpool, where I was making a film about the 'Fifth Beatle', Pete Best, who was replaced as their drummer by Ringo. He was a gentle chap, happily married, worked in a Jobcentre and played rugby on Saturday afternoons. I was getting dressed when on television the news was broken of Duke's death. 'That's a shame,' I thought, and began to do up my sneakers. And then I choked. And broke down in tears, an experience I've rarely had before or since. I don't know why; it wasn't as if we were friends or anything. Maybe it was because it was the end of an era. When you cry, you often do it, not for the departed, but for yourself.

8

On Location, Holland ...
A Bridge Too Far

In the second half of the twentieth century, no force was more formidable in British films than Richard Attenborough: a well-known film star, an Oscar-winning director (for *Gandhi*), head of BAFTA, the BFI, the National Film School, the British Screen Advisory Council and sixty further worthwhile bodies. If you wanted to assemble a meeting of the Great and the Good, you would only need to invite Dickie into the room.

Everybody in movies knew Dickie Attenborough and Dickie Attenborough knew everybody. Not necessarily by name, hence his widespread use of the epithet 'Darling'. But he knows me by name, not least because we nearly came to the steps of the Royal Courts of Justice in a bitter legal dispute. But it was settled, and forgotten and forgiven. I know this because he bumped into my wife in a supermarket near his home in the south of France the following year and personally guided her to the iceberg lettuce whilst solicitously asking her about me.

He has been lampooned on television, first by Monty Python and taken up by *Spitting Image*, as a man who cries a lot at award ceremonies, but today his life is blighted by genuine sadness. He and his wife, Sheila Sim, who had met at RADA and were in the original production of *The Mousetrap* sixty years ago, lost their daughter, Jane, and their granddaughter, Lucy, in the Thailand tsunami of December 2004. At over ninety, in ill health and wheelchair bound, his recent years have been a tragic contrast to his glittering past.

In 1976 Attenborough was to form an unlikely partnership with the maverick producer Joseph E. Levine, who engaged him to direct *A Bridge Too Far*. Joe Levine was every lack of inch a movie mogul. Short, Jewish, imperious, tough talking, he was the polar opposite of Dickie who was polite, friendly, articulate and a gentleman – except for the fact that they were both, in their fashion, ruthless. Joe had made his name in the early sixties by buying the Italian sword-and-sandals epic *Hercules* starring Steve Reeves, dubbing it and submerging it in publicity for its American distribution. It opened simultaneously in 175 cinemas in the New York area alone. Joe was on record as saying: 'It was one of the worst movies I had ever seen. But you can fool all of the people if the publicity is right.' And it was; he was one of the first distributors to use extensive television advertising. *Hercules* cost him $120,000 to buy and made him $15 million.

He observed the success of Darryl Zanuck's *The Longest Day* a couple of years later which earned more than five times its budget. This owed not a little to the fact that Zanuck had crammed the movie with star names: John Wayne, Robert Mitchum, Henry Fonda, Sean Connery, Richard Burton, Peter Lawford, Kenneth More and Paul Anka (who also wrote the theme music).

Joe cunningly courted Cornelius Ryan who wrote that book and followed it up with *Bridge*. Irish-born Ryan had been a war correspondent and interviewed hundreds of men who had participated in Operation Market Garden to provide a comprehensive history, seen not just from the generals, but from the grunts on the ground. After D-Day in June 1944, the Allied advance on Berlin had been slow with strong German resistance. It was essential to get the tank corps across the Rhine and, to this end, General Montgomery proposed a mass parachute jump to liberate the German-held bridges. The operation was code named Market Garden.

Joe Levine's art was to fill the proposed film with thirteen major stars and pre-sell it around the world on the strength of their names. When he got to Japan the auction was won by a distributor who offered him X million dollars up front, but added 'if Redford's in it, I will give you two times X'. So the Magnificent Thirteen became the Magnificent Fourteen as the screenwriter, William Goldman, expanded the part of Major Julian Cook, and Redford's reported $500,000 for two weeks' work was easily covered by the $2X Japanese advance. (When Sean Connery learned of this deal he went on strike until his own salary was upped to parity.)

Thus, during the long, sweltering summer of 1976, the Magnificent Fourteen – Robert Redford, Sean Connery, Dirk Bogarde, Ryan O'Neal, Gene Hackman, Edward Fox, Michael Caine, Maximilian Schell, Elliott Gould, James Caan, Liv Ullmann, Hardy Kruger, Anthony Hopkins, Laurence Olivier – and me – turned up at various times at the small Dutch town of Deventer which was to play Arnhem in the film. At Dickie's suggestion, Gordon Arnell, the film's publicist, tempted me with the promise that not only would I be able to interview all the stars but also most of the officers and men who had actually participated in the Battle of Arnhem and would be invited to the location. It was an attractive offer, not least because I would be paid at American rates. (I didn't know at the time that Joe had already sold my documentary to NBC for a million dollars as an 'educational film' – part of his package for the overall TV rights.)

The main man missing was General Frederick 'Boy' Browning who had died in 1965. His widow, the novelist Daphne du Maurier, subsequently attacked Dirk Bogarde for his slightly camp portrayal of her late husband, although Browning was given to flourishes, such as designing his own uniform made of *barathea* with a false Uhlan-style front. It was Browning who commanded Operation

Market Garden in 1944 under Montgomery's plan to speed up the Allied liberation of Europe by an airborne drop on the Germans at Arnhem. The paratroopers would liberate the bridge over the Rhine there, enabling the Tanks Corps to drive onwards to the German border.

'Boy' was sceptical of the scheme. He asked Monty how long his men would have to hold the bridge. His commander assured him it would be two days, by then General Horrocks's tanks would arrive and take over. 'We can hold it for four,' Browning replied. 'But I think we may be going a bridge too far.'

His words were tragically prophetic. Of the 35,000 men dropped at Arnhem, 17,000 didn't come home: dead or taken prisoner.

Dirk Bogarde told me he had actually served in Arnhem as one of Monty's intelligence officers, chosen for the assignment because he spoke fluent Dutch: Derek Jules Gaspard Ulric Niven van den Bogaerde.

People were quartered in the one-storey Keizerskroon Hotel in Appeldoorn. On one of my trips to the location I was given Laurence Olivier's old room. Across the corridor were Ryan O'Neal and his then paramour, Anjelica Huston. A wonderful, fragrant, intoxicating aroma came from under their door in the evenings, a couple of sniffs and your worries evaporated. I wondered if Larry had taken a few.

The modern reader may wonder how Ryan, playing Brigadier General Gavin, happened to be part of this galaxy of stars. The fact is that after *Love Story* and *What's Up Doc?* with Barbra Streisand, in 1973 he came second after Clint Eastwood in the Annual US Top Ten Box Office Stars. One may equally wonder why an actor aged thirty-six would be playing a general. The fact is that 'Jumping' Jim Gavin was only thirty-six when he was made Brigadier General in command of the US 82nd Airborne. Gavin had led the successful jump on Sainte-Mère-Église on D-Day (he was played by Robert Ryan in *The Longest Day*) and he and his men took the vital bridge at Nijmegen over the River Waal which fed into the Rhine. It was the last bridge before Arnhem.

President Kennedy subsequently made Gavin his Ambassador to France where he played a vital part in healing the rift with de Gaulle. Still in his sixties, Jim now ran Anderson Consulting in Boston and arrived on set, youthful and slim, in a dapper business suit.

I sat beside him and his wife, Jean, in a camouflaged hideout to watch the ground action following the jump (which would be shot later). He told me about his life which epitomised the American Dream. An orphan who was adopted by a coal miner and his wife in Pennsylvania, he had a rudimentary education and left school at fifteen to work as a miner and later in a shoe store. He felt the army was the only place where he could get an education and lied about his age to enlist, later making corporal. He would get up at 4am to revise in the basement latrines, making it into West Point. It was there, studying German tactics, he became more and more convinced of the importance of airborne operations.

'At the Market Garden briefing in General Browning's room, I was amazed that [Major General] Urquhart was going to drop eight miles from the bridge at Arnhem,' Gavin told me. 'I had been through three parachute operations before – Sicily, Italy and Normandy – and I was really concerned. If they had landed nearer, it was a takeable bridge. I intended to land as near to Nijmegen Bridge as possible. We jumped near a triangular patch of woods which – we didn't know it from our intelligence – had about a thousand Germans in them. A machine gun opened up on us and one of my captains took out the gunner with his rifle. I asked him how he managed it and he said: "Training, General.

I could see the white spot between the line of his helmet and the sights of his gun. Took the top of his head off."'

Gavin had had a lot of experience in fighting over bridges. He knew that if you managed to back the Germans up, they would withdraw and blow them up. 'There's only one way to get a bridge in war and that's to get both ends of it. So I contacted General Horrocks who was advancing with the XXX Tank Corps and said: "You must have some boats somewhere down the column." He had and our men from the 3rd Battalion crossed the River Waal, under fire and against the tide. They showed the greatest heroism of any of my men. We got the bridge intact and waved the tanks across. When we finished this battle I talked to the old-timers who had been through the war with me, because there is a certain drainage point of your courage and yourself. They were keen to do a fifth jump to take Berlin, but this had been our toughest battle. I guess it was the most satisfying moment in my life.'

As I said goodbye to Jim I realised I had been in the company of a brave man and a brilliant soldier. If his advice had been heeded, the tragedy of Arnhem might have been averted and also that of The Battle of the Bulge in the Ardennes the following winter which cost more American lives than any other in the war.

Major General Roy Urquhart, who had commanded the British 1st Airborne's drop on (or near) Arnhem, had been an infantryman and this was his first jump. He was a tall, debonair seventy-five year old when I met him and much resembled his friend, David Niven (an ex-Commando), in speech, manner and moustache. Dickie had asked him to be an advisor on the movie, sending him William Goldman's script in advance. 'I didn't care for it in some places at all,' Urquhart said. 'I'm not being disrespectful but it was obviously written by an American. One conversation I had with General Browning couldn't have been less real. I couldn't imagine either of us using the words or expressions in the script. I think Sir Richard Attenborough incorporated most of my suggestions.

'I don't think Market Garden was a folly. I don't accept the criticism that it was a complete flop and waste of lives. The two American divisions got their objectives. We didn't do so well at the top end. We figured that it wasn't on to drop people on the bridge at Arnhem in daylight. So our dropping zone was a hell of a long way away. Far too far I think. Doing it again, one would have thought differently.'

Major General Urquhart was played in the film by Sean Connery but he had never heard of the actor, despite the fact that Connery had by then played James Bond six times. 'I'm not a great cinema-goer,' Urquhart told me. 'In fact I'd never seen him in the cinema at all. But my wife and daughters were thrilled when they heard he was going to play me. When we met, I thought there was a remarkable resemblance in some ways ... especially from the back.'

Even among a cast as star laden as *Bridge*, one man stood out: Robert Redford. He was regularly feted as the world's most handsome man and, after achieving movie immortality as The Sundance Kid, came to Holland as the number-one star with his picture, along with that of Dustin Hoffman as Carl Bernstein, on the cover of nearly every magazine as Bob Woodward in *All the President's Men*.

Redford was escorted on to the set by our location manager, Norton Knatchbull, and greeted like royalty by Sir Richard. (Actually Norton, now Lord Brabourne, was a bit closer to royalty, the Queen having spent her honeymoon at his parents' house and Prince Philip being his godfather.) At forty, Bob was a little old to be playing twenty-seven-year-old Major Julian Cook, who led the

Robert Redford on his way to war in *A Bridge Too Far.*

Waal crossing, but one suspects that even if he had been seventy he would still have got the part.

Redford was conscious of how much his looks contributed to his fame and even brought his make-up man with him. Before the shot where he was to lead his men across the Waal, he checked his hair and make-up in the reflected lens of our documentary camera. 'Are you running?' he finally asked my cameraman, Martin Bell. Martin nodded and Redford immediately turned away.

A furious Attenborough took me to one side. 'Can't you understand?' he remonstrated, 'Redford's meant to be a butch soldier in this scene and you show him checking his make-up. Now piss off.' We pissed off.

Meanwhile, back at the lake near the Keizerskroon Hotel, a lesser sort of trouble took place. Ryan O'Neal's nine-year-old daughter, Tatum, had pinched a boat, rowed to the middle of the lake and lost her oars. It was the first episode of a week of wild misbehaviour from the girl whom Gordon Arnell, the film's publicist, renamed Tantrum O'Neal, a name that stuck.

I sensed Redford would have welcomed some company in Holland. I was chatting to him on the set on another day and an American lady came up to him and said: 'My friend really fancies you.' 'Well, I wish she was here,' Bob replied. He went to the production office that evening and invited Gordon's astonished assistant, June, out to dinner.

There was only one man missing on that September Sunday morning in 1976 when they stopped the busy Rhine-bound traffic of the Waal for an hour to recreate the gallant action. That was the commander, Julian Cook himself. I asked Dickie why he wasn't there. His reply was diffident: 'We gather he's rather a grumpy fellow today. This is difficult enough without him complaining. I wouldn't bother with him, if I were you.'

But I did. Cook had remained a regular soldier and had retired only a few years previously. I contacted the Pentagon pension department and they said they'd see what they could do. When I got back to my hotel three days later there was a message that a Colonel Cook had called me from his home in South Carolina. I rang him back. He didn't sound at all grumpy. He had done a long interview with Cornelius Ryan for the book. He'd even had a letter from the production company telling him about the film and had offered his services as a consultant. But then nothing.

By chance a neighbour was sent Dutch newspapers which included a piece about the film. 'Guess who's playing me?' Cook, now sixty, asked his children. 'Gabby Hayes? Walter Brennan?' they variously replied. 'No,' said their father, proudly. 'Robert Redford.' We talked on the phone about his role as Battalion Commander and he made it clear that he hadn't volunteered any of his men to make the crossing. But they all did it anyway.

I didn't ask him directly why he wasn't here in Holland but it was soon apparent. 'Gavin didn't particularly care for me. He had no respect for me. He relieved me as liaison officer.' It was clear that this movie set wasn't big enough for both of them. But Julian could still cherish his Distinguished Service Cross: the second highest medal for extreme gallantry in the US Military.

Very much the main drama in the film was, of course, at Arnhem. As Roy Urquhart mentioned: 'We didn't do so well at the top end,' namely the attempt to hold on to the bridge. It was largely British with a backup of Polish troops. William Goldman had managed to squeeze five top American stars into the story (with Gene Hackman, admittedly, playing a Pole), but this may have proved the film's undoing.

Obviously the movie's parachute drop had to be done by professionals and the British 16th Airborne Division volunteered for the job as a training exercise. Today their numbers would have been multiplied in post-production by Computer Generated Imagery (CGI) but, thirty-five years ago, mattes (the blending of two pictures together) were the most that could be done and a lot of that was to put missing gliders into the scene (they were an extinct breed and too expensive to build). To help cover the jump I took an additional camera and my place on one of the camera planes, a Dakota C47 with a side removed to enable us to film. A large oil slick began to make its way towards me down the floor from just behind the cockpit.

'We're in trouble,' I shouted to the pilot. 'There's oil all over the place back here.'

'Of course there's oil all over the place,' he shouted back. 'It's a fucking Dakota.'

Although nobody was jumping from our plane, I felt so airsick I certainly felt like jumping. We had a parachute-training instructor on board who mentioned: 'You look a little white, sir. Would you like one of these pills?' I swallowed it gratefully. 'Bumpy old things, Dakotas,' he said.

The 16th Airborne were a little braver and jumped into simulated German fire from 800 foot, much lower than their accustomed 1,200 foot in training. With multiple cameras, the result was spectacular.

But back then, on 17 September 1944, the trouble began. General Browning had told the 1st Airborne they would be greeted by 'Hitler Youth and old men on bicycles'; instead they were met by two crack SS Panzer Armoured Divisions, the 9th and 10th. It had been planned that 9,000 troops would hold the bridge at Arnhem for two days until XXX Tank Corps arrived. In the event, only then Lieut-Colonel John Frost and about 400 of his men made it to the bridge. The Germans expected them to surrender but Frost and his men held out for an incredible four days and nights before they ran out of ammunition. Around 250 wounded men were removed on subsequent days during two-hour truces granted by the Germans, but only 100 British Paras were left at the end. A wounded Frost became a legend amongst his men and throughout the army.

Johnnie Frost came to watch the recreation of those days of hell thirty-two years later and I asked him if it was upsetting. 'Surprisingly, not really,' he said. 'I always found in life that you forget the bad things and remember the good things. And there was a wonderful sense of glory, if you like, here.'

Anthony Hopkins played him in the movie. 'He seems to be growing a little bit more like me every day,' Frost told me. 'He seems to be biting out his orders better all the time.'

Hopkins recalled: 'I was doing a scene where I was running across a street under gunfire. And Lieut-Colonel Frost said to me: "You're running too fast." I said: "I'm running too fast?" "Yes," he said. "You wouldn't run that fast. You'd have to show the Germans and your men contempt for danger."'

Attenborough directed the combat on the bridge with flair and energy, greatly aided by his camera operator, Peter MacDonald. With Peter on board, almost anybody can direct a movie. (Indeed, throughout the *Harry Potter* series, Warner Bros, after viewing the rushes, would send him in to pick up the extra shots the studio thought necessary.)

I was intrigued by the truces. Why? It was a bit like the Christmas Day football in the first world war. After the movie had finished filming I flew to Stuttgart to meet that man who had agreed to these compassionate truces for the British wounded. *Obersturmbannführer* Walter Harzer's study was devoted to the war: pictures, citations, books and files of letters (some, I noted, from South America.) A sturdy man with a duelling scar, he greeted me with polite formality. At thirty-two he had led the 9th Panzers on the harsh Russian front, 'Where,' he said, 'there were no rules.' He had been a student in England before the war and told his men at Arnhem: 'Now you are fighting the British and must behave with honour. You do not fire on their stretcher-bearers. They have neither the medical staff nor equipment to deal with so many wounded. So I ordered the two-hour truce on successive days. My men helped take the British wounded to the St Elizabeth Hospital where British and German troops were treated by English and Dutch and German surgeons.'

At the end of the war, Harzer was taken prisoner by the Russians to face his inevitable fate. Then, to his surprise, an order came through that he was to be the prisoner of an American general. 'Gavin had heard what I did at Arnhem and saved me.' As I left Harzer's house, he shouted after me: 'You tell Jim that you met me and give him my regards.'

Montgomery had little experience of parachute operations but this one had been postponed sixteen times and, to save face, he insisted on it going ahead. Browning was shown conclusive photographic evidence of the Panzer divisions in the area by an intelligence officer. But Montgomery ignored it and fired the messenger who had brought the bad news. Arnhem was a catastrophe waiting to happen.

The film was not a great success, either. It cost $25m and brought in much less than that at the American box office. Cinema owners there and distributors abroad, who had paid advances, lost a lot of money. The official reason was that Americans, especially, didn't want to see a movie about a British defeat. But it went deeper than that. *The Longest Day* had worked because it was made a mere fifteen years after the war, an event still seared in people's memories. In 1977, Arnhem wasn't. Moreover the day of multi-story war epics was over. If Goldman had focussed on an involving, emotional human story then it might have worked. Spielberg showed how that could be done in *Saving Private Ryan* twenty years later.

Oh, and that spat between me and Dickie and Joe Levine. When they learned I was going to publish my diary of that summer, they threatened to sue for breach of copyright. That meant I would have to pay my publisher more money than I had to pulp the books. Eventually Dickie mediated a truce. If I removed any photographs and stopped a second print run, they would drop the case.

Instead, Joe published the photographs in a book of my interviews written by William Goldman. I am sure William would have been intrigued to have talked to Frost and Horrocks and Harzer in the flesh.

9

Richard Whiteley … Close Encounters with the Salkinds

At the weekends I would frequently stay with Richard Whiteley in Yorkshire. He had returned to his roots from ITN and now fronted YTV's nightly programme, *Calendar*. To begin with I stayed with his parents and his bubbly sixth-form sister, Helen. The Whiteleys had been opulent mill owners in Bradford for three generations but the textile trade went into decline with the arrival of synthetic fibres and Richard's father, Kenneth, had to sell up. As Richard put it: 'One day he went to work in a Bentley and returned home in a Volkswagen.'

Helen was never one to acknowledge any fall in fortune. When Richard was the subject of *This Is Your Life* in 1996 she told the story of how his pet hamster, Kimi, died while he was away at school and she buried her in the garden. She wrote to her brother informing him of its sad demise. Richard rushed to the phone and shouted: 'She's not dead, she's hibernating!' Helen told Michael Aspel how she dug Kimi up and, as instructed by her brother, put Kimi in the Aga where the hamster revived and went on to enjoy a longish and happy life. 'Typical Helen,' Richard said to me after the show. 'We were never able to afford an Aga. It was a cheap Esse stove.'

But that was more than thirty years in the future. He bought a cottage outside Masham, home of the unique beer, Theakston's Old Peculier. I helped him do it up, fortified by healthy walks in his beloved Wensleydale and unhealthy evenings with too much Old Peculier. Richard built up a firm body of local friends, none of whom

Richard Whiteley on Ilkley Moore bar tat.

was in the media. One in particular was a much sought-after physiotherapist, Charley Barley. Richard succeeded in winning her affections through her mother. In the summer Mrs Barley liked to end the day by contemplating the North Sea from her bright-blue beach hut in Filey, near Scarborough. On occasion, Richard would join her, bringing with him a bottle of British sherry, Mrs B's favourite tipple, and she became convinced of his charms – and soon her daughter was too. Richard would have liked to marry Charley but he delayed too long and she went off with a footballer, a prototype WAG.

He quickly married his next girlfriend, a curly-haired, well-proportioned interior designer called Candy, the daughter of a wealthy heart surgeon. I was his best man and in my speech joked how Richard had tried to bribe the vicar to cut the 'forsaking all others' promise out of his marriage oath. The wedding reception was held in Candy's parents' garden and her mother spent much of the afternoon washing up paper plates and drying them in the oven. This love of paper plates seemed to run in the family. When Richard returned home to their Leeds flat after doing *Calendar*, only eight months later, it was to discover a note from Candy, indicating that she had not forsaken all others and was gone, taking most things with her save for a paper plate on which she left a small amount of instant coffee for his breakfast.

In Soho, I screened *The Arnhem Report* for Joseph Levine and Dickie Attenborough and rather too many of their colleagues. Addressing them beforehand, I began to explain that there were shots still missing, it hadn't been colour-corrected ... but Joe cut me off with the words: 'Ah, the director's speech.' At the end, it seemed to have gone down OK: nobody wanted any changes and some actually thought it rather good. One was a short young man who seemed to have grown a moustache to make himself look older. He introduced himself with the words: 'My name is Ilya Salkind.'

Of course, I knew the name as it had been on the guest list, for one thing. I was a bit staggered that Ilya looked so young. (I later learned that he was twenty-nine to my thirty-three.) But he and his father, Alexander, were famous in the industry for releasing *The Three Musketeers* in 1973 and then *The Four Musketeers* in 1974 without remembering to tell the actors, including Oliver Reed, Richard Chamberlain, Charlton Heston and Raquel Welch, that they were actually making two films on the same shoot, not just one. They had been contracted, probably legally, to do a certain number of weeks on location playing named parts. But writs flew and settlements were reached although the Salkinds triumphed as the stars were paid much less than they would have been for two movies. This caused the Screen Actors' Guild to put 'The Salkind Clause' in all future contracts to prevent such chicanery happening again.

Ilya treated me to lunch and told me he and his father had bought the rights to the *Superman* comics. I had already known about this from the trade magazines. They had hired Mario Puzo (Oscar winner for *The Godfather*) to write the script. He had come up with a classic structure but unfortunately it was 400 pages long (most film scripts are 100 to 150 pages) so Hollywood writers Robert Benton and David Newman had been engaged to make it manageable. They had actually written a (not very successful) Broadway musical: *It's a Bird ... It's a Plane ... It's Superman,* although Benton went on to cop a couple of Oscars for *Kramer vs Kramer* for both his writing and as best director.

The search for an actor to play Superman generated its own publicity. They tested the Olympic Gold-winning athlete, Bruce Jenner, later to find fame as Stepfather Kardashian, but thought he was too young. Redford turned them down and Ilya even auditioned his own dentist. But, after seeing the usual hundreds of candidates, they settled on a twenty-four-year-old Broadway actor, Christopher Reeve. He did a screen test that was quite brilliant in his transformation from Clark Kent to Superman.

I think that it was at this point I was about to confess to Ilya that I had never read a *Superman* comic and probably wasn't the best man to make a TV special, when he mentioned that Marlon Brando had agreed to play Superman's father and he would guarantee me an hour-long interview with him. This was the promised land for a star scalp hunter so I said: 'Where do I sign?'

Little did I know that this would lead to five years of Close Encounters with the Salkinds.

They had been going to shoot *Superman* in the Cinecittà Studios in Rome and had already spent hundreds of thousands of dollars building sets there, but the Italian unions had become greedy so it was switched to England. This meant losing the Bond and *Battle of Britain* director, Guy Hamilton, who was a British tax exile, and hiring an American director, Dick Donner, who had cut his teeth on *Kojak* and had had a hit with his first major movie, *The Omen*. As Ilya walked me round the sets at Shepperton Studios he told me: 'On every film there are two camps: the producers' and the director's. You have to decide which one you want to be in.' He was right. By the end of the shoot Donner and the Salkinds were only communicating with each other through Dick's agent. I chose the money.

Amazingly, they built the *Superman* sets, or some of them, in three successive studios: Cinecittà, Shepperton and Pinewood in Buckinghamshire which was better able to accommodate a production which was to employ more than a thousand people. I doubt if students studying film at university will be told that this is the most economic way of starting a production.

When I stepped on to the Fortress of Solitude set in Pinewood at the end of March, it was a bit like an *A Bridge Too Far* reunion. The Salkinds seemed to have bought us as a job lot: Geoffrey Unsworth and Peter MacDonald on camera, Dave Tomblin and Roy Button as assistant directors, Vic Armstrong and Alf Joint doing the stunts, Gordon Arnell and June Broom publicity and even Gene Hackman, who had been a Polish general at Arnhem, now transformed into Superman's nemesis, Lex Luthor. We had all been together for the end of the epic World War II films and now, without knowing it at the time, we were in the vanguard of the comic-book films era, which shows no signs of abating.

The 007 Stage, all 60,000 square feet of it, had been built to house a warship and a harbour in *The Spy Who Loved Me* and went on to become Meryl Streep's mountain village in *Mamma Mia*. There's a saying in cinema 'people don't go home singing the sets' but this one was certainly worth an aria or two. John Barry, who had cut his teeth in the art department on *Cleopatra* and designed *Star Wars*, had surpassed himself on the Fortress, a vast crystalline cavern, constructed from Styrofoam, plastic, polyethylene and mirrored glass. John rightly won an Oscar for *Star Wars* but was unable to collect his BAFTA for *Superman* as he died from meningitis in 1979, aged forty-three.

So the sets and the script were top drawer and the *Star Wars* special effects team did the best that was available thirty-five years ago with poor Chris Reeve dangled for endless weeks in a harness in front of a blue screen. But what really made the movie such a hit were the leading actors.

Despite his crummy part in *Bridge*, I knew Gene Hackman was a formidable character actor from his Oscar-winning 'Popeye' Doyle in *The French Connection*. But I had no idea of his supreme timing as a comedy performer. He played off his henchpeople, actors Ned Beatty and Valerie Perrine, as if they were The Three Stooges. Donner cleverly brought in a sixth writer, Tom Mankiewicz, who had done three recent Bonds, to polish Gene's lines. 'It's Kryptonite, Superman. Little souvenir from the old home town. I spared no expense to make you feel right at home.' Tom was instrumental in casting Margot Kidder as Lois Lane and the pair became a temporary couple.

Chris Reeve had the looks and the height to play the lead but to get the shape was put on a special diet and beefed up at the Grosvenor House gym under the supervision of bodybuilder Dave Prowse, who

Chris Reeve pumping iron to bulk out for Superman.

had played Darth Vader in *Star Wars*. (Prowse was a bit put out when James Earl Jones revoiced his lines, but his West Country lilt had earned him the soubriquet of 'Darth Farmer' on that set.)

The thing about Christopher D'Olier Reeve wasn't just that he was a superb actor – in 1973, out of 2,000 applicants, only he and Robin Williams were selected for Juilliard's Advanced Programme – but, at twenty-four, he was a true American WASP. He was an accomplished pilot, he spoke fluent French, he rode competitively and was an all-round sportsman. Although he claimed he hadn't lifted a tennis racquet since Cornell, and I played every weekend, when we had games at Queen's he would trounce me soundly. We weren't particularly friendly – Chris was in the Donner camp who ate at San Lorenzo and partied at Tramp at the weekends but he did invite me to the thirtieth birthday dinner that Dodi Fayed gave for him. Chris dated an English girl, Gae Exton, and they had two children.

So my *Bridge* cameraman, Martin Bell, and his crew filmed the filming and I would do the odd interview, knowing that my main contribution would be in the script and cutting room.

I had no idea of the widespread American popularity of *Superman* until we hit New York. It was known that Chris was to be filmed in front of the Solow Building, a towering concave skyscraper, made of glass and metal. A burglar was climbing the building with suction pumps on his hands and knees and Superman, his flying rig on the end of a giant Chapman crane, flew in to arrest him. As Chris swooped, the crowd on packed West 57th Street whooped in unison, as if a second Messiah had arrived. The next day this was the lead on virtually every local newspaper and TV news programme. I filmed Andy Warhol talking to Chris for his *Interview* magazine. It was less of an interview; more a prolonged piece of fan worship. Andy purred that he loved the silver buckle on his belt and Chris told him he had made it himself 'in shop' at school – another of his talents!

New York was brutally hot and humid. At 8.30pm on 13 July the temperature was still in the nineties when the five boroughs, with their ten million inhabitants, were plunged into darkness. Con Ed could cope no more. I was eating at the apartment of Sarah, my former literary agent, in the Village, more than fifty blocks from the Mayfair Hotel where we were billeted. It seemed best to stay the night. I was about to suggest this when, out of the dark, the not-yet Poet Laureate, Ted Hughes, arrived with a similar, though more romantic, idea.

I actually managed to find a night bus going north. Progress was extremely slow as various loonies who had the dream of becoming traffic cops were manning every intersection, adding to the chaos.

Worse than that, there was widespread looting that night. Looting is possibly too mild a term: fifty brand-new Pontiacs were stolen from a dealership in the Bronx. Five thousand people were arrested and the police had to reopen The Tombs, a former house of detention in Lower Manhattan, to accommodate them. It seemed to confirm Plato's theory that, if we could become invisible, people would turn to crime.

In the morning, power was switched on over three hours, area by area in order of criminality. The Mayflower Hotel, on the Upper West Side, was an early choice and, from bed, I watched on live TV people smashing shop windows, jumping in and removing televisions and other portable goods. The Big Bad Apple was certainly in need of Superman.

At the other end of the social scale, I learned a little bit about Manhattan 'society' when I met a perky television reporter, Kristi, who was covering *Superman* in New York. She had rented a beach house for the summer in The Hamptons and invited me for the weekend. I jumped at the idea of escaping muggy New York and threw my swimming togs and toilet stuff into a bag and caught the coach. Kristi was at the Quogue bus stop to greet me but her face fell. 'Where's your jacket?' I only had a short-sleeved rugby shirt on and thought the forecast indicated no need for a jacket this weekend. 'There is a need,' she remonstrated, 'We're going to dinner at the Lichtensteins tonight.' Ooops. Much of the rest of the day was spent searching through thrift shops until we found a blazer that looked vaguely respectable.

She was right: most of the other male guests were in blue blazers, pink trousers, no socks and Gucci shoes. Roy Lichtenstein was very welcoming and friendly. I told him a print of his painting, *This Must Be the Place*, had hung above my bed in Boston. He was genuinely interested in the Superman film, having painted many images of the Man of Steel himself. 'Poor Joe Schuster didn't make enough out of him,' he mused. (Siegel and Schuster had sold the rights to *Action Comics* for $130 in 1938, but were looked after by Warners, who took over the rights, in their later years.) Roy Lichtenstein's own works sold for about $5 million each in his lifetime. After he died in 1997, one was auctioned for $43 million.

I was placed beside Lee Radziwill, Jacqueline Kennedy's sister who was an Anglophile, having lived for long periods in London. She and Jackie had grown up on an estate not far away from Roy's with riding stables and a jumping paddock. 'Jackie was braver than me, a great horsewoman. She once thought she had killed me when she hit me on the head with a croquet mallet. I was out cold for several hours.'

In truth I didn't feel particularly comfortable with The Hamptons set and was relieved to get back to the city furnace on Sunday evening. Kristi and I did not pursue our relationship. I read in a social column some years later that she had married a rich man called Tyler.

Dick Donner had a television career stretching back to the fifties and his nostalgic streak came to the fore when he shot a missile hijack scene in the Canadian Rockies. It was guarded by Marines who included Kirk Alyn – he had played the first Superman in 1948 (not a fact that he let anyone forget since his visiting card read 'Kirk Alyn – Superman'). Larry Hagman vouchsafed to me that Dick Donner drafted him in as he was pretty hard up. Hagman hadn't had much decent work since *I Dream of Jeannie* in the sixties. His luck was to change a month later when he was cast as J.R. in *Dallas*, a part he played for the next thirteen years. Hagman was immensely amusing and, after the shoot, entertained his fellow guests in the baronial Banff Springs Hotel by finding a pair of bagpipes and serenading them into dinner.

We ordinary mortals were quartered in Calgary, some seventy miles to the east. I offered the unit photographer, Bob Penn, a lift there, suggesting we drive through the Stoney Indian Reserve where many of the Sioux had retreated after the Massacre at Wounded Knee. 'Are you quite sure?' asked Bob nervously, although he had fought with valour in World War II. He put up the car windows and checked that all the doors were locked. 'I just don't want to get scalped,' he said – and I don't think he was joking. We weren't. In fact we didn't see many Indians, just dozens of abandoned cars by the side of the road. In Calgary I asked the hotel receptionist why there were so many breakdowns. 'The Indians buy these cheap second-hand cars and, when they run out of petrol, they think they've broken down and they just leave them,' he explained.

Superman, like Dorothy, came from Kansas, only he landed there from Krypton whereas she took off from there for The Emerald City. To obtain Commonwealth film tax concessions, Kansas was played by the wheat fields of Alberta in Canada, and Pa Kent was played by the veteran star, Glenn Ford. Canadian-born Glenn, now somewhat forgotten, had made his name in the fifties with *The Big Heat* and *3:10 to Yuma*. In a fifty-five-year career he was never even nominated for an Oscar, possibly because he always played the same character: himself. He continued to do this in *Superman*, rejecting the wig prepared for him with the words: 'People will just say, "That's Glenn Ford in a white wig."'

At dinner, he asked me if I knew the British journalist Roderick Mann (who covered showbiz for the *LA Times* and the *Sunday Express*). I said I was passingly acquainted with him. 'Well, next time you see him, punch him in the face from me. He came to my place a few Saturdays back. I was sitting by my pool with a glass of water, waiting for my dinner guests to arrive, so I was anxious to get rid of him. But he was a bit drunk and in tears, sobbing because Kim Novak, whom he'd been living with, had kicked him out. Eventually he went but two Sundays later he wrote a story that began: "Glenn Ford sits by his pool sipping neat vodka, a lonely, sad and broken man." He had turned himself into me.'

I agreed that this was a bit off, and I did encounter Roderick about a decade later at a friend's house in LA. He was charming: married to an attractive travel agent, Anastasia, and in a very good mood that night as it had just been made public that his friend, Cary Grant, had left him all his suits in his will. 'It's going to cost me a bit to have them taken in,' he confided. I decided not to punch him in the face.

We returned to London and started editing. Donner's film was a hit, grossing more than $300 million worldwide. My documentary seemed to do its promotional trick, with the added bonus of becoming the first part of three successive *Superman* Sundays on ABC TV. It aired in the early-evening 'educational' hour; presumably ABC persuaded the Federal Communications Commission that it would teach people how to make Superman films. Ilya was pleased because he was able to put all of its profits in his pocket and did not have to share them with Warners, as he did with the feature.

Chris Reeve became a face known throughout the world. There are quite a few people in this position, but Chris's was slightly different. We were once having lunch in New York. People recognised him in the restaurant and there were a couple of autographs. He suggested a game of chess afterwards at his apartment on West 74th Street. I was happy to do so. As we walked up Broadway, he asked me what the time was: 2.45pm. 'We have five minutes,' he said, urging me to quicken my step. 'Why?' I inquired. 'School's out at two-fifty,' he replied. 'It's not possible for me to be on the streets between then and five.' He explained that Superman was so pestered on the street that progress was impossible, so for two hours each day he became the prisoner of 74th Street.

Ilya was good to me. We repeated the process with *Superman II* and *III*, with the usual law of slightly diminishing returns. Richard Lester (not Dick; his friends know he prefers Richard) took over as director. He is a friendly, most companionable man and the Donner divide did not recur.

I was kindly included in most of the treats. There was that Washington brunch at the home of Sargent Shriver and that dinner at the White House. As an encore The Beach Boys did 'Surfin' USA'. In fact Brian's brother, Dennis, was the only Beach Boy who actually went surfing but he drowned in the Pacific in 1983 after a day's drinking at Marina del Rey.

It's sad to end *Superman* on another tragic story. On 27 May 1995, Chris Reeve was competing in an equestrian cross-country competition in Virginia. His horse refused at the third jump. Chris fell and was paralysed from the neck down. His valiant work for the disabled and stem-cell research has been well chronicled. I wrote to him, to express my admiration and recall the good days. A handwritten letter (he had dictated it to his wife, Dana,) came back some time later, expressing fond memories of those years and suggesting that maybe I would like to come and stay in Westchester where we could talk about those times.

It was not to be. He died two weeks after his fifty-second birthday.

10

An Evening with Marlon Brando

On Sunday 21 March 1976, Richard Donner, Ilya Salkind and his co-producer, Pierre Spengler, had gone to see Marlon Brando at his rented mansion in Surrey prior to his first day of shooting. He had jet-lag and a severe head cold but promised he would turn up at Shepperton the next day.

Marlon had been thinking about his part on the plane over. He said he liked to surprise audiences and, since Jor-El was an extra-terrestrial, he didn't want to be a traditional alien with a big bald head but would play the part as a green suitcase that emitted electronic bleeps. They all laughed convivially, but Brando assured them he was deadly serious. In the limo back to London, Ilya put his head in his hands. 'We're paying the world's greatest actor nearly four million dollars for twelve days' work and all we get is a fucking suitcase. Anybody could be inside it.'

It was, of course, one of Marlon's notorious practical jokes. When he arrived in make-up the following morning, he dutifully put on his white wig and the extended costume that had been created to cover his 300 or more pounds.

On set – the crystal ice palace – it would be nice to say he was word perfect. But he wasn't. In fact, he didn't know any of his lines at all. So they had to be written with a felt pen on cue cards for the actor to read. When tracking shots were used, the words would precede him, with a grip nervously holding up card after card.

I had been introduced to Brando and asked if he minded me filming this. 'Not in the slightest, dear fellow,' he replied in the

Captain Bligh English accent he had decided to adopt for the part.

The crew, in the main, thought his not learning lines was just laziness. A privilege to be enjoyed by a man whose salary was so absurd that, it was calculated, if he ordered a new Rolls-Royce from Jack Barclay's in central London, he would have earned enough to pay for it by the time it was delivered to Shepperton.

Later on I asked Marlon about the cards. 'There's nothing more boring than an actor going to a door, turning back and saying "Martha, goodbye."' he explained. 'It's death to the actor if the audience can second-guess you. But if you don't know what the words are – you just have a general idea – you can glance at the cue card and give the audience the feeling that you're searching for what you're going to say.'

On set Brando approached his part with a Shakespearean flourish, whether condemning Terence Stamp and fellow rebels to an eternal living death or recording a tender message for his infant son, Kal-El, later Clark Kent, subsequently Superman, to explain his history and his mission when he struggled with his identity. Fortunately, Susannah York had a small part as Kal's mum. When they came to make *Superman II* the director needed further messages from Jor-El but Marlon demanded the usual exorbitant sum for doing so. (He had already made about $14 million in his profit share from the first one.) So Susannah did it.

The British crew liked Marlon and he liked them. 'On an American set,' he told me, 'the size of the smile you get when you arrive in the morning depends on how much you're getting paid. Two teeth for a regular fee, ten if you're getting paid a million and, if you're getting more than two million' (here he bared his teeth in illustration) 'the full Flatbush Cemetery.'

Filming on a feature frequently runs into the night to get the day's schedule completed. This clearly did not appeal to Marlon as, at 5pm every day, he would shake the hands of the director and senior members of the crew and simply leave. Ilya didn't mind; he was delighted to have snared the star. 'When you get someone as big as Brando to commit to a film, all the other casting falls easily into place. All actors want to be in a film with him.'

And Ilya was as good as his word with regard to my interview. Before he left England, Marlon invited me down to his Surrey mansion to do it. Alice Marchak, his longtime secretary, seemed in charge of things, keeping an eye on his teenage son, Christian, and daughter, Cheyenne. (Christian was later to murder Cheyenne's boyfriend, Dag Drollet, and spend six years in jail. He died of pneumonia, aged 49. Cheyenne committed suicide in 1995.) There were also two young Chinese girls (possibly the star's masseuses) who giggled a lot.

Marlon ordered drinks for all while his personal make-up man, readied him for the interview. Then he summoned my cameraman, Martin Bell – with whom he had become on joking terms during the previous weeks on set. 'What did he want?' I asked Martin.

'He told me to stick to a 70mm (narrow) lens, just to stay in a head and shoulders close-up.' Although the star was wearing a black polo-neck jumper, it was evident he was self-conscious about his spreading bulk.

Marlon was most friendly and accommodating, almost eager to be interviewed. I started by asking him why he had taken the part. 'They offered me a lot of money and that's as far as my interest went.' Did he feel guilty about earning so much for twelve days' work?

'Not guilty at all. There's a market rate. They pay vast sums to rock groups who inflate balloons from their ears. The money buys me the time to make a television series on American Indians. I once spent six not-very-pleasant months in Colombia making a film about a slave revolt in the Antilles. I think it was released, if it was released at all, as *Burn!* It was an enormous flop, but I found it very satisfying. So for every commercial movie, you can still make something that's worthwhile.'

Of course, Brando's career got off to a scorching start with the play and film of *A Streetcar Named Desire* when he was only twenty-five. He capped that with an Oscar for *On the Waterfront* which he actually collected. 'I remember pulling on my tuxedo trousers in the back of the car and thinking, "This is silly, but let's do it once." Oscars are manipulative nonsense.' True to his word, when he won another, nearly twenty years later for *The Godfather*, he sent Sacheen Littlefeather in her Apache costume to collect it and protest about the treatment of native Americans.

But there had been a major dip in the star's career in the sixteen flop films before that, including *A Countess from Hong Kong*. 'I had wanted to work with Charlie Chaplin,' he told me. 'He asked me to be funny but I found out that I was not a very good comedian. The film was the biggest bore ever presented before a viewing public. Chaplin had been a genius. I don't know where talent goes. Maybe where elephants go to die.'

It is known that Brando was only offered Don Corleone after Laurence Olivier was too ill to play him. At first Brando, a fit forty-seven year old at the time, told the director, Francis Coppola: 'What the hell do I know about a sixty-five-year-old Italian who smokes fat cigars?' It was the stuff of Hollywood legend that Brando created Don Corleone on his own, dyeing his hair, pencilling a moustache and stuffing his cheeks with cotton wool to give himself a jowly look which won over a reluctant Paramount management.

'There is no art to find the mind's construction in the face,' he quoted to me [Duncan in *Macbeth*]. 'My look did not betray the ruthless evil of that old man. Nor did I need to shout and rant: powerful people don't need to do that. They can speak as softly as they like.'

Paramount, still wary about the fallen star, wouldn't pay him for his work on the film, only a percentage of the subsequent box office, which they had expensive cause to regret. Marlon thought the story, ostensibly about the Mafia, in fact fundamentally dealt with the corporate mind. 'The Mafia may be the best example of capitalism we have, not that much different from General Motors. We worship before the goddess of success in America. Success equals worth. If you are unsuccessful, you are unworthy. I consider *The Godfather* to be one of the most powerful statements made about America.'

Any actor, even a major star, is a gun for hire and Marlon was holidaying in Paris when he was contacted by Bernardo Bertolucci. He was prevailed upon to see the director's anti-fascist film, *The Conformist*, which chimed with his views. He was also impressed by the fact that both the author, Alberto Moravia, and Bertolucci were poets. Bernardo had an idea for a film that might interest him, so Marlon invited the director to his home on Mulholland Drive in the Santa Monica Mountains.

Last Tango in Paris evolved from Bertolucci's fantasy of a man having three assigned days of uninhibited sex with a young woman whose name he never knows. The nineteen-year-old French girl, Maria Schneider, who agreed to be the naked plaything, was not quite the innocent she has been painted. She was into heroin, cocaine and Warren Beatty. The film proved a good career move and she moved on to leading roles playing opposite Jack Nicholson in Antonioni's *The Passenger*. But she subsequently maintained she had been violated by *Last Tango*. 'Marlon said to me: "Don't worry, it's just a movie," but during the sex scenes, even though what Marlon was doing wasn't real, I was crying real tears. I felt humiliated and to be honest, I felt a little raped, both by Marlon and by Bertolucci. After the scene, Marlon didn't console me or apologise.' Schneider later turned lesbian. She died of cancer when she was fifty-eight.

'I never could figure out what that movie was about,' Brando laughed. 'I was as mystified on the last day of shooting as I was during the first conversation with Mr Bertolucci at my house. Perhaps he was receiving messages from afar and was unable to communicate them. Reading the interviews he subsequently gave, his interpretation seemed to change with every interviewer.'

'I wrote a lot of it. I would decide if I wanted this particular quality or thrust.' He paused, and laughed again. 'Maybe thrust is not a good choice of words.'

'Jolly good thrust,' I couldn't stop myself saying, knowing that the lubricating of Miss Schneider with some Burro de Parma had been Marlon's idea and guaranteed the film's widespread notoriety.

He disagreed. 'Scenes don't make a film. Just as colours don't make a painting.'

Last Tango premiered in New York on 14 October 1972 to enormous public controversy. The media frenzy surrounding the film generated intense popular interest as well as moral condemnation, landing cover stories in both *Time* and *Newsweek* magazines. *Playboy* published a photo spread of Brando and Schneider 'cavorting in the nude'. *Time* wrote: 'Any moviegoers who are not shocked, titillated, disgusted, fascinated, delighted or angered by this early scene in Bernardo Bertolucci's new movie, *Last Tango in Paris*, should be patient. There is more to come. Much more.' Columnist William F.

Buckley and ABC's Harry Reasoner denounced the film as 'pornography disguised as art'.

Others disagreed. The director Robert Altman said: 'I walked out of the screening and said to myself, "How dare I make another film? My personal and artistic life will never be the same."' The critic Pauline Kael pronounced: 'Bertolucci and Brando altered the face of an art form.' And the Academy nominated Bertolucci and Brando for Oscars. (It was to be the last of Brando's eight Best Actor nominations.)

Some writers have suggested that the reason that Brando didn't set foot on a film set for another five years was because he had painfully drawn so much out of himself in extemporising in the film: his childhood on a farm, his drunken father (true) and his current middle-aged anguish and melancholy. A more relevant reason might be that the movie was made for about $1 million and earned $100 million, not a little of which went to the star.

But, by the time we spoke, he was definitely disenchanted with acting. 'It was never something that I wanted to devote my whole life to. That would have been unpleasant and not very interesting. It was, on occasion, a wonderful way to make money. But I'd rather clean out stables than be an out-of-work actor.'

But what about men like Olivier and Gielgud? (Brando played a memorable Mark Antony to Gielgud's Cassius in the 1953 film, *Julius Caesar.*)

'These are men that are keeping alive a tradition. We have no sense of language that the English do. In America we talk in grunts – although I'm not one to talk about grunts! I was introduced to Shakespeare by Laurence Olivier. He is an artist: a cultured and talented man. The foremost actor in the world. He has made a mark that history will not soon forget.'

'How's your flock, Mr Brando?'

Since he didn't want to be labelled an actor, I asked him how he described himself on his passport.

'When they wanted to induct me into the army, I had to fill in some questions which I found offensive. So when they asked for "Race", I put "Human". And for "Color" I put "Seasonal", as I go darker in the summer. In my last passport, for "Occupation" I wrote "Shepherd". They never look at it. Except this last time, at Heathrow. The Immigration Officer handed it back to me with the words: "How's your flock, Mr Brando?"'

I concluded our conversation with the sort of question you might ask nowadays of a local TV presenter. But, in Marlon's case, I felt it might be a weighty encumbrance. 'How do you deal with your celebrity, with other people?'

'Well, I've sacrificed my anonymity. It does make me cynical the way some people change when they meet me and go into a different gear. That's why I like to be in Tahiti. They have no sense of notoriety there.'

There we left it. Well, not quite. He asked me and the crew if we would like to have dinner and got Alice to book a local restaurant. It was called Lucio's, just outside Epsom.

At the table it was the same Marlon as the interviewee but now he could engage Martin and the sound man and the electrician not as the people who had had to remain silent but as fellow human beings. I haven't experienced that much with stars. He joshed them about English names he had seen such as 'Cock and Company' and 'Turnbull and Asser'.

As the wine went down, the conversation became a little more serious. Brando said there were no major living American writers. Martin suggested Truman Capote. 'Capote said he'd invented a new art form,' Marlon countered, 'but I don't think we've yet been overwhelmed by it.' I chipped in 'Saul Bellow', just for the sake of an argument. 'In the panoply of artists of the last fifteen hundred years,' he argued back, slightly unfairly, 'Bellow is a midget. What do you think caused the Italian Renaissance in the fourteenth century? Or the Flemish Renaissance in the sixteenth? What brought about the sublime German composers in the eighteenth century?'

Now it was his turn to ask the questions and he was winding me up, I knew, but I was saved by the bill. I reached for my wallet to pay but Marlon insisted, passing me his American Express card. I looked at it. It read, logically enough, I suppose, MARLON BRANDO.

I presented it to the waiter. After a while another man, Lucio himself, arrived at the table, brandishing it. Here we go, I thought. Perhaps he's going to comp us the meal. But, no. Lucio fixed me in the eye. 'I am very sorry, Mr Brando, but we have sold the restaurant and next month there will be a different owner. And American Express takes three months to pay us.'

Marlon's hand went back to his pocket and he handed me some £20 notes. I could see the bill came to £24 so I told him two would be enough. 'Give him three,' said Brando, 'I get these for my daily allowance.'

I did as I was bid. A £36 tip would make it a good day for Lucio. It had been quite a good one for me, too.

11

Born in Brooklyn: Barbra Streisand and Woody Allen

Barbra Streisand had long wanted to do a re-remake of *A Star Is Born*. It had already been a film in 1937 and 1954 (with Judy Garland and James Mason). An aspiring Hollywood actress is helped on her way by a declining, drunken star. But Barbra wanted to do it about singers. She had even gone to Vegas to ask Elvis to be her co-star but the Colonel vetoed the idea. Mick Jagger was considered – and discounted, so Kris Kristofferson got the gig. But the stories of verbal fights on the film had crossed the Atlantic and I had a hunch that Miss S might want to put her side of the story. This proved correct. Through Warners, I secured an interview.

Her assistant answered the door to her mansion at 301 North Carolwood Drive, Holmby Hills and showed Marcia, me and the three-man crew into the ground-floor living room where I would talk to her. It was hardly an appropriate place to film as it was so immaculate and expensive: Shaker chairs (not much change from $5,000 for each of those), innumerable small tables bearing delicate pieces of Minton and Limoges, some of them small teacups, a couple of Klimts (worth about $100 million today, if she's been wise enough to hold on to them) and a pair of parakeets in a cage. Their chirping would not make for a very satisfactory soundtrack. It had been good of Barbra to invite us into her home, rather than the suggested studio, but now I wondered if she wanted to intimidate me a little.

The process had already begun a few days previously when someone at Warner publicity had called me at the modest Le Parc Hotel where I was staying and suggested I might like to move to the five-star Beverly Wilshire where, of course, they would pay for everything. Somewhat taken aback, I asked why. (Le Parc had a smashing tennis court on its roof.) The publicist explained that if Miss Streisand were to telephone me to talk about the interview, it would be better if she called the Wilshire.

Undoubtedly, an aura surrounded Streisand. Some years later, when she agreed to go on Jonathan Ross's show to plug a new album, he got rid of all the other guests, even his Four Poofs, had the show moved to prime time and the BBC announced it as: 'Jonathan Ross secures a sensational world exclusive interview with Barbra Streisand.' She certainly had a diva reputation, obtained by raw talent and a refusal to be pushed around. Her accelerated rise from lounge singer Barbara Joan Streisand to Fanny Brice in *Funny Girl* on Broadway and on film, winning her an Academy Award for her first movie (she collected another five years later for Best Actress in *The Way We Were*) and the deluge of Grammies that attended her multi-million-selling albums, put her up there with Sinatra and maybe, when you consider her brilliant comic timing (*What's Up, Doc?*), a little higher. She was on the cover of *Time* when she was twenty-two and seemingly never left it.

I had read that she always kept the price tags on the bottom of her objets d'art and suggested to Marcia she pick one up to see if this was true. My usually fearless PA declined. Streisand was upstairs making a call and when she came down she announced: 'I've been talking to Jon in London. He says it's raining. Does it always rain there?' I assured her we enjoyed the occasional sunny day. She was petite, surprisingly attractive, wearing a simple pink jumper and a pair of jeans and radiated a woman in love. We had hit on a good day. Her romance with her hairdresser, Jon Peters, was seldom out of the gossip columns and now he was the producer of her film.

I wondered why she had wanted to make *A Star Is Born* for a third time. 'I was never fond of the passivity of the woman in the other two films, I wanted my Esther to be proactive, to save this man. I have a scene where I propose to him and I'm wearing a man's suit. I'm not a radical feminist or anything, but I do believe in women taking hold of their own strengths.'

Speaking as much of herself as the character, she went on: 'One has to have one's inner life together, not just be reliant on the audience's approval. Life is short. You must take risks. You must grow, even if growth is failure.'

The parakeets had been removed from the room but there was an elephant that remained: Frank Pierson. Best known for writing the screenplays for *Cool Hand Luke* and *Dog Day Afternoon*, he had been hired by Barbra and Jon to rewrite *Star* but insisted that, if he did, he wanted to direct as well. He was now better known for writing a long and venomous article about the vitriolic, often hysterical, battles between him and Barbra and Jon and Kris. (Kristofferson was not a man to get into a physical battle with: at Oxford he had got a Blue for boxing.) This had been published in *New York* and *New West* magazines prior to the film's US premiere.

'What made him do it?' I asked. Streisand shook her head. 'I don't really know. It was destructive to the film and to himself. He could have waited.' Was it perhaps because she took the film away from him and edited it herself? 'It was in the contract that he had first cut, but I had final cut.'

So the piece was all smoke without any fire? 'I'm not saying that,' Barbra replied. 'The film was a nightmare. Pierson may be a good

Barbra seems friendly enough.

director but he and I had ... er ... different chemistries. I would come up with suggestions about a detail on a set or a look for a costume and he implied I was being meddlesome. Well, a producer can meddle. There were a couple of major rows with Kris, especially when we were filming the live concert which I knew couldn't be reshot. But we're good friends. He gave up drinking after the film.'

And the editing? 'I'm intuitively editing in my head while we're filming scenes. There'll be two characters in the landscape with vast mountains in the distance and then we'll go in for close-ups to capture their emotions. Pierson wrote that I cut Kris out of some early scenes. Not true. I actually put in more shots of him. But that article polluted the reviews. In New York the critics reviewed the rows and not the movie.'

It's just possible that the article had the effect of making more people want to see *A Star Is Born* rather than having any destructive effect. It was the second most popular film in the States that year.

And Barbra won an Oscar for writing the song, 'Evergreen'.

Pierson had written that at one stage he suggested to Streisand that she direct the film herself. And that's exactly what she did – six years later. Even before *Star*, she had been keen to make a film out of 'Yentl the Yeshiva Boy', a short story by Isaac Bashevis Singer. He wrote the original in Yiddish. It was about a Jewish girl in nineteenth-century Poland who disguised herself as a boy in order to go to a yeshiva (an orthodox Jewish school) and study the Talmud. A 1975 Broadway version quickened her interest and she wrote a forty-page outline.

In 1979, Barbra saw Mandy Patinkin singing as Che in *Evita* and was determined that he would be her male lead, Avigdor. Mandy, the foremost interpreter of Sondheim musicals, read her script, hated it and turned her down three times. But Streisand is not a woman to be rejected and she cajoled Patinkin into helping her improve the script, even persuading him to go to a yeshiva, where women were still not permitted, and film it with a hidden camera.

The late Jack Rosenthal, who wrote *Bar Mitzvah Boy* and was married to Maureen Lipman, worked with her on the final script and *Yentl* began filming in Lee Studios in north London in 1982. Jane Lush, a BBC producer, saw it as a good opportunity to make a documentary about Streisand at work and brought me in to do the interviews and script.

This time, with Barbra in command, the production went harmoniously. After some sniping in the *Sun*, the British crew even wrote a letter to the press saying: 'She has shared jokes, chats and pleasantries with us every day ... she appears to have no temperament.'

Well, maybe a little. When I turned up in her dressing room for the first in a series of interviews, she threw a major wobbly at her publicist, Allen Burry. 'You never told me Iain was coming today,' she screamed. (He had.) 'I haven't prepared for this. I'm not ready to talk about the film.' I told her that this was the first in a series of running chats that Jane had planned and it would be nice to see her dressed as a boy. But we could easily do it another day.

Like a ship that has emerged from a squall into tranquil waters, she sat down with the words: 'Let's do it.'

I said I had observed her on set finessing the smallest details, even rearranging bread rolls in a basket. Barbra nodded. 'I love detail – it's the difference between right and wrong. I always think that everything can be better. Schedule and budget are the enemies of perfection. That's why I'm called difficult. Some people think I'm crazy.'

The year before shooting started she had travelled with a friend and a home movie camera to the intended locations in Czechoslovakia. She even dressed up as the 'boy' Yentl. 'I wanted to see how my character would look, say, framed in an archway, whether it would look better backlit. And how the colours of my costume fitted with the buildings. And the light. Maybe especially the light. Every country has its own light.'

Prudently, she had engaged Peter MacDonald, the top camera operator. But what had made her want to direct? 'I wanted an artistic challenge and to stretch myself as a human being. Doing this is a wonderful shaker-upper: it puts you in your place. I wanted to do this film after *Funny Girl* but the studio didn't think I should do two ethnic roles in a row. In the end we had to turn it into a musical for the finance. But that's elevated the piece into something magical. I call this a realistic fairy tale.'

Not wishing to risk a return to her earlier outburst (maybe that's why she did it?) I didn't mention that although she had cast the mellifluous Mandy, she got to sing all the songs.

In subsequent conversations, Streisand revealed a deeply emotional side. Her father, an English teacher, had died when she was a baby and that was why she wanted to emphasise the father–daughter love in the early scenes when he, illegally, teaches her the Talmud. I wondered if maybe the film was too personal to be popular? But Barbra was adamant: 'When an artist contacts his own self, that's when you reach most people.' And she was right. *Yentl* was a worldwide success; most of the critics were favourable – *Newsweek* called Streisand's control over the aesthetics of the film 'a delight and at times an astonishment' – and she became the first woman to win a Golden Globe for directing.

At the end of filming she confessed to me: 'I can't wait to just act again. This has been hard labour camp. Acting is getting paid for having fun.' Which, indeed, she has had, playing Mother Focker even as she approached her seventieth year.

Six years before Streisand, another star was born in Flatbush, Brooklyn: Allan Stewart Konigsberg. He told me he changed his name to Woody because he didn't want fellow students at school to know he was contributing jokes to newspapers. Starting as a stand-up comedian he, too, was attracted to America's indigenous art medium. At seventy-eight, he has directed forty-nine films and should make his half century. Such prodigality of output has led to wavering results, although a bad Woody Allen movie might be preferable to a Mel Brooks comedy.

Just when it seemed he might have lost his gift, along came *Midnight in Paris* in 2011 which was widely popular and profitable and gained him his fourth (uncollected) Oscar. Hollywood has long ceased to back him so his sister, Letty Aronson, goes round Europe getting the finance. In 2013 *Blue Jasmine* proved an even bigger hit.

Every comedy-film maker has a period when he hits top form – and then continues to make movies because that's what he does. Chaplin, after the advent of sound, made *Modern Times* (1936) and *The Great Dictator* (1940) followed by little of note. Allen made *Annie Hall* (1977) and *Manhattan* (1979). Both, not uncoincidentally, had Diane Keaton as his female lead and were co-written with Marshall Brickman.

Annie Hall had swept most of the board at the Oscars: Best Film, Best Actress for Diane, Best Screenplay for Woody and Marshall Brickman, and Woody was acclaimed as Best Director, beating both George Lucas for *Star Wars* and Steven Spielberg for *Close Encounters of the Third Kind*. They'd turned up at the ceremony; he hadn't, preferring to play his clarinet with his New Orleans Marching and Funeral Band at Michael's Pub in New York.

I asked him why he hadn't bothered to go, especially as he was the first man since Orson Welles in 1941 to be up for three Oscars. 'They do nothing but give out awards there,' he said. 'They don't mean too much. How can you measure *Annie Hall* against *Star Wars?*'

So he didn't believe in awards? 'I certainly believe in them for track, where you see physically that someone has won outright. I got a few of those when I was a kid. My mother keeps them.'

Annie Hall achieved almost perfection in its integration of Woody's clever stand-up wit – 'I was thrown out of NYU in my freshman year for cheating in my metaphysics final. I looked within the soul of the boy sitting next to me' – with an involving and funny love story – 'that sex was the most fun I've ever had without laughing.' He also managed to settle some scores, not least against Los Angeles – 'I don't want to move to a city where the only cultural advantage is being able to make a right turn on a red light.' When

Annie observes: 'But it's so clean out here.' 'Alvy comes back: 'That's because they don't throw their garbage away, they turn it into television shows.'

Another target was know-alls in cinema lines. Alvy turns on the man loudly pontificating behind him and says: 'You don't know anything about Marshall McLuhan.' 'It just so happens I teach a class at Columbia called TV, Media and Culture,' the bore retorts, 'So I think my insights into Mr McLuhan have a great deal of validity.' In a piece of near universal wish-fulfilment, Alvy then pulls a listening McLuhan out from behind a poster. 'You know nothing of my work,' the guru reprimands the 'expert'. 'How you got to teach a class in anything is totally amazing.'

'I had hoped to get Fellini but he was working on a film in Italy,' Woody recalled. 'I think the favourite subject guys use to impress their dates is Fellini.'

And, maybe, Woody Allen. He seems to have abandoned his serious, 'Bergman' films like *Interiors* (1978) and *September* (1987) largely, perhaps, because his audience abandoned him. But when he inserted his unique humour into an examination of marriage in *Husbands and Wives* (1992), the result was both entertaining and insightful.

Woody is droll and amusing company whether recounting how he attempts to keep the pigeon population down on his balcony by shooting at them with his BB gun or the tricks he will go to to stop people following him in the street by looking in store windows or pretending to tie his shoelaces. His stand-up material is as fresh and funny today as it was more than fifty years ago, such as the story of his taking a moose to a fancy-dress party and it winning second prize to a couple dressed as a moose. His first wife even took out an injunction to stop him telling jokes about her: 'My wife is an immature person. She'll march into the bathroom while I'm in the bath and sink my boats.' A later partner, Mia Farrow, was to allege that he sexually abused their adopted daughter but the judge found her allegations inconclusive.

Allen once said that 'My one regret in life is that I'm not someone else.' I asked him why and he told me that this had been taken entirely out of context. 'My publisher had drafted a list of my credits to put on the back of a book and they looked so pretentious that I just added those words underneath them.'

But if he were to be someone else, who? 'Maybe Louis Armstrong, Sugar Ray Robinson, Marlon Brando.' I suggested that Brando wasn't the most contented man in the world but Woody insisted: 'I like his looks, his nose, the way he talks, his acting sensitivity.'

As one of his characters says: 'I believe in sex and death, things that only come once in a lifetime, but at least after death you don't feel nauseous.'

12

Cleese in Greece ... The Pythons in Africa: *Life of Brian*

In the mid-seventies John Cleese and I had fallen into the habit of eating dinner together a couple of times a month. We lived only a few hundred yards from each other in Notting Hill, an area at the time deluged with Italian restaurants, none very different from the other. We were both single, John having broken up with his wife, Connie.

John is a curious combination of the very silly and the very serious. He gave himself the middle name 'Otto' and his mother Muriel used to complain to me 'I don't know why he does that. He's got a perfectly good one in Marwood.' Sometimes he went by the name of Nigel Farquhar-Bennett or Kim Bread. On the serious side he attended weekly Gurdjieff meetings to try to achieve a higher state of consciousness and personal potential. They were convened by the director, Ron Eyre, who went on to make an insightful study of world religions in *The Long Search* on TV. John continually encouraged me to come but they were held on the night I played tennis with Ted Croker (of the FA), his son and Jimmy Hill. I might have become a better person if I had gone – but a worse tennis player.

John had persuaded Connie to go to a marriage-counselling group run by a psychiatrist, Robin Skynner, and his wife, Pru. Robin and John were later to write a supremely successful book together called *Families and How to Survive Them*, but, alas, not in time to save the Cleese marriage. John was always better at theory than practical and had a technique of trying to solve emotional problems intellectually, not always a good idea in marriage arguments. I once pointed out to him that family counselling had clearly not worked for Connie and him since they ultimately divorced but he robustly replied that it had indeed worked since it pointed to the correct solution. I've always wondered about that; I know he hankered after Connie for a very long time.

They had, of course, achieved considerable success with the first series of *Fawlty Towers*. It had not had an easy birth. When they sent a specimen script to Jimmy Gilbert, Head of Comedy at the BBC, his reaction was that it was full of clichéd situations and stereotypical characters. 'I cannot see it as being anything other than a disaster.' And when they approached Bridget Turner, who was playing Tom Courtenay's wife in Alan Ayckbourn's *The Norman Conquests* in the West End, to play Basil's wife, Sybil, she turned them down. The

John Otto Cleese aka Nigel Farquhar-Bennett or Kim Bread.

fall-back position was Pru Scales who had done a one-off comedy as Ronnie Barker's nagging wife in *One Man's Meat* on BBC2. Although she was seven years older than John, she seemed born to play Sybil.

At the time of the Queen's Silver Jubilee in 1977, John had been loaned a villa on the Greek island of Hydra and he generously asked me along. Our group was made up of mutual friends, Andrew and Maxine, John's six-year-old daughter, Cynthia, who in *A Fish Called Wanda* would play his screen daughter, Portia – 'Who would name their daughter after a car?' asks Otto – and Georgie, Cleese's semi-girlfriend. 'Semi' because she was simultaneously having an affair with a chap who worked backstage at the National Theatre. John referred to him as 'The Primate' and would do imitations of him swinging from rope to rope. These did not give Georgie great pleasure.

Their fragile relationship took a turn for the worse when we embarked on the hydrofoil to Hydra. As the vessel gathered speed from Piraeus harbour two objects were clearly visible on the quay. 'You did remember to put my suitcases on board?' Georgie asked John. Something was simmering in her voice. 'You didn't ask me to,' he replied. 'Well, how come you checked them in at Heathrow, picked them up at the carousel and put them in the taxi this morning?' to which John responded, 'That doesn't make me your valet.'

That apart, life at the villa was passingly relaxed. We lazed around the swimming pool although John didn't really do 'laze' and would get a two- or three-day-old copy of *The Times* from the local store and try involving us in the crossword. We were, unfortunately, at the height of the backgammon boom and Andrew had brought along his set with which to fleece everyone else. It was bad enough losing drachmas but to lose them in such a boring fashion rubbed salt in the wound.

about the series and she had been reluctantly pressured into appearing. 'The trouble is, Iain, I didn't actually write *Fawlty Towers*.' I knew that after they worked out the characters and plot, John would do the lines. Such modesty was typical of her but I was able to tell her – because he had told me – that John could never have written the shows without her. She had been inspired in terms of ideas and construction and he found himself completely unable to write the female characters so he relied on her. The battleaxe that is Sybil Fawlty sprang from the imagination of the shy, self-deprecating Connie Booth. She gave up acting later in life and put her insight into human nature to use as a psychotherapist.

In the late summer of 1978, the Pythons shot *Life of Brian* in Tunisia. They always liked slightly unfashionable Christian names. One suggestion for the Flying Circus itself had been 'Ow! It's Colin Plint'. Michael popped up more than once in the series as Arthur Pewty. And John's highwayman had been Dennis Moore. 'It was just such a silly name,' he told me. 'Dennis Moore, Dennis Moore, riding through the glen.'

John asked me to come out and stay – he tended to get bored on film shoots. 'Why not bring a camera crew for some of the time? That way the BBC can pay for your holiday.'

I worked out that the movie would be released around the tenth anniversary of Monty Python. Fortunately, Bill Cotton, who had been Head of Comedy at the BBC for *Python* and *Fawlty*, had just been made Controller of BBC1 and he gave me the green light for two weeks' filming in Tunisia.

Thus on Thursday 28 September 1978, I found myself in the sweltering heat of the market at Monastir on the north African coast. It was a completely surreal experience as bewildering to me as to the Berbers and Arabs who had been corralled as extras. Terry Gilliam, entirely covered in mud, was berating them from a plinth. 'The eyes will be red with the blood of living creatures and the whore of Babylon shall rise over the hill of excitement and throughout the land there will be a great rubbing of parts.' Even those with a slight command of English found this utterly incomprehensible and to confound matters Michael Palin took up the dire warning. 'And there shall in that time be rumours of things going astray and there will be a great confusion as to where things actually are and nobody will really know where lieth those little things with the sort of raffia-work base that has an attachment, they shall not be there.'

The idea, I think, was to illustrate a diversity of religions. Terry Jones was directing and, although he and Gilliam had done this jointly on *The Holy Grail*, there was quite a difference in approach with Jones more interested in the comedy content and Gilliam the visual look. During one scene in that film Terry G had obliged John to crawl through Scottish mud in full body armour several times. 'Just one more take, John,' he called. 'Why?' demanded the bedraggled, angry Cleese. 'Because the sun's coming round the mountain and it's going to look just great reflecting off your helmet.' 'Oh, fuck off,' yelled Cleese, rising to his feet and stomping off to his chair.

Gilliam was the production designer on this one and delighted in a little Eric Idle-baiting. Eric had recently turned vegetarian and for his scene where he sells an artificial beard to Brian (so that his mother can go to the stoning) –'Aren't you going to haggle?' – Terry had dressed Eric's stall with the carcasses of dead sheep, pungent and rotting in the powerful sun.

Eric had by then parted from his wife, Lyn, but evidently her influence over him in matters of vegetarianism and feminism had been considerable. She was thick with another feminist, Marty Feldman's wife, Lauretta. So in the film Eric played a revolutionary, Stan, who wanted to be a woman, who insisted that he be addressed as Lauretta and demanded the right to have babies. Cleese, as Reg, pointed out that this might be difficult as he didn't have a womb. 'Where's the foetus going to gestate? You going to keep it in a box?'

Unlike the others, Eric had brought a glamorous new partner with him to the location: Tania Kosevich, a model whom he had met at a *Saturday Night Live* party in New York. He was greatly envied as people thought of him and this long-legged beauty whiling away their evenings in their suite at the Meridien Hotel.

John Goldstone, the producer, had promised both cast and crew that he would provide videos to entertain them in the evenings but the consignment never seemed to come. Curiously, Eric was the most vociferous in complaining about this. 'Where are the fucking videos then, John?' were frequently his first words to the producer each morning. At lunch I asked Goldstone if he didn't think it strange that Eric was always complaining about the videos when he had the delicious Tania. The producer shook his head sagaciously: 'I knew that sooner or later he would want the real thing,' he said.

I hadn't known Goldstone before the film but, after we discovered we were 'twins' – by date, at least – we held a joint hundredth birthday party in April 1983. I remember Alan Coren couldn't come but sent us a hundredth birthday card he had found, adding the Corenish words: 'I wonder how many of these they sell?' More, nowadays, I suspect.

I had met Eric years ago in Bristol, but was only passingly acquainted with the others. They were on good form: the script was superb, the days were sunny and so was the atmosphere on set. Allegedly by chance Gilliam and Goldstone had stumbled upon the sets where Zeffirelli had recently filmed *Jesus of Nazareth* for Lew Grade and so adapted them for *Brian*. 'I'm sure Lew would have wanted us to do this,' smiled John.

In fact, Lew's brother, Bernard Delfont, had initially intended to back *Brian*. EMI, Britain's main studio, had made a lot of money from distributing *Holy Grail* and the managing director, Barry Spikings, creased himself when he read the script of *Brian* and agreed to finance it completely.

But when his board got wind of this, Delfont, the Chief Executive, who didn't read scripts, deputed board director Sir James Carreras to do so. Carreras, a man of pretty low taste (he had made such films as *Slave Girls* or Hammer horrors such as *The Satanic Rites of Dracula*) didn't so much read it as misread it entirely and deemed it blasphemous. So Bernie withdrew the financing.

Eric, as John once remarked to me, 'knows a lot of very famous people in the rock industry'. Indeed Keith Moon, outrageous drummer of The Who, was due to play a prophet in the film and had already learned his lines before his untimely overdose and death. Looking for money in Los Angeles, Eric bumped into George Harrison, a devoted Python fan – he always claimed that watching their TV shows helped him get over the break-up of the Beatles – and told him of their plight. George said that he would find the money, which he did from his own resources. Mortgaging his house, he came up with $4m – the equivalent of nearly $40m today. George said he just wanted to see the film; Eric maintains it was the most expensive cinema ticket ever purchased, and George was rewarded with a fleeting part as Mr Papadopoulos.

John very much wanted to play the part of Brian but the others were opposed to this. In Python, Cleese was usually an authority figure but the whole point of Brian is that he is a complete innocent and has no desire whatever to be a leader. Terry J astutely argued Cleese out of the role by pointing out that he would have to forfeit many of the meaty character parts on offer. This proved true on the very first day of filming which was the stoning. Who else but John could berate the culprit who broke the stoning embargo? 'Come on. Who threw that stone? There's always one, isn't there?' Or deliver the speech of the revolutionary leader, Reg, with such pungency that it has fallen into the English language: 'What have the Romans ever done for us?' (followed by another J.C. list).

Graham Chapman very nearly didn't become a Python or have a career in show business at all. At Cambridge he read medicine and went on to St Bartholomew's Hospital in London to complete his studies. He managed to be a medical student by day and appear in the Footlights Revue, *Cambridge Circus*, by night. But then an offer came for the revue to go on tour to New Zealand and Gra was faced with a tough choice. 'I was secretary of the Students' Union,' he told me, 'and one day the Queen Mother came to open a new building and I was obliged to take tea with her. She had beautiful skin. More to fill in time than anything else I mentioned to her that I was having difficulty making this decision and she said: "Oh you must see New Zealand, the mountains are so beautiful." So I told my parents that the Queen Mother had ordered me to go to New Zealand and that was pretty well that.'

Although he never obtained a practising certificate to prescribe medicines, Gra arrived in Tunisia with cases full of drugs, none of them obtained legally. He used to drink far too much, to the annoyance of John, who found it hard to write in the afternoons with someone who had fallen asleep, and to the amusement of Eric who fondly recalled the days when Graham would crawl around the floors of pubs barking like a dog.

Evidently, he played King Arthur in *The Holy Grail* fairly pissed and had difficulty remembering his lines and, on occasion, even standing up.

But he cleaned up his act for *Brian* and used the time regained from the bottle to act as unit doctor. His hotel room was an open door to cast and crew alike. Graham's early miracles included curing Terry Jones's stomach upset and alleviating the art director's sunstroke. When the lighting gaffer, Chuck Finch (whom I knew from *A Bridge Too Far* when he fell from the top of a ladder after eating a piece of cannabis cake cooked by Ryan O'Neal) went to see him, he whispered: 'Graham, I can hardly speak.' Gra shone a torch into his mouth and weightily pronounced: 'I think you've got a sore throat.' 'I know I've got a fucking sore throat,' Chuck responded, 'that's why I can hardly speak.'

I had my own experience of Dr Gra in action when I was playing in the second round of Monty Python's International Tunisian Tennis Tournament. This had been organised by the first assistant director, Jonathan Benson, in the sure knowledge that he would win it himself and collect the kitty (in London he knocked up with Vitas Gerulaitis and had his old racquets). My opponent was Andrew MacLachlan, a friend of Terry J's from Oxford, who had come to play a Giggling Guard, an Official Stoner's Helper and other versatile roles. The temperature was well over 100 degrees and Andrew had possibly enjoyed a little too much Thibarine (a Tunisian liqueur which is about 140 per cent proof) the night before.

Taking advantage of this, I managed to win the first set. But at the changeover Andrew just collapsed on to the ground, out cold. I tried to rouse him but he appeared to have fallen into a deep coma. Jonathan, who had been watching, went to get Graham who arrived with two suitcases and his pipe firmly clasped between his teeth. I

Dr Graham Chapman with his nurse in Tunisia.

ventured to suggest that Andrew might be dead, he lay so still with his breathing barely perceptible. 'He'll be fine,' Gra assured me, 'We'll soon have him up and about.' He produced a saline drip from one of his bags and plunged it into Andrew's arm. Within less than five minutes Andrew was on his feet again, picked up his racquet and asked me what the score was, as if nothing had happened. 'Should he play on?' I asked Graham. 'I don't see why not,' said the unit doctor, 'but make sure he takes plenty of water. You too, Iain.'

So we did and Andrew bloody well beat me. Talk about Lazarus.

I genuinely believe Graham got more pleasure from his role as doctor than he did as Brian. His acting seemed so effortless; he sailed through the film hermetically sealed in this bubble of incredulity at what was happening to him. As Terry J observed: 'Of all of us, I think Gra is the one most likely to be Monty Python.' Only when he was obliged to open his bedroom window and appear stark naked before a multitude of Muslims (playing Jews) did he break out of character and roar with laughter as all the women screamed and scuttled away, their religion forbidding them to cast their eyes upon a foreign member.

The BBC film crew arrived in Tunisia with bad news ... and good. The bad was that their union had failed to get a pay deal with the Beeb and so all crews had been ordered to work to rule. The good was the production assistant, Mo Hammond, who was devastatingly attractive: already tanned from a holiday in Ibiza with a model's figure and a smile you could see in the dark.

John, the cameraman, took me aside and said he had hoped they could have come to some sort of a deal with me but, unfortunately, the appropriately named Dave, the assistant sound recordist, was a shop steward and would insist on doing things by the book. This meant strict clocking on and off time (I didn't dare ask if this was London or Tunisian time), meals and tea breaks at the appointed hour, a long list of who could operate and carry what equipment (I hoped this let me off carrying the tripod – every director's nightmare chore), and no overtime.

Well, always look on the bright side, I thought, at least that freed up my weekends and maybe Mo would like to go swimming ...

Dave was a man in his fifties who, being unable to progress from assistant sound recordist to sound recordist during his thirty years in the job, found his métier as a hard-line, Fred Kite-type trade unionist. But fate, to an extent, was on my side. The first scenes we covered were in the tunnels beneath the Ribat (fortress) at Monastir where rival fanatics (The Judean People's Front, The People's Front of Judea and the Campaign for Free Galilee) clash as they find they are all hell-bent on kidnapping Pilate's wife. Reg, in a very Fred Kite manner, had spelt out his group's demands: 'We're giving Pilate two days to dismantle the entire apparatus of the Roman Imperialist

State and if he doesn't agree we're going to cut off his wife's head. Also we're demanding a ten-foot mahogany statue of the Emperor Julius Caesar with his cock hanging out.'

Dave was curiously muted after that satire on excessive demands. Also I had arranged with the Italian caterer, Signor Memmo, that the BBC crew be brought tea in china cups at precisely four o'clock. The main feature was still shooting so while their Oscar-winning cameraman, Peter Biziou, was hard at work, the BBC stopped for tea. Or didn't. The embarrassment was just too great and thereafter there was an outbreak of common sense.

Spike Milligan turned up on the set one morning and he was immediately written into the script, playing a character called Spike. All the Pythons had been avid *Goon Show* listeners. Spike and Sellers had undoubtedly opened the door for British surrealist humour. 'Our aim was to get as much past the BBC censors as we possibly could,' Spike told me.

Placed in the vanguard of the believers charging after Brian, who loses a sandal in his desperation to get away, Spike is witness to the argument as to whether the sandal is a 'sign' and terminates it with the ad-libbed words: 'Let us pray.' He was due to do his close-up after lunch but he just disappeared. Mo pointed out that we had failed to get him to sign a release form for his appearance in our documentary. I doubted if he would mind and later caught up with him in the BBC bar in London and he didn't. He was sitting on his own. 'I'm waiting for Johnny Speight,' he said. 'He told me he had a surprise for me. The surprise is: he hasn't turned up.'

When John recruited the other five for Monty Python he certainly knew he didn't want it to be serious satire – surreal satire, maybe – and he wanted to build on Spike's liberating influence on freedom from conventional sketches and punchlines. Then it was up to the others. Terry Jones felt: 'We were not philosophers. Our only claim to people's attention was that we could make them laugh.' Eric added that in some of the material they put a modern consciousness on history, certainly true of the Spanish Inquisition.

Michael was very much aware of their middle-class backgrounds in which the serious professions beckoned as careers, or so their parents hoped. Sometimes their rebellion was only too apparent as in the sketch where he played a chartered accountant who found the job 'dull, stuffy, tedious and boring' and went to a headhunter to apply for a job as a lion-tamer. Cleese informed him: 'Mr Anchovy, your report says that you are an extremely dull person: unimaginative, timid, lacking in initiative, spineless, easily dominated, no sense of humour, irrepressibly drab and awful. In most professions these would be a considerable drawback but in chartered accountancy they're a positive boon.' (As I've mentioned, the hallmark of many a Cleese script is a long list – see 'Dead Parrot' or 'Cheese Shop' – with a thesaurus sometimes not too far away.) John was nervous when the chartered accountant item was transmitted as he had to go and see his own accountant the next day. The man had loved it. 'People rarely see themselves from outside,' John reasoned.

Although the Python television series had ended with a degree of factionalism with Cleese backing out of the last, foreshortened, series, in Tunisia the atmosphere was harmonious and fraternal. It was fun to film a lunch table with such lively minds, surrounded by moaning camels. Gilliam: 'A camel is a horse designed by a committee.' Palin: 'A camel is a bus stuffed by a blind taxidermist.' Idle: 'If it's a double-decker then it's a dromedary.' Cleese: 'A donkey is a camel without a hump.' Palin: 'A camel is a lolly seen through a huge magnifying glass.'

Terry Gilliam tended to be the good-natured butt of some ribbing from the Cambridge boys. As Cleese observed: 'Being American, Terry is not very good at language. In fact he has only two phrases: "yeah, I really like that" or "yeah, it really pisses me off". So life is divided for Terry into two clear and distinct categories: things he really likes and things that piss him off.' Chapman recalled: 'I remember we were flying over the Great Lakes once on a Python tour of Canada and Terry pointed out of the window and observed, "Look, a whole bunch of water."'

In fact, Terry Gilliam was probably the most popular Python among the group. He was good-natured and seemingly always on a high with his infectious giggle resonating around the Roman courtyard. He recalled how, many years ago, an English writer was being flown first class to Los Angeles to do some work on a screenplay. The man drank rather a lot on the plane and left his wallet in the car-hire building. Driving erratically towards Freeway 101, he was stopped by a motorcycle cop and asked for proof of ID. He had none but pleaded that he was an English writer who had just landed. 'If you're British, name the American in the Monty Python team,' said the cop – somewhat surprisingly as the series was then unknown in the States. But the writer did and the cop let him off, since he happened to be Terry's brother.

With his fine-art background (the crashing Python foot was taken from Bronzino's Cupid), Terry relished the idea of super-imposing slapdash Doric Roman columns on Zeffirelli's Hebrew temples and decorating the interior with mosaics and frescoes.

Although Terry Jones was the director of *Brian*, he collaborated closely with Gilliam on the look of the film, with the designer frequently framing a shot with the camera. Jones was a democratic director, managing to absorb input from the others and consulting

Terry Jones, collaborative director of *Life of Brian.*

them on whether a scene had worked. This was not born of insecurity but confidence. Too much is made of the auteur director in cinema; this was auteur direction, design, writing and performance by a team of men who knew what they were trying to achieve.

Jones and Cleese had engaged in a good deal of head-butting in the television days but here, with the script in place, harmony prevailed. Terry J is the most intellectual of the group. After the film he wrote a book, *Chaucer's Knight: The Portrait of a Medieval Mercenary,* which challenged the gentle, academic world of Chaucerian literature by attempting to prove that the 'perfect gentle knight' of *The Canterbury Tales* was actually a brutal, hardened killer. At the time of filming he and his wife had, he assured me, an 'open' marriage – something that was borne out when I came across him on a day off frolicking in the Med with one of the actresses from the film, both of them stark naked.

How different from the home life of his longtime writing partner, Michael Palin. 'Michael is appallingly normal,' Graham confided. 'There he is with his wife and two children, all very happy together in not too large a house not too small a house in a not too nice a part of London that's not too awful either with moderately terrible neighbours who are really quite pleasant really when you get to know them.'

Niceness has long been Michael's crime but he is, for men and women alike, the childhood friend and adult companion they would like to have had: clean-cut, cheerful and funny. John Cleese thinks that Palin can produce a spontaneous, witty stream of consciousness better than anyone save Peter Cook. In his memorable performance as Pontius Pilate – 'I have a vewwy great friend in Wome called Biggus Dickus' – he would have both cast and crew in stitches as he ad-libbed a different silly name for Biggus's wife on each take (they ended up using Incontinentia Buttocks). I asked him how on earth he managed this and he confessed that he had made a list of names in his hotel room the previous evening.

For the tag of the BBC documentary, I questioned Mike on what he did at the end of a day's shooting. He came back immediately: 'We usually have a drug-based orgy of some sort with women, politicians – anybody who's good at an orgy. A lot of stuff to smoke, three kinds of orangeade and Ribena for the children – there are children – and, obviously, straw for the animals.'

His wit aside, he is the most watchful and observant Python. He would talk to the extras, learning that it was not wise to speak critically of President Bourguiba of Tunisia who had deposed the Bey Muhammad VIII al-Amin who had assumed the title of King twenty years ago and ruled the country with an iron fist. Or he would delve into the history of Carthage, which once dominated the Mediterranean, and observe how its Roman and Punic heritage had been built over to make it the Beverly Hills of Tunisia. No wonder his later travel series set new standards.

Few people would guess that Michael is possibly the most obdurate of the Pythons. Many years later when the others had been tempted by a $10 million offer to do a two-week tour, he refused, fearing the work of men nearing sixty would tarnish the carefree abandon that characterised their television series.

His joviality in public cloaks a darker character. 'There are times in the middle of the night when I wonder how I'm going to face the next day. I've occasionally contemplated walking to the end of the plank but never jumped off.' Tragically, his elder sister, Angela, did. She committed suicide in 1986, leaving behind a husband and three children. Both of them had grown up in a Sheffield household with a father who had a bad temper and a stammer. Michael winces at the memory of how he would have embarrassing scenes with waiters in restaurants. Resultingly shy as a child, he used to escape to Sheffield public library where he would devour travel books and go on fictional journeys.

Even before the BBC asked him to go around the world in eighty days, he was a committed lone traveller. But sometimes a black cloud would hang over him. He told me how he was once sitting at a café table in St Mark's Square in Venice when a frightening feeling of unease came over him, chilling his spine. He took the next flight home. He has always kept a diary. I asked him why. His reply was telling. 'So that the days have some meaning and don't just slip off the side of the world.' I was to get to know Michael better in the years to come as we worked on *Wanda* and *Fierce Creatures* and his company was to be treasured.

Most evenings in Tunisia I would eat with John, and frequently Mo. Sometimes we were joined by other members of the cast and crew. We always seemed to end up eating *brik à l'oeuf*, the local delicacy which consisted of egg in pastry with a hint of cheese. It seemed to be as ubiquitous as mullet on Hydra. Dr Gra counselled us against eating the local fish, saying it came out of 'one of the most polluted seas in the world and was full of men's excrement and intestinal flora'. Terry Jones ignored him since he preferred 'natural' foodstuffs and Graham maintained he had to give him little pink pills to enable him to direct.

I had rarely seen John in better humour than he was during those weeks in Monastir. The only thing missing in his well-ordered life was sex. He had invited a girlfriend to the next Tunisian location at Gabes after we had left, with the hope of rectifying this situation. There, it was reported, his good humour temporarily deserted him and he became somewhat irritated while being crucified although whether this was due to a cold or a cold girlfriend is not a question I have ever put to him.

The BBC shoot went well with the Pythons creatively co-operative, thanks, in part, to the fact that the contract said they owned the documentary after two BBC transmissions. It now adds 'extra value', as they say, to the DVD. Professionally, everything that the team did was always divided by six – not something that pleased Eric when it came to the publishing royalties for 'Always Look on the Bright Side of Life'. But, on this occasion, they divided the documentary earnings by seven and gave the seventh part to me. There was no need to do that but I was touched. It was like becoming a temporary fifth Beatle – well, almost.

Towards the end of our shoot, Mo came to the balcony of my room to go through notes of what we had shot so far and cables to go to London the next day. Maybe the BBC strike was over, but they would probably have told us.

Then: crack! A terrifying bolt of lightning followed by a loud, iridescent firework display put on by heaven itself. Followed by thick rods of rain that would have floated Noah's ark. A true African storm, exciting and intimidating.

We put away our papers and watched in awe. I had played Casca in a school production of *Julius Caesar*; nobody put it better:

> I have seen tempests, when the scolding winds
> Have rived the knotty oaks, and I have seen
> The ambitious ocean swell and rage and foam,
> To be exalted with the threatening clouds:
> But never till to-night, never till now,
> Did I go through a tempest dropping fire.

Such storms are auguries of life-changing events. Caesar, I recall, turned into a human pin cushion later that day. For us, matters took a little longer. Mo had a chap in London.

13

Alien … The Shining with Kubrick and Nicholson

Nobody on the planet had a greater desire to be in two places at the same time than David Frost. He loved doing chat shows in London and New York in the same week. To his delight, the advent of the Concorde flight from Heathrow to JFK in November 1977 at least enabled him to arrive in New York, in local-time terms, before he had left London. His nightly *The David Frost Show* had been cancelled by then, but he persuaded NBC to put on *Headliners with David Frost* in prime time. The programme was something of a conveyor belt, with David interviewing as many celebs as possible within the hour, while Liz Smith of the *New York Daily News* provided the gossip.

Even with the supersonic plane, Frostie was unable to knock off star names in Europe and the States simultaneously, so he asked me to 'be him' in Europe and he would insert himself in my place in the editing. His American producers organised everything and I would drop in on film locations and the like and interview the stars. It was much easier to work *for* David than, on paper, being the BBC producer who contracted him.

Thus I would arrive on the Greek island of Rhodes, where they were making *Escape to Athena* (a pretty dire film) and Roger Moore, Telly Savalas, Stefanie Powers, Claudia Cardinale, Richard Roundtree, Sonny Bono, Elliott Gould and David Niven would all become *Headliners* in a couple of days' shooting. I cannot recall anything anybody said save for David Niven who retold his favourite story of Prince Rainier asking him with whom he had had the best sex in Hollywood and David replying: 'Oh, Grace ... er, Grace ... um ... Gracie Fields.' I had a list of questions – great loves, favourite characters, etc – so that the producers could montage these back in New York. This somewhat came to grief when I was obliged to ask Harrison Ford (on *Hanover Street* – an even direr film) how he liked to relax after filming. 'Smoking dope and having sex,' came the honest, but not prime time, reply.

Sadly, *Headliners* came to grief after one brief season. Bad ratings. 'It wasn't me who scheduled you to follow *Grizzly Adams*,' Fred Silverman, the president of NBC, apologised to David. (Grizzly was an innocent fugitive who nurtured an abandoned bear cub in the wilderness, successfully putting it, and the viewers, to sleep each week.)

Rather more stimulating was the sci-fi film *Alien* – 'In space no-one can hear you scream'. But we could hear the screams on the Shepperton set when the slimy creature shot out of John Hurt's chest and the rest of the cast genuinely hollered. The director, Ridley Scott, had omitted to inform them what was about to happen. Ridley, who had been at the Royal College of Art, was fanatical about the film's design, so Fox commissioned me to make a documentary about the movie's two contrasting concept designers. In those pre Computer Generated Imagery (CGI) days, Ron Cobb used NASA blueprints to design an almost fully functional spacecraft interior, Nostromo (named after Conrad's novel). When you walked along its sculpted corridors from the control bridge to the med lab to the cocoons where the crew slept to the old workshop, you sensed it was more of an old space tub, part futuristic flat screens, part cobbled together workshops (made, in fact, from bits of Lancaster bombers). Even the signage had a logic: a black symbol warned you the next chamber was a vacuum; a red one signalled an area of artificial gravity.

In complete contrast were the unknown planet and the Alien. When Ridley was shown the scary visions of the Swiss artist, H. R. Giger (a dark Swiss surrealist whose actress wife had committed suicide), the director was captivated by one drawing, Necronom IV, and this informed the design of the planet. Giger and his new girlfriend/assistant stayed in a B & B near Shepperton Studios, and churned out fearsome images. Giger told me his style was biomechanical, the creature's eggs were fertilised by the planet. The Alien emerging from Hurt's chest was a model, but then a skinny seven foot two Nigerian, Bolaji Badejo, was put inside the suit with the terrifying head with its huge tongue-like proboscis and lethal jaws. Film buffs pore over the material but most male fans will carry a visual memory of Sigourney Weaver's pert bottom in her white knickers.

At the same time, another memorable film set had been created in Elstree Studios in north London: The Overlook Hotel, the location of Stephen King's thriller *The Shining*. Stanley Kubrick had built its vast interior using several sound stages. Snippets had crept out in the press, but it was well known that Kubrick films were closed sets. I got a call from a mutual friend asking if I would sign Vivian Kubrick's (Stanley's daughter's) ACTT card; nobody could work on a film then without belonging to the technicians' union. This seemed strange since the director's daughter would certainly be able to get sufficient signatures from her father and his crew.

Vivian turned up at our house in Fulham the following night. She was only eighteen but clearly had a determination that had been chipped off the old block. I duly signed and then she revealed the true purpose of her visit. She was shooting a documentary about Stanley at work and needed somebody to do the interviews for her. She had seen some of my stuff and thought I might be right. I didn't exactly need a lot of persuading; *Dr. Strangelove* had long been my favourite film: clever, hilarious and quite brilliant in the way Peter Sellers played all three main parts. 'Will I get to interview your father?' I asked. 'No,' she smiled, 'but he wants to meet you.'

And there he was, the reclusive film legend, in his blue boilersuit, beard, rimless specs, standing in the vast ballroom of The Overlook. 'Want to take a look around?' he inquired in his soft Brooklyn voice. Kubrick had a proprietorial pride in the hotel he had created: the vast and intricate Colorado Lounge, long interconnecting corridors to the enormous hotel kitchen with aisles separating the stoves and storage racks. On the upper level, the narrow Torrance family apartment and the elegant and ominous Room 237 where the revenants would be manifest. He told me the hotel was based on The Timberline Lodge on Mt Hood in Oregon (a huge replicated frontage had been constructed on the Elstree lot). The owner had asked him not to use Room 217 as King had in the book for fear of putting off potential visitors. I would have thought it might have attracted them. The Timberline had no room 237.

I dutifully expressed my awe at this complicated structure and asked him why it had not been built as individual sets, as was the case in most films. 'He's the reason,' said Stanley, indicating a man, tall enough to play the Alien, with a portable, hydraulic camera attached to his body. This was Garrett Brown, inventor of the Steadicam – a new toy that Kubrick was experimenting with on the movie. Hand-held shots inevitably had a slight wobble, magnified on a large cinema screen. The hydraulic Steadicam eliminated this. Garrett later told me that the exacting director insisted on seeing exactly what he was seeing as he made his way through the set so Garrett had also invented a makeshift transmitter to enable Stanley to monitor the shots. Stanley had also insisted that the camera shoot

Stanley Kubrick is always looking for an original angle.

from the point of view of little Danny in the film, as he tricycled through the forbidding hotel. Kubrick was good at pushing technicians beyond what they thought possible and it led to the invention of a low-mode bracket so Garrett could shoot from below his waist – an innovation now frequently used in movies.

In King's book, the hotel's garden consisted of topiary animals which came alive. Today that would be no problem for special effects' houses. But not then, not even for Kubrick. So instead a complex hedge maze had been built on the backlot. So complex that crew members were given a map of it attached to their call sheets on the days and nights they shot there, but many still found themselves lost. It was easier to find the centre since that had been built to one side of the set. The plan was for part of the maze to be dismantled and assembled inside on the vacated Stage One. There it would be winterised with dendritic (sodium chloride) dairy salt and Styrofoam snow and, to capture the atmosphere the director wanted, dense oil-smoke would be pumped in. And up your nose if you were unfortunate enough to be on set.

So, what was Stanley Kubrick like? Almost avuncular. Stanley adored his little girl so any friend of Vivian's couldn't be all bad. In his dealings with his cast and crew he was polite, quietly spoken (as anybody with such power and respect can be) and always got his own way in the end. It is known that he did multiple takes, as many as seventy-five if need be. I was to be on the receiving end of that later. Stanley was always looking for a little bit more. One of his favourite actors, Murray Melvin, told me that Stanley would see something – a gesture, perhaps – in an early take which was imperfect in other respects, so he would get the actor to do the scene again and again in the hope that he would repeat it and the rest of the action would be up to scratch. But if he told the actor what he was looking for, the result might look artificial.

Garrett Brown said Kubrick also did it because he needed to know he had three perfect takes when he started editing at the end of the shoot. My own feeling was that he did it because he could. And, whether he knew it or not, he was employing a technique top tennis players use: they practise every stroke so thoroughly that they develop a muscle memory, so in a match the body plays the shot and the mind is free to consider the tactics. Thus actors, through repetition, would forget they were saying lines or, indeed, playing a part, but were freed to just be that person. Nobody would question Kubrick, not Warners, not the crew, maybe occasionally an actor – Jack Nicholson, on one occasion, asked Stanley to call a halt as seventy-six-year-old Scatman Crothers began to wilt. It was hard to divine what might be going on in the mind's eye of this perfectionist director.

In *The Shining*, Jack Torrance (Nicholson), a writer, takes a year's job as caretaker of an empty Colorado hotel. He brings his wife, Wendy (Shelley Duvall), and little son, Danny (Danny Lloyd), who is possessed of the 'shining' – the psychic ability to see and communicate with the hotel's ghosts. The previous caretaker had killed his wife, his twin daughters and then himself. Encroaching madness eventually drives Jack down the same path.

I dutifully did my interviews for Vivian. It has been said that Shelley Duvall, who played Jack's put-upon wife, had been bullied by Stanley. If so, I didn't witness it, although he did get a bit testy with her one day. Unknown to most, Shelley was pretty ill for most of the shoot, a condition made worse by the oppressed and then terrified role she played. Less prominent today, Shelley (Robert Duvall's daughter) was a considerable talent and arrived on the set having won the Best Actress Award at Cannes for Robert Altman's *3 Women*.

Vivian had formed an almost maternal bond with little Danny. She delighted in getting him to perform the croaking voice of his invisible friend, Tony, represented by his little finger, who warns Danny of his destiny. The five year old had great fun shooting the movie – what child wouldn't? – not least because he had no notion of its sinister content. He didn't continue as an actor, but now in his forties Danny is a science professor, arguably a more worthwhile profession.

Jack Nicholson was forty-two and in his prime when he made *The Shining*. Already nominated for five Oscars and Best Actor winner for *One Flew Over the Cuckoo's Nest*, he was Stanley's favoured choice for Jack. No wonder: few other major stars could communicate madness and chilling danger as he could.

Jack had agreed to do my interview on his Saturday off. I turned up early at his suite at Elstree to go through my questions. But I was not alone. A familiar figure in a blue boiler suit was putting Perspex on the windows to filter the natural daylight. 'He's going to talk about more than *The Shining*, right?' Stanley asked me, as he started arranging the lights. I should have guessed he'd be there; he had a compulsive need to micromanage everything to do with his films, whether rewriting newspaper advertisements for them in Peru or getting New York cinemas screening them to paint their walls black.

Vivian had placed her camera in Jack's dressing room to shoot through the open door. Or, more likely, Stanley had. The star arrived in great good humour, as he tended to every day. He had a warm rapport with the director, eager to experiment with variations on each take and to offer ad-libs.

We started with how he and *The Shining* had come together. 'I'd just finished a summer writing a script and I made a few calls to see if there was any work around. One of them was to Stanley and he said: "That's a coincidence, I've just been working on a project where the leading character's name is Jack." So he sent me a copy of the book. It wasn't that necessary; I would have done anything Stanley wanted.'

Is Jack a psychopath?

'Definitely. You know, in the book it says that Jack used to be a teacher but he pummelled a student. When we were discussing the script I would say: "Well, Stanley, nobody would ever do this in this situation," and he'd reply: "But you're insane." You can't play insane, as I learnt from the people when preparing *Cuckoo's Nest*. It doesn't look like anything in particular. It's all in the actions, what people actually do. With Jack, it surfaces whenever he's thwarted. He's as far over the line as anybody I'll ever play.'

When you go home in the evening, is it easy to divest yourself of the character?

'Heeeeere's Johnny!!!'

Jack, pointedly to Stanley: 'Well, we get home so late in the evening from this job that there isn't much time to divest. But it's an occupational hazard for actors, although my first teacher always said: "If you can't dump the character in three minutes, you'd better re-examine your work."'

Nicholson had grown up in New Jersey where his early talent emerged in a school play. 'I was rather flamboyant for a seven year old and I sang 'Managua Nicaragua' – a hit song of the forties – in a red-and-gold crepe-paper cape and bellboy's monkey hat.' His first job was in the cartoon department in MGM where he could observe movie making. 'I was sort of star-struck at that time, still am.' He was spotted on the lot by Joe Pasternak, a leading MGM producer in the fifties, who asked him to do a screen test. It didn't go well. 'You've got to get rid of that high-pitched Jersey accent,' Pasternak told him. 'Take some acting lessons.'

The MGM talent department sent him to work at night at The Players' Ring Theater, a little showcase theatre in Los Angeles, where he rose from cleaner to bit-part player. 'I got to see everybody read for parts and almost no-one read well – it's the toughest thing to do. So I always read well. I know part of my mystique is that I had a very hard beginning to my career, but it's simply not true. I only started to work in films because I liked doing it and wanted to do it well. I wanted to do something in life well. I'm still working on it.'

'Although early on I was in some of the most dreadful pictures of all time, so were all the people I was working with, trying to do their best under the circumstances. It's not that bad for you. There's an old acting cliché: "You can only be as good as you're willing to be bad." You know, I've always felt I was lucky. If I'd been successful early on, I'd be trying to make a comeback now. When I was around twenty-two I was doing a play with Michael Brandon. And he got the lead in *Bonanza*. Everyone was envious but he was in the series for the next fourteen years while my career was getting on. That was very good for him, but I wouldn't trade places with him.'

Nicholson got his movie start as a juvenile delinquent in *The Cry Baby Killer* in 1958. There was not much chance of even a retake in a Roger Corman quickie, shot in ten days. It would be a decade before his big break came as a drunken lawyer in *Easy Rider*. 'I had taken LSD under clinical supervision to write *The Trip* for Peter Fonda and Dennis Hopper and when Rip Torn dropped out of *Easy Rider* they asked me to do it. The character was Texan and I didn't have much time to prepare but LBJ's speech pattern was familiar to me so that was something I could refer to. Doing the camp-fire scene I obviously did get stoned. I took the Nick-Nick-Nick gesture from a guy called Gypsy Bill, who had been a mechanic on earlier motorcycle films.'

Nicholson got an Oscar nomination for that and another the following year (1970) for his failed pianist in *Five Easy Pieces*, undoubtedly fuelled by the monologue where he breaks down in front of his wheelchair-bound father. 'Carole Eastman, the writer, didn't want it to be in there. She thought it was the obligatory summing-up scene and you shouldn't pander to the audience that much. But the producer wanted it, so I wrote it myself the morning we shot it.'

Was it true, I wondered, that Miss Eastman had taken the 'hold the mayo' scene from something she'd seen Jack once do in a Sunset Strip café? 'Oh yes,' he laughed, 'and other times as well. Not any more, but I was more prone then to acting out my emotions in public.'

Nicholson's career then accelerated like a neutrino: *Carnal Knowledge, The Last Detail, Chinatown*, Antonioni's *The Passenger*, culminating in his first Oscar for Randle P. McMurphy in *One Flew Over the Cuckoo's Nest* in 1975.

'I had tried to option the book with a friend ten years earlier when I was twenty-six. I knew it would be a success. It was a classic like *From Here to Eternity*. You were carried by emotion for the people involved as opposed to the theme. Milos Forman [the director] and I went to the Oregon State Mental Hospital while we were doing the script and decided to film it there. The research was all around you. We could drop into a ward at any time during the day. I had to watch the shock treatments because it is not something you can conceptualise out of your imagination. We were all there all the time. A very close group – not like the usual shoot where an actor comes one Wednesday and you don't see him again for two weeks. That's one of the reasons the work got to such a good depth.'

It was the first film since Frank Capra's *It Happened One Night* in 1934 to win Oscars in all major categories and it made Jack rich; he took a substantial percentage of the film's $200 million gross.

And then came *The Shining*. We had been talking for two-and-a-half hours by then, interrupted only by Vivian having to change film magazines every ten minutes. I suggested that maybe we had covered pretty well everything but Stanley, inevitably, wanted more. Jack lit up a joint and whispered to me: 'That man just doesn't know when to stop.'

But something unexpected happened halfway through the next mag. The phone rang and Jack answered it. Vivian kept the camera running and captured an exchange between Jack and his girlfriend, Anjelica Huston. He was tender and loving and chatted to her about plans for that evening and then, somehow reinvigorated, continued to chat to me about his acting.

'An actor usually wants the character he's playing to become as real as possible. But lately I've gotten interested in not necessarily creating characters you might expect to see in the grocery store the next morning. Maybe someone who's never existed. Someone who could be real but is an unreal person. Stanley sometimes says of a take: "Yeah, it's real, but it's not interesting." When I come up against a director who has a concept that I don't agree with or maybe just hadn't thought of, I'd be more prone to go with them than my own because I want to be out of control as an actor. I want them to have the control. Otherwise it's going to become predictably my work and that's not fun.

'I would say unequivocally that I have always done the most pragmatic, adventurous, creative choice that was available to me at the time. I don't want to be the same guy they saw in the last picture. I believe in change – that's why I ended up in this occupation. The really tasty part of this craft is that you can just be somebody else. I think it's silly to think there's not competition on every movie. In reality you have to work together as a unit, but there's still that inner,

I think, positive competition. I would be afraid to be openly competitive with Marlon Brando as an actor. That would be crazy. I call him "The Big Man on the Hill".'

'Why do you call him that,' I asked.

'Because he lives up the hill from me,' Jack grinned.

And that was that. I asked Vivian if she had any film left and there was one last mag. So I suggested to Stanley that maybe he would like to talk on camera for ten minutes. Jack joined in, insisting that it was a great idea. But, as ever, the director demurred saying we should get back to his house for lunch. The family had only recently moved to a huge Victorian mansion, Childwickbury Manor, in Hertfordshire. It had a pillared façade and Stanley had converted the stable block into a mini studio with cutting, recording and projection rooms, functioning offices and, outside, satellite dishes so he could watch television from all over the world. Pride of place was a shortwave radio where he could eavesdrop on conversations between pilots and Air Traffic Control at Heathrow Airport. 'You'd be amazed how many near-misses there are,' he warned me. Although a qualified pilot himself, he had resolved never to fly again.

In the baronial kitchen there was a vast refectory table groaning with cold cuts, soup and salad, bread and wine – and books and boxes. We were joined by his wife, Christiane, whom he had met when she sang '*Ein treuer Husar*' in the last scene of *Paths of Glory*. She is a warm and chatty woman – and an accomplished painter. I think she knew that by living in a place where Stanley could work when he finished shooting, she and Vivian and their other daughter, Anya, would see more of him. The family were expansive hosts.

I recall the conversation turning to what happens after death. Stanley really believed in his revenants in *The Shining*. 'If you can be frightened by ghosts,' he argued, 'then you've got to believe in supernatural beings, and they come from beyond the grave.' He didn't think that Stephen King would like the film, not least because he had rejected the author's screenplay. 'Stephen's script was too cut and dried,' he said. 'Art isn't about giving answers, it's about asking questions' – thereby explaining much of his work. He had moved the story away from sheer terror to a more psychological examination of Jack's mind. How Stanley would have reacted to the 2012 documentary *Room 237* which argued that his film was about: (a) the persecution of American Indians, (b) the Nazi holocaust or (c) Kubrick's guilt at faking moon footage purportedly brought back by Apollo 11, can only be left to conjecture.

As he cleared away his plate, Kubrick purposely put his knife and fork sharp end down in the dishwasher. 'I do this in case the cats jump on them,' he explained. When I was leaving, he took me aside and sort of apologised for not doing an interview, quoting the science-fiction writer, H.P. Lovecraft: 'In all things that are mysterious, never explain.' It was up to his audience to draw meanings from his work, not for him to spoon-feed them. It also preserved the enigma and mystique of Stanley Kubrick.

In the late nineties he persuaded Steven Spielberg to direct *A.I.* with Kubrick producing. Steven told me that his wife, Kate, was driven to remove their personal fax machine from the bedroom of their house in Brentwood, Los Angeles, as Kubrick would fax them endless brochures during the night from local estate agents so that they could rent a place near him in Hertfordshire.

But the collaboration was not to be. Stanley, aged seventy, died of a massive heart attack on 7 March 1999. Nobody expected it. He didn't go to doctors because he didn't believe they were fully informed.

Steven and Kate and Tom Cruise and Nicole Kidman (who had spent nearly two years with him on *Eyes Wide Shut*) flew in for the funeral. Stanley had wanted to be buried in his own garden, beside his dogs and cats, to keep his grave away from prying, or venerating, eyes. He intended to remain secretive, even in death. Jan, Christiane's brother, had got the local undertakers to dig a plot behind the house. One of them asked him if he had council permission, something that had never occurred to Jan. As executive jets from Hollywood were landing at London Elstree Aerodrome for the funeral, Jan was pleading with St Albans Council to be allowed to bury his brother-in-law. Fortunately, compassion rather than strict adherence to the book ruled that day.

Vivian, too, came from LA, but with a minder from the Church of Scientology which she had joined during her time with the Cruises. She was greatly changed from the enthusiastic teenager who had bounced into my kitchen twenty years earlier. Bowed by grief, she found it difficult to meet anybody in the eye. Seven years later her sister, Anya, died of cancer. But this time she did not return to England for the funeral.

14

Friday Night ... Saturday Morning ... The Bishop Attacks

The BBC, as David Frost was wont to say, is alma mater to us all. And for his and, to an extent, my generation that was certainly true. When Frost emerged fully formed from the chrysalis in *That Was The Week That Was* in 1962, ITV was a mere seven years old. You pretty well had to have learned how to make television programmes at the Beeb.

Although I had left the place when I was thirty, my heart still belonged to Auntie so it was intriguing to get a phone call when I was thirty-five, inviting me to come and see the new Controller of BBC2, Brian Wenham. I knew Brian from ITN and, again, when he was my boss at Current Affairs. And I didn't particularly like him. He was a game player, whether with Corporation politics, or, more cruelly, with people's careers.

So when, in February 1979, I went to have a cup of coffee in his office in Television Centre, I made sure that I had a long spoon. At first it seemed as if I had been summoned to hear a lecture on BBC history. He said how BBC2's *Late Night Line-Up* – a show which began by assessing the evening viewing and ended up doing pretty well anything it liked – had been axed by his predecessor seven years ago. Wenham thought this had been the right decision. 'It had lost its focus, no control.'

He then went back to the time of *That Was The Week* and said how that had come from Current Affairs and was much tighter programming. But he felt that satire had died in the sixties (wrong! *Spitting Image* was to run triumphantly from 1984 to 1996) and what he needed to end the week on BBC2 was a 'new sort of programme'.

'You were never a real television news journalist, you know,' Wenham told me, flattery being his chosen weapon. I wondered what a 'real television news journalist' was: somebody who arranged stories in order of importance or a producer who telephoned pundits to come in and talk about them? 'But that film programme of yours isn't too bad and some of the Frost shows were OK. There's nobody in Current Affairs at the moment who can do the entertainment stuff, so you may as well have a go.'

He didn't even make it an offer. Perhaps he knew that any producer would jump at the chance to start with a blank sheet of paper.

'When will it begin?' I asked.

'End of September. There's a fifty-minute slot from eleven-thirty on Fridays.'

'What's the programme called?'

'Up to you,' Wenham replied.

Much tempted by this, I also had another temptation to set up a new nest in Television Centre (TC) which was the thought of seeing Mo again. I knew she was there because the black mini she bought from John Cleese's secretary was cheekily bumped up on the pavement outside TC, with the commissionaires keeping a watchful eye out for cops and traffic wardens. After seeing Wenham, I felt intrepid enough to call her. We went for lunch in the BBC canteen. It transpired that her boyfriend had been sent to New York but she had decided to lay down roots in London and had bought a flat in Chiswick. She seemed pleased when I said I was coming back to the BBC.

It is said that the Chinese logogram for 'opportunity' can also mean a 'crisis' and the blank piece of paper that now confronted me was more of the latter. I knew I couldn't do a conventional chat show – Parky had cornered that market. But I wanted good conversation to be the lifeblood of the programme. The variation, it seemed to me, would be to get some guests who wouldn't usually be chat-show fodder and the solution lay in having a presenter who could corral such friends and acquaintances. But he or she would soon run out of them, so the art would be to rotate presenters, say every fortnight. That also gave me the chance for a bit more producer power; as I've mentioned, in television once the performer gains some fame, the producer's role is commensurately decreased.

I wanted the show to have a louche, late-night feel to it. So I trolled round a few cabaret clubs at the Beeb's expense before honing in on Sponooch – a girl dance troupe who had recently left the popular Hot Gossip (which, at one stage, featured the Italian-born British dancer, Bruno Tonioli). There was, in particular, one dancer called Donna for whom the word louche might have been invented.

Then it was time to visit Ned Sherrin. He had, of course, devised *That Was The Week That Was*, following the injunction of the then Director General, Hugh Carleton Greene, that he wanted to be reminded of the sort of cabaret shows he had seen in Berlin in the fifties. Ned had had a big budget for performers, writers, actors and even an orchestra, plus a male troupe known as the 'Vietnamese dancers' whom he spent much of the week rehearsing. I had a small budget but, I reckoned, if I asked him to host the first two shows, I could, at least, pick his brains.

Although I had never met Ned at the BBC, I had encountered him a couple of times at dinners given by the Bishop of Southwark, Mervyn Stockwood, at the Bishop's Residence. These were fairly gay affairs for what Mervyn termed 'young people'. I was taken along by Cathy McGowan, a mutual friend, who had presented *Ready Steady Go!*.

Ned, now producing movies, had been very witty in his *Side by Side by Sondheim* stage show. While he cooked me lunch at his flat in Chelsea, he dispensed advice as liberally as he did dry Martinis. 'The cheapest way to fill up airtime, dear boy,' he said, 'is a quiz.' He had never quite forgiven the BBC for dropping *Quiz of the Week* which he had hosted in the late sixties with various members of *Private Eye*, notably John Wells and Willie Rushton.

'Isn't that a bit expensive, I mean labour intensive?' I queried. 'Oh, no,' Ned replied airily. 'Willie will set the questions.' 'But won't he be one of the panellists?' I asked. 'Makes it even better,' said Ned. 'He doesn't usually answer them. He's happy to lose provided he can get in a few prepared jokes. Makes him look clever.'

Indeed, we included a 'Quiz of the Week' in all the shows Ned did in the six seasons of the programme. On one edition Arianna Stassinopoulos and her sister, Agapi, played against Willie and John – and won. Ned announced it as a contest between 'The Greeks' and 'The Rest of the World'. The following evening Agapi was at a concert at the Royal Festival Hall. She felt a tap on her shoulder and turned to see ex-King Constantine of the Hellenes. 'You did well for the country last night,' he told her.

After Ned, who? I think I may have been a little over-ambitious at the time. I was fleetingly acquainted with Harold Wilson from *The Frost Interview*. After almost eight years as Prime Minister he stepped down rather dramatically in 1976, saying he had always intended to retire at sixty. I contacted his assistant, Marcia Falkender. She remembered me and I got an appointment to see him in his office in the former New Scotland Yard building. He was still an MP and working on a history of Israel. By now my programme had a name: *Friday Night ... Saturday Morning*; it had seemed glaringly obvious and stood out from the list of prospective titles on my office wall.

I didn't think quizzes would sit well with Sir Harold. If he agreed to present two shows it would be enough of an event to have him in the chair. He was dubious about this but I said that, having chaired Cabinet meetings for eight years, chairing a TV interview programme was a doddle. Also he could read an autocue better than any professional TV presenter. Flattery will sometimes get you what you want and, slightly to my surprise, he agreed to do it. Two dates were pencilled in for October 1979.

Having pulled off this coup, I returned to Wenham's office. He, too, was slightly surprised, but, giving me the green light, he said he would come and see Wilson's second show. (He didn't.)

So I assembled an initially lean team: Frances Whittaker who had been my assistant producer on *Ask Aspel* (Michael, once a newsreader, had brought warmth and wit to *Miss World*), John Burrowes who had directed *The Old Grey Whistle Test* and whom I pinched from *Parkinson*, and David Turnbull, a sharp General Trainee.

I wanted the set to look distinctive, so that if any clips from the programme were shown they would be instantly identifiable, and suggested to the designer that it should look as if *Desert Island Discs* were on TV. He took me at my word and came with a cyclorama of a Pacific sunset and so many green fronds that we had to denude half of them so that the audience could see the guests. Using the words *Friday Night ... Saturday Morning*, I composed a little ditty (mercifully forgotten) and took it to the composer, André Jacquemin. He worked in a studio owned by Michael Palin in Neal's Yard, hidden behind the sign 'The Holy Roman Empire Pension Fund Ltd'. Terry Gilliam owned the building next door and tried to outdo Mike by calling it 'The British Film Industry Ltd', but Companies House turned down the name so I think he registered it in Panama. The opening titles of *Friday Night* of a man and a woman in bed about to make love but turning on the programme instead still make me wince.

If this all sounds a bit 'my bat, my ball', well, it was. I think I reckoned I would never again get such freedom from a TV company – and I was right. It was to be, to paraphrase Charles Dickens, 'the best of times, the worst of times'.

But, before any of that, tragedy struck. I went with Mo to Sadler's Wells on the evening of 11 July 1979 to see Ballet Rambert's *The Tempest*. When we got home (Mo had moved in with me only days before) there were more than a dozen messages on my answering machine from my brother-in-law, David Allen, asking me to ring him. I did so. My mother, Gillie, had been hit by a car on the way home from the shops in West Kirby. Gillian, my sister, had already gone north. Gillie was still alive when the ambulance took her to Clatterbridge Hospital. A surgeon had drilled two holes in her skull to try to alleviate brain damage. But it hadn't worked. She was dead.

I drove to West Kirby the following morning. My father, Jack, and my sister were going to visit Gillie in Quinn's Funeral Home at the bottom of the hill where the Volvo had hit her. But I just couldn't bear to. The shock and grief were too overwhelming. Also, my parents had come to London less than a month previously and that was the image I wanted to retain. Gillian said, when she came back, that it didn't look like Gillie at all: they had put an unnatural wig on her to cover the surgery and her face had been over-made-up in a fashion she never did.

She had lived to see her grandchildren, Hugo and Charlie, grow into a loving family. We held a small service conducted by the

Reverend Rosie, the minister at the church she devoutly attended. And then she was cremated.

I stayed with Dad for a few days to try and sort things out, but I was probably more of a hindrance than a help. Ironically, he knew the driver of the Volvo that had killed his wife as they were both members of the Royal Liverpool Golf Club at Hoylake. We were fired by a primal lust for revenge on the man – as if that would bring Gillie back. His solicitors subsequently offered Jack £500 compensation. He wrote back, contemptuously, saying the only compensation he wanted was a promise that the man would never drive again.

I joined Hoylake myself, as a country member so when Dad went back there would be no danger of him meeting the man alone. But the chap was to die a few months later. In the months to come I would go home and partner Dad at the club, usually hitting the ball along the ground.

Gillie had been a stern and loving mother. She had wanted so much for me that I would never have done decently at school without her. But I had let her down by failing to go through with the law and by getting divorced. My punishment was that she would never see my children. A friend, who had recently lost his father, told me that the period of extreme grief lasted for three months and mine did exactly that, the depression lifting like a dispersing fog. I don't think I realised how profoundly I loved her until she was no longer there to say it to.

I was sustained through my grief by Mo. She had never met my mother and so didn't come to the funeral. She must have wondered what sort of a basket case she had hooked up with. But, without her, I don't think I could have continued with *Friday Night*. We went to France for a while to stay with some Canadian friends who lived in two converted windmills in the Dordogne. But you cannot run away from grief.

So, back to showbiz. I had eleven shows to fill in the first series of *FN ... SM* and so far had only nailed down four. No, that's not true: I had agreed with John Cleese we'd do something when *Life of Brian* came out in November. There was a chance of finding something or someone new on the Fringe at the Edinburgh Festival. I travelled to Scotland and about the first person I bumped into in The Meadows was Rowan Atkinson. I'd met him through Cleese and he was already established as a comedy star. Sadly, he couldn't do my show as he was working on one of his own called *Not the Nine O'Clock News*, due to start on BBC2 a month before we did. 'Have you seen anything good?' I asked him, probably the most used question in Edinburgh. 'Not really,' Rowan replied. 'I'm always looking for "the performance" and there doesn't seem to be anybody.' Except for him: he was doing his 'one man' show with Richard Curtis. 'By the way,' he mentioned as we parted, 'they say the Cambridge Footlights aren't bad this year.' As an Oxford man, the words came reluctantly from his lips.

They weren't bad. They were brilliant. If not all the material but the performers: Hugh Laurie and Robert Bathurst (talented toffs); Simon McBurney (incredible body language) and Emma Thompson (sexy and funny and a splendid singer).

So I met the director, Martin Bergman, the very next day and immediately signed them up for a slot in November. We agreed we could do an adapted version of their revue, *Nightcap*, which we could work on in the BBC rehearsal rooms in Acton. Martin had so much confidence that I asked him to front the show and maybe do some interviews.

Thus Ned kicked the whole thing off on 28 September 1979 with a few of my friends: Arianna, Chris Reeve and Alan Coren (who used to ask me to the occasional *Punch* lunch). Willie came up with the less-than-honest 'Quiz of the Week' which got more laughs than if it hadn't been rigged. We recorded in front of an audience at 8pm 'live-on-tape' at the Greenwood Theatre near the London Dungeon, with Frankie back at Television Centre having a couple of hours to do some edits. (The BBC had leased the theatre as one of its big studios was being refitted but Robin Day kindly tried out the arrangement earlier in the week with another new show called *Question Time*.)

Then it was everybody back to our place in Campden Hill to watch the transmission. People brought wine and Mo served a very edible concoction she called 'Gorbals Chicken' which is not to be found in any recipe book but apparently expands to feed any number of people. Just as well as there were more than twenty of us.

With Ned's second show in place, it was time to return to New Scotland Yard and discuss guests with Sir Harold. He wanted *Coronation Street*'s Pat Phoenix who played Elsie Tanner, fellow Yorkshireman Fred Trueman, Tony Benn, the Goon-turned-singer Harry Secombe and Brian Clough.

All accepted except Clough. He was the current miracle man of English soccer, having taken Nottingham Forest from thirteenth in the Second Division to Champions of England. He invited me up to Nottingham where he was performing in a nightclub: largely a question-and-answer affair with Brian displaying the plain speaking and acerbic wit for which he was famed. Afterwards we had some drinks. Although rumoured to be an alcoholic, he just sipped halves of bitter and I followed suit. But he levelled with me and said he couldn't do an evening TV show in case it turned out to be a 'drinking day'. He asked me to keep this to myself, which I have – until now. But in 2003 he had a liver transplant, dying the following year at sixty-nine.

Curiously, when I went to pick up Harold for his first show (as a former Prime Minister he had a government car) his driver, Bill, made a drinking sign to me, indicating that his boss should be kept away from the bottle until after the show. We rehearsed at the Greenwood Theatre with me playing all the guests and indicating to Harold when he should use the scripted pieces on autocue, ending with his 'good night'.

'That's it, we're in good shape,' I told him. 'Now all we have to do is do the show.' The former Prime Minister then uttered this blood-chilling question. 'Haven't we just done it?' He wasn't joking. I think my heart stopped.

The programme started merrily enough with Harry Secombe bouncing on first. All went well for two, maybe three minutes. Then Harold, well, ran out of questions. Harry just sat there and then, unforgivably, began to whistle to get a laugh. I certainly never forgave him. Nor myself. Of course, Harold could chair Cabinet meetings but television was different. Nobody, especially the host, is allowed to pause and think. You have to keep *speaking* and think.

I rang Frankie at Television Centre. 'Houston, we have a problem.' 'You're telling me,' she replied.

Things hardly improved with Pat Phoenix but at least she didn't whistle. The show staggered along like a wounded antelope. Things got a little better with Tony Benn as the fellow ministers traded anecdotes. (Amazingly, in his memoirs, Benn said he thought the programme had gone rather well; he must have missed the first half-hour.)

Frankie did womanfully in the short time she had to tighten things up but it was a near-impossible task. The lean gathering at Campden

Harry Secombe about to humiliate Harold Wilson on *Friday Night*.

Hill that night was more of a wake. The press, of course, had a field day and the programme went down in Channel 4's annals as one of the *100 Greatest TV Moments from Hell*.

When I went to pick up Harold the following week, he told me: 'Y'know in my eight years as Prime Minister I never lost a night's sleep. But I've hardly slept at all for the past six nights.' Me, neither. This time I addressed the assembled guests – Mike Yarwood, Robin Day and Winston Churchill – in the Green Room beforehand and told them that since Sir Harold was more used to answering questions than asking them, perhaps they could fill any gaps by doing that. But my nerves were so frozen that evening that I have never been able to look back at that show and have always assumed it just stopped short of being the disaster the first one was. It was a revelation to discover for this book an old cutting from Philip Purser, the veteran TV critic of the *Sunday Telegraph*.

The second show found Sir Harold in a greatly more genial and relaxed mood. He responded in kind to Robin Day's playful combativeness, added an avuncular twinkle when young Winston Churchill, MP joined them and, miraculously, abstained from trying to be funny with Mike Yarwood. Finally, dear Lady Wilson came on to read a sentimental poem, and it's no good pretending that the host did not carry off the whole occasion with aplomb.

My nerves settled a little thanks to Tim Rice who fulfilled the brief of rounding up his mates: Bob Willis, fellow cricket fanatic Tom Stoppard, Tim's former lover Elaine Paige and George Martin. But for his second show I apologised to him as I already had a plan in place. I suggested to John Cleese that rather than the Pythons just being interviewed about *Life of Brian* by Tim, it might be more fun to have something more controversial. He agreed and fielded Michael Palin for his team as he was 'the most respectable Python'.

I called Mervyn Stockwood, the Anglican Bishop, and he was game. He called me back to ask if he should wear his bishop's garb. 'Full drag, sir,' I disrespectfully replied. It wasn't hard to get Malcolm Muggeridge on the telly; it was harder to keep him off. He had once been an agnostic and a womaniser and was now a Christian and a womaniser. I was pleased to hear from the make-up girl on the night of the show that St Mug's hand had found its familiar path up her flimsy smock.

The religious team went to see *Life of Brian* on the afternoon of the programme and were in agreement as to their reaction, although they didn't give much away beforehand. You may have seen it or seen part of what happened on the show – an unholy, or holy, battle of words. It started intellectually enough with Malcolm claiming

The Bishop of Southwark denounces the Pythons on *Friday Night*.

Christianity had been responsible for more good in the world than any other religion and Cleese coming back with: 'What about the Spanish Inquisition?'

The men of God, certainly on the back foot as far as the studio audience was concerned, turned to insults. 'I wasn't the vicar of Cambridge University for nothing,' said Mervyn, 'and I'm familiar with undergraduate humour. I was also a governor of a mentally deficient school.' Malcolm dismissed the film as 'a little squalid tenth-rate number,' managing to rile even the mild-mannered Michael who riposted: 'You started with an open mind, I realise that.' But the Pythons kept their cool, taking on the nose the crucifix-waving Bishop's final insult: 'You'll get your thirty pieces of silver, I assure you.'

Tim Rice came up to me afterwards and apologised for not keeping order by intervening more. I assured him his silence had

Rowan Atkinson as the Bishop of Southwark.

been golden. It was the most satisfactory piece of studio television I had ever produced.

And there the matter might have rested. But Rowan Atkinson, a long-time Cleese fan, had been watching and on *Not the Nine O' Clock News* a few weeks later there was a clever parody of the show. Even the set was parodied, although the team were not to know that it was pretty well what our original had been before we attacked the foliage. In the satirical sketch, they said the General Synod had made a movie of *The Life of Christ* with Mel Smith, as a film critic, expostulating: 'Jesus Christ is quite clearly a lampoon of the comic messiah himself, our lord John Cleese.' Rowan, the defending director in bishop's gear and waving his viewfinder, insisted: 'The Christ figure is not meant to be Cleese – he's just an ordinary person who happens to have been born in Weston-super-Mare at the same time as Mr Cleese.' Mel countered: 'The final scene is set in a Torquay hotel where literally hundreds of Spanish waiters are being clipped about the ear by this Jesus Christ.'

Their show had several million more viewers than ours and I've often wondered, with multiple repeat showings, what people who hadn't seen the original made of the sketch. But matters didn't end there. In 2010, an independent drama producer contacted me saying she would like to make a *Frost/Nixon* drama about that evening. I offered to help with the research but that wasn't required because what was transmitted on BBC4 the following year was a fervid fantasy of what might have happened. Called *Holy Flying Circus*, the result was marginally amusing with the producer of the show called Harry Balls and his assistant Alan Dick, their surnames being a fair example of its level of wit. Bizarrely, the Pythons themselves were portrayed in such an absurdist fashion that there was little risk of libel. But I was on the record as the producer of the original programme and was portrayed as an incompetent idiot. Clearly, lawyers had been at work and there were liberal references to 'Iain Johnstone' or 'Iain' being a distant and absent executive producer. Mike Palin said I should have sued them anyway, but life's too short for some things.

I had fun with the Footlights programme. Emma, though barely out of her teens, was wonderfully feisty at rehearsals; she certainly knew her own mind. Hugh Laurie arrived two hours late, waving his arms and delivering an absent-minded-professor speech about how he had driven from Cambridge but had got lost at Harrods, nowhere near our Acton rehearsal room. 'He's often like that,' Martin Bergman explained. Bergman distinguished himself on the show with a deft interview with Peter Cook, who had been president of Footlights exactly twenty years before him. 'You hosted a chat show some years ago,' Martin asked him, 'what was the public reaction to it?' 'The public reaction,' Peter replied, 'was that I should desist from hosting chat shows. One of the main problems was that I had no interest whatsoever in anything people had to say.'

Friday Night marched confidently on and was recommissioned for another series (and four more after that). But I was born under a wandering star and left it to Frankie and Ned and, later, Tim. Mo cooked her final Gorbals Chicken four nights before Christmas for thirty or more people. Some of the Footlights continued to come on Fridays, including Stephen Fry and Rory McGrath, who wrote for the programme. As I look back from the isolation of the keyboard, those were good days. I did not abandon a buoyant ship with any joy. But, even before it had started, I had an assignation with the Earl of Snowdon.

15

Travels with Lord Snowdon ...
Marriage to Mo

Anthony Charles Robert Armstrong-Jones, 1st Earl of Snowdon, Knight Grand Cross of the Royal Victorian Order, was fifty when I met him in 1980. I knew quite a bit about him. His turbulent marriage to Princess Margaret was well chronicled, true or false in the gossip columns – he allegedly told her she looked like 'a Jewish manicurist'. It had ended two years previously (the first royal divorce since Henry VIII and Anne of Cleeves in 1540). Tony had coxed a winning Boat Race crew for Cambridge, designed an aviary at London Zoo and married Lucy-Lindsay Hogg who had worked with him on the BBC documentary he made in Australia about the explorers, Burke and Wills.

He had also been in at the launch of *The Sunday Times* colour supplement and Will Wyatt, who had somehow gone from being my assistant to my boss, invited *The Sunday Times* editor, Harry Evans, and Tony and me to Au Jardin des Gourmets in Soho to discuss a TV series on photography. I think the idea was that Harry would write it, Tony would front it and I would direct. This seemed a bit strange as Snowdon was an accomplished director himself.

All I recall from that meal was Tony telling us to close our eyes and then describe various things about the restaurant. He wanted to make the point that observing things was more essential to the photographer's craft than merely clicking the button. I did terribly, being the only one who had never been there before.

I called Harry the following day and he explained he didn't really want to do any writing for Tony but had been happy to make the introduction and assure him he'd be fine as a TV presenter. He said if I really wanted to learn a bit more about him before we started planning the programmes, I should meet Mark Boxer. He was the same age as Snowdon and they had been at Cambridge together. It had been Mark, the first editor of *The Sunday Times* colour supplement, who had brought him on board. I duly contacted Boxer and we had lunch at Le Caprice the following week – a bit outside the BBC expenses zone. He didn't seem much interested in talking about Snowdon; it wasn't clear whether he even liked him. Perhaps they had had a tiff. Mark was a dandy and a social animal, more interested in relaunching *Tatler* and dropping the names of his famous literary friends, such as Martin Amis and Clive James. He didn't send me a thank-you letter after the lunch but an invoice for £70 for his time.

It was time to tackle Tony himself. He was rather nervous, smoked a lot and kept insisting photography wasn't 'art' and he was just a snapper. He had a mischievous enjoyment of his status, however. When *The Sunday Times* sent a journalist to do a profile of Paul Johnson, at the time editor of the Fabian magazine the *New Statesman*, the then socialist Johnson invited the writer to lunch in his house with his wife, Marigold, and booked a table in the local pub for the photographer. When the Queen's brother-in-law turned up, arrangements were hastily changed and another place laid at the Johnson table.

When Tony left Margaret and Kensington Palace he moved to a nearby house in Launceston Place so that he could be near their children, David and Sarah. I confessed I had little knowledge of photography and he invited me there to borrow some books. He had a photographic studio built on the ground floor where he could do his portraiture. He demonstrated to me how he was a natural-light photographer, adjusting black curtains to control the light coming in from the large side and top windows and occasionally using a silver reflector board to fill in any shadows. It was a technique that had stood Vermeer in good stead (although there wasn't even the possibility of electric lights in the seventeenth century) and certainly Snowdon deserved his reputation as one of the leading English portraitists of his time.

We met again to brainstorm with my assistant producer from India, Adam Low, and a very sharp researcher, Charles Miller. Adam wanted to deal with the remarkable rise in the sales of 'photography as art' market which had happened in the States in the past five years. Charles wanted to look at advertising and the technical side and Tony was anxious to prove how simple photography actually was. What we all shared was a common sense of mischief: these programmes were meant to be fun.

We certainly started with that. Madame Harlip was an eighty-year-old portrait photographer in Bond Street. She specialised in doing debs with the hope they might make the 'Girls in Pearls' photo in the frontispiece of *Country Life.* (This later happened to my daughter, Holly, who was snapped by a stranger one Sunday in Hyde Park.)

Madame Harlip doughtily informed Tony that photography was art and his daylight style was wrong: 'I would call that a snapshot.' She demonstrated this on a young woman, saturating her in artificial light and even waving a spotlight at different angles as she summoned an ancient retainer from her back room to operate the enormous camera. 'Give me a Rembrandt, Mr Heller,' she commanded, to make her point.

Tony was good with people, asking impish questions that might be considered cheeky if not coming from a noble lord. And he was game, blocking out most of the lights with anoraks in a Waterloo Station photo-booth to come up with a stylish portrait of himself. 'Let's see if we can get a Rembrandt,' he said wickedly to camera.

He was famous and he knew it and liked it and got a more eager response from people than a professional reporter. The programmes are something of a time warp since the microchip has replaced the negative. But in 1980 people sent eighty-five million rolls of film to be processed at Kodak. The typical one containing thirty-six frames would begin on Christmas Day one year, cover a couple of holidays, maybe a wedding or a christening, and end on Christmas Day the next year. However 18,000 people would forget to put their name on their film and Kodak had a division of women who would track them down by questioning the sender, hoping they might just have snapped a recognisable landmark. They usually succeeded. All gone today, though.

So, too, with newspapers: since Wapping, their offices became quiet rooms with people staring at silent screens. But then we filmed at noisy, smoky, messy newsrooms with everyone on the phone, especially picture editors negotiating with photo libraries and the latest photos coming continuously down the line from the wire agencies.

We covered advertising with Tony insisting we use his old friend, Bob Belton, who 'photographed frocks'. We shot a muffled, gay Bob being pulled backwards on a wheelchair as he pictured a model by the lake in Hyde Park. Not a great believer in modern methods, Bob kept his focal length consistent by attaching a stone to a string which the model had to walk one pace behind. Nor had he any truck with lightmeters. 'I only use one if there's a client watching. The sun's always the same distance from the earth, so today I set my camera at cloudy-but-bright,' he explained.

My troubles with Tony began in Venice. Through a friend of Princess Margaret, Billy Hamilton, Snowdon, ever the operator, was able to get us free rooms at the expensive Hotel Cipriani if Billy could give the *Daily Mail* diary the story of Snowdon filming in Venice. The problem was that I ended up in the Presidential Suite. I didn't realise it: I assumed all the rooms were like this. But Tony and the crew had comparatively humble single rooms and, when we discovered this, it was too late to change.

Adam persuaded a museum to lend us Canaletto's camera obscura which had his name, 'A. Canal', carved into the wooden frame. Tony explained how it was just a simple reflex camera with a reflex lens, but with no means of keeping the image so it would have to be sketched with eighteenth-century tracing paper. He delighted in using the camera our researcher Charles Miller had created by making a hole in a biscuit tin. With a paper negative on the opposite side, Snowdon managed to take a creditable snap of the Venice basilica, the Santa Maria della Salute.

He urged amateur photographers to get up early, take pictures that are different from the postcards and, if lucky enough to go to Venice, shoot during the winter when the atmosphere is almost eerie. I ended the first programme with a montage of magnificent scenes Tony had taken there for a book in 1972 – but he insisted we did not say they were his.

Our relationship worsened when we went to New York. 'Where's your tie?' he hissed at Heathrow. 'In my bag,' I replied. 'Put it on,' he ordered, and then at check-in asked the girl if the flight was full. She said it was full in economy where we were seated. 'So if you move us up to first class, you'll be able to resell our seats to people on stand-by,' She demurred but gave us passes for the executive lounge.

An American lady there asked Tony for an autograph. He replied: 'I'm afraid I'm not allowed to.' She apologised profusely without working out who on earth it might be who didn't allow him. Tony worked the lounge, asking everyone in a BA uniform for an upgrade and, eventually, we got one. A whiff of royalty and a lot of persistence equals success.

We had a day off the following day and the BBC New York producer, Peter Foges, asked me to brunch at the Café des Artistes. This was an in-place (since closed) on the Upper East Side with vast murals of sylvan nymphs on the wall. 'I've never been able to get a table here in two years,' Peter confided to me when I arrived, 'so I said it was for Lord Snowdon and it worked.' An hour later Tony turned up with a friend. 'They told me at reception I already have a booking here,' he said as the waiter laid two extra places. It was not a comfortable meal. He had phoned my PA, Janina, and asked where I was. Later on he was to tell her: 'Iain's going around booking restaurants in my name.' I wasn't, but it was probably unfair to land Peter in it.

We did an interview with the famous portrait photographer, Karsh of Ottowa, who had a place in New York. If you haven't seen the portraits of this legendary Armenian–Canadian it is certainly worth looking them up. His wartime photograph of Churchill on the cover of *Life* magazine made his name; Karsh claimed he got the famous scowl by removing Churchill's cigar without his permission. But his pictures of Ernest Hemingway, Humphrey Bogart, Edmund Hillary and others are in a class of their own. Twenty-six million copies of his portrait of Pope Pius XII were printed.

'Do you just photograph famous people?' Snowdon asked him. 'It is in the capricious nature of human beings to be interested in the famous,' Karsh replied. He, like Madame Harlip, painted with lights.

A Karsh was instantly recognisable in any gallery: why was that? 'I try to get into the very soul of my subjects, the depth of their consciousness,' the great man said. 'Rembrandt had no need to sign his paintings.'

My assistant producer Adam's research led us to the redoubtable Tennyson Schad, the lawyer who first had the idea that contemporary photography was collectible and founded the Light Gallery on Madison Avenue to prove his point. It was deliberately packed on the evening we came to film. Tony argued that whilst a photographer retained the negative, a print was only worth the paper it was printed on. Tennyson countered that it was the art medium of today; there had been a societal change and an aesthetic revolution. Even *The New York Times* had appointed a photography critic three years ago. The proof was there for us to film with collectors paying thousands of dollars. (John Szarkowski, the director of photography at the Museum of Modern Art, told us he had put on an exhibition of the photos of Hungarian photographer André Kertész. Collectors grew interested. His prints initially sold for $250 and, by 1980, ten times that.)

Tony pointed to what looked like a photo of a black Rorschach inkblot on the wall. 'How can that be art?' he asked. Tennyson smiled: 'It depends on what you take from it. The photographer was making a statement, but nobody listening to Mozart says "What was he thinking when he composed that?"'

We went to New York University to talk to postgraduates doing their masters in photography. This was anathema to Snowdon who had learnt his trade in a six-month apprenticeship with the society photographer, Baron. Tony threw a loaded question at a student: 'What have you learnt during your three years here?' 'I have explored the philosophy of photography,' the young man replied. 'It's a reflection of myself. I find something in myself and use my camera to get it out.'

Our last New York location was Sotheby's and a spirited auction of work by contemporary photographers. The highest price was $20,000 for *Moonrise, Hernandez* by the great landscape photographer, Ansel Adams. 'How can it be worth that?' a genuinely incredulous Snowdon asked the auctioneer afterwards. 'Adams does his own developing,' the smooth young man replied, 'and this is a unique platinum print.' (In 2010 *Clearing Winter Storm, Yosemite National Park* by Adams sold at Sotheby's for $722,000.)

So we travelled to Carmel, California to visit Adams in his studio. Possibly overwhelmed by what he had learnt in New York, Tony drank a lot of wine on the plane to San Francisco and fell asleep in the back of our hire car. He awoke with the words: 'Where's Barney?' 'Barney who?' I inquired. 'Barney Wan. I want to see Barney Wan. He's here somewhere.' 'I don't think we can find him,' Adam assured him, telling me that Barney was the art director of *Vogue*. Perhaps he had a place in the Castro area of San Fran, the gayest place in a gay city.

Any thoughts that Lord Snowdon might have had a relationship with Barney were allayed later that night. Maggi Weston, daughter-in-law of the famed photographer, Edward, and founder of the first West Coast photo gallery in his name, gave us a party to which she invited Carmel's elite. Towards the end, Tony disappeared into the night with a well-groomed and very tanned female admirer. I was happy to talk to Ansel on an informal basis and he said he had met Snowdon once before when he and Princess Margaret had made a state/trade visit to LA. They hosted drinks on board the Royal Yacht *Britannia*. Important Californians were invited to stay to dinner, but Ansel and his wife were among those escorted off the ship after drinks.

We met again the next day at his house where he had his studio. He had told me he relaxed by playing the piano so I filmed him playing a Bach fugue – as much an artist at the keyboard as he was behind the camera and in his laboratory. He told Tony that, as far as he was concerned, the negative was the score and the print the performance. 'Printing can give it the sonority of a full orchestral performance. It can express what I saw and what I felt.'

We covered him developing a large negative, exposing various parts of it to the light at different times. 'The negative carries the information required for my expression. It's not a rigid thing. Just as you can play a Chopin nocturne with a different insight over the months and years, making a photograph can be performed differently.'

This was how he had composed *Moonrise, Hernandez*. 'I'd had a fruitless day in the Chama River Valley. I couldn't see any pictures and was driving back to Santa Fe when I glanced out of my left window and I saw the picture immediately. I nearly put the car in the ditch. I set up my 8x10 camera but I couldn't find my lightmeter. I had no time: the low sun was trailing the edge of the cloud and I'd lose the white crosses. But I happened to know how bright the moon was so I set my exposure by that. I knew I had an unusual photograph and made a note for a water-bath development for the negative.'

If ever I had any doubts about photography having the potential to be art, they were dispelled by the philosophy and the very presence of Ansel Adams.

The Pacific that afternoon was turbulent and I wanted a back shot of Snowdon and Adams on the edge of the ocean so I could put their edited conversation on the soundtrack. And I knew the rocks where to set it up; I had been there four years previously with Clint Eastwood. Which brings me to a running sore that had often made filming uncomfortable. Tony was much better at visualising set-ups

Sellers and Snowdon play chess with camera lenses.

than I and would try and convert the cameraman to his view. No director likes that. But I got my own back when it came to scripting the films. Tony couldn't write. So I wrote them for him.

We had only one serious disagreement over content. Snowdon was a great friend of Peter Sellers who was a photography nut. The star was staying at the Dorchester Hotel in the suite designed by and named after Tony's uncle, Oliver Messel. Peter had more camera equipment than a small branch of Jessops so we laid the lenses out on a table where he and Tony played a silent game of mock-chess with them. After eight moves Tony said 'check' and, waiting a beat, an incredulous Sellers mumbled: 'That's it.' We also filmed some fun footage of Peter and Tony trying to snap pigeons on the vast balcony of his suite overlooking Park Lane.

Tony thought we shouldn't use it. I thought we should: Shakespeare would always put in a comedic scene, even in his tragedies. But Snowdon insisted that it might stop people believing these were serious films. So I took it out. And he was right. Clive James, probably the country's best TV critic, wrote in *The Observer*: 'A first-class two-part documentary about photography *Snowdon on Camera* could well serve as a model for fledgling TV producers of how these things should be done. It was closely argued, richly filmed, tersely cut.'

I was nominated for a BAFTA as Best Documentary Director of the year. There were three other candidates; one of them, Eddie Mirzoeff, was up for his film *The Ritz*. Eddie, evidently, suffered from a very nervous disposition at awards ceremonies and told his head of department that he couldn't attend unless he knew in advance whether he had won or lost. The head duly contacted Paul Bonner, the chairman of the BAFTA awarding committee and explained the problem. Bonner replied: 'I'd tell Eddie not to get too excited.' 'Really,' asked the head, 'which film did you personally like?' 'I thought Iain Johnstone's was rather good,' said Bonner.

The bush telegraph brought word to me of this exchange. So Mo and I dressed in our evening clothes and tripped up the red carpet into the Talk of the Town. I even had a few words in my pocket about the brilliance of my team, Adam and Charles. We had reached the main course of our dinner when an uninvited guest arrived. Tony. The man could talk his way into the Pentagon. Again, another place was laid and as the cameras roamed the room they lingered on him. Tony said that Prince Charles had phoned him to say he liked the films. When the moment came for our award, the screen was quartered into the faces of the four nominated directors. I tried not to look too confident which proved fairly prudent when the presenter, Jan Leeming, read out: 'And the winner is Eddie Mirzoeff for *The Ritz*'.

I think the only time I heard from Tony again that century was when he sent my newborn daughter an exquisite little cardigan and an extravagant bouquet of flowers for Mo in hospital. But in 2001 he rang out of the blue and said: 'Why don't we do something together?' He suggested we could have lunch in the House of Lords. I was surprised, as most of the hereditary peers had been kicked out. But the 1999 Act made an exception in the case of six first-generation hereditaries and Lord Snowdon had now added the title of Baron Armstrong-Jones of Nymans in the County of West Sussex to his name.

In the event we lunched round the corner from his house in a restaurant which, he told me, Margaret used to refer to as 'the Italian cesspit'. He said he wasn't doing much and we had had so much fun together. We played with a few ideas but the television world had changed and unless we could come up with a cookery programme (not a likely prospect as neither of us could cook) I doubted if we would get a hearing.

But we had a mutual love of wine and that has fuelled lunches two or three times a year ever since. Tony always suggests we have one – usually on the day – and I inevitably pay. When I suggested that he might, he said he had no money. I pointed out that Launceston Place must now be worth more than six million pounds but he said the house belonged to the Queen.

He also told me that when she had guests for lunch at Windsor Castle, the rest of the royals would play a game of taking a small piece of bread from their plate and rolling it into a tiny ball every time a guest uttered a cliché. The favourite ones were, 'It's not the M4 that takes the time but it's getting out of London.' Or 'I believe a royal swan can break your leg with its wing.' The winner was the one who had spotted most.

Today, unfortunately, the polio that afflicted him as a child has returned with a vengeance and he bravely hobbles with a stick. But the calls keep coming and I welcome them.

In 2006, Tony had a change of heart about selling photos. You can now buy his silver gelatin print of Princess Diana with wet hair for £3,500. His ex-wife is worth slightly less at £2,250. He did exhibit a rather intimate one of Margaret in the bath but somebody, probably the Palace, told him George VI's naked daughter was not for sale.

Mo and I got married that August. Alan Riding and Don Bennetts were the witnesses at the (now deceased) Kensington Register Office. I told a sad Richard Whiteley he couldn't be my best man again as that might bring us bad luck. As a consolation prize we took him on our honeymoon to Ibiza. Dickie was always better at talking to strangers than I. When we changed planes at Valencia a fellow Yorkshireman came up to him with his suitcase. He patted it. 'I bet you don't know what I've got in here, Richard?' he said. Dickie presumed it was clothes for his holiday. 'No,' said the man, opening it proudly. 'Individual meat pies. I don't trust that foreign rubbish.' It was full of them.

We had rented an apartment in Santa Eulalia on the coast. Dickie's radar quickly led him to Sandy's Bar. He discovered that most of the clientele were 'resting' British actors, some of them Cybermen and Weeping Angels from Dr Who. Bar owner Sandy Pratt was the possessor of a commodity more popular than Tetley's Bitter ... a phone. As Dickie nursed his 11 am lager, men would arrive and uniformly ask Sandy: 'Has my agent rung yet?' If the answer was no, several would angrily turn on camp Sandy and scream: 'Well, why not?'

Mo and I left a few days early and Dickie made me promise to call him from London when I got back. I duly did the next morning. 'Who is it?' snapped Sandy. 'It's the *Dr Who* production office for Richard Whiteley,' I lied. Sandy didn't bother to cover the mouthpiece as he yelled out: 'Richard, it's Dr Who for you.' Heads turned in envy as Dickie walked proudly to the phone.

16

Barry Norman on Broadway ...
Paul Newman

On arrival in New York on 26 December 1981, Mo and I became powerfully aware that this was virtually a city in mourning. Twelve days earlier a wake of a quarter of a million people had gathered in Central Park. For ten minutes every single radio station in the city had gone silent. It was the shock reaction to John Lennon's murder and the shock had certainly not subsided.

I had signed up to direct *Barry Norman on Broadway*. Barry had a few weeks free before he started the new season of *Film '81*, so we had to shoot the documentary in January, certainly New York's most Siberian month. An icy wind came off the Hudson and was channelled through the city's streets and also through your body. But Mo and I had a warm week together. She had not been to New York before so we did the tourist attractions from the World Trade Center to the Metropolitan Museum. Added on to the Met was a vast conservatory which contained the 2,000-year-old Temple of Dendur which Arthur and Jillian Sackler had shipped, stone by ancient stone, from Egypt. I used to play tennis with Jill (now Dame Jillian) at Campden Hill so I made contact and she invited us to lunch at their Fifth Avenue apartment, a modern art gallery in itself. Arthur was absurdly rich from drugs – the legitimate kind – and tended to endow museums wherever he went.

We bumped into Richard Curtis and his little brother, Jamie, at the Rockefeller Center ice rink and went for dinner together. I had known Richard as the other performer in Rowan Atkinson's one-man show. Later he got his own back by writing *The Tall Guy* in which Dexter King (Jeff Goldblum) plays straight man to unpleasant comedian Ron Anderson – sportingly played by Rowan himself. Richard was obsessed with Woody Allen and demanded to know all about him. He matched his idol in 1994 when he wrote *Four Weddings and a Funeral.*

Naturally, Broadway beckoned in the shape of *A Day in Hollywood/ A Night in the Ukraine.* The second half was a dazzling display of Chekhov's farce *The Bear* as if it were acted out by the Marx Brothers. It was by the London-based American, Dick Vosburgh, whom I was to work with for eight years on Radio 4's film quiz, *Screenplay.* On the night we went, the curtain was delayed for twenty minutes by paramedics attending to a sick man in the front stalls. They wheeled him out on a stretcher assuring the audience: 'He's fine. Nothing to worry about.' I told Dick about this when we met for rehearsals for the radio show. 'Oh, you went the night the guy died,' he said.

Manhattan Plaza on West 42nd Street was an apartment block rented out only to performing artists. A friend of Ned Sherrin's invited us to his New Year's party and when Mo went into the kitchen at midnight to get a view of The Times Square Ball Drop, she also got a view of a man dressed as a Village Person performing what the papers call 'an obscene act' on a chap in similar garb. At 2am we went out into the dark and dangerous Devil's Kitchen in search of a cab, but there were none. However, a truck, with three tough-looking guys in the front, roared to a halt beside us. The driver banged the side of the vehicle and yelled through the open window: 'Where the fuck's the Midtown Tunnel?' We explained that we were tourists (and that we didn't want to be murdered), so they roared off back into the night.

Mo left for London the next morning and I joined Charles Miller who had already embarked on his research. In those days, before today's microchip technology, a fifty-minute documentary took a few weeks to research, three weeks to shoot and then three months in the cutting room. So the next five months of my life were pretty well accounted for.

Ned had also given me an introduction to Milton and Arnold. Milton Goldman was vice-president of the theatrical agency, ICM, and represented Lillian Gish, Ruth Gordon, Albert Finney, John Gielgud and Laurence Olivier. Arnold Weissberger was a theatrical lawyer whose clients included Igor Stravinsky, Olivier, Martha Graham and Orson Welles. 'The story is that, twenty years ago, Arnold stopped his car at a Long Island filling station and, after Milton, a young attendant, had filled it up, Arnold said: "Jump in" and they've lived together ever since,' Ned informed me. 'Is that really true?' I asked. 'I've never asked them in case it wasn't,' Ned replied.

Milton asked Charles and me to drinks that night. They had an apartment, decorated with a few Monets and Manets, in Turtle Bay on the East River, near to Katharine Hepburn. It transpired they served cocktails most weeknights at 6.00pm and visiting firemen from England just dropped in, only to be pushed out again by Milton at 7.40 so that they could get to the theatre in time. The assumption was that everybody was going to the theatre. The night we went was something of an all-male event, but Milton assured me he would round up a few stars if we came to film with Barry Norman. He later vouchsafed to me: 'I mistakenly thought that you and Charles were a couple.'

Two weeks later, Milton did us proud. I kept Barry in another room and asked the cameraman to just stick with him when we let him in. Milton's hobby was introducing people to each other so, within three minutes, Barry was introduced to Otto Preminger, Sir Robert Helpmann, Lilli Palmer, Myrna Loy (twice), Alger Hiss, the alleged spy, John Lindsay, former Mayor of New York, George Rose, Mrs Sean O'Casey (three times) and Ian McKellen who told an unhearing Milton that he already knew Barry. As Nicol Williamson said: 'He'd introduce you to yourself.' Indeed at Milton and Arnold's London party at the Savoy, Sheridan Morley told me Milton introduced him to a fellow guest with the words: 'Do you know Robert Morley?' 'He's my father,' Sherry replied. 'But have you met him tonight?' Milton continued, undaunted.

The sequence in his apartment made for memorable and funny television. Elsewhere we were more serious about the New York theatre which was a major reason people visited the city. Musicals dominated. We filmed the party after *The Pirates of Penzance*, which went ecstatic when they got the call from the typesetting room at *The New York Times* that it was a rave review and then turning on the local TV to see the same at 10.45pm on the news. Instant gratification. *Pirates* was meant to be sold on the pop stars Linda Ronstadt and Rex Smith but was hijacked by Joe Papp regular, Kevin Kline, who gave a giddy and breathtaking performance as the Pirate King, holding the audience in the palm of his hand. (I was to work with Kevin on a couple of films; actors don't come any more versatile than he does.)

At the other end of the spectrum, *Frankenstein* at the Palace Theater opened on a Sunday night and closed the following Monday morning. There used to be Seven Butchers of Broadway (theatre critics) when there were that many influential Manhattan papers; now there was only one: *The New York Times*. Their critic, Frank Rich, had deemed *Frankenstein*: 'Lead-footed – a talky, stilted mishmash that fails to capture either the gripping tone of the book or the humorous pleasure of the film.'

We had arranged to film David Dukes, the star of the show, in his suite overlooking Times Square the morning after the premiere. He didn't let us down, telling Barry how they had taken away the drinks at the after-party when they got word of the killer review. David put on a very good performance of dolefully packing his good-luck telegrams and bottles of champagne. Inside, however, he was overjoyed. His agent had just called him to say they had kept the main role in television's *Winds of War* open for him and he was going to make a fortune.

I filmed Chris Reeve who had the star power to keep a straight play open, although he was playing a gay man. With a shuddering irony, Chris's 'Ken' in Lanford Wilson's *Fifth of July* was a paraplegic veteran.

Broadway ads, many of them incorporating the 'I Love New York' song, blasted at you all day on the television; it was still a realm where master showmen ruled supreme. Impresario David Merrick once, when he had a show with universally bad reviews, went through the phone book and found people with the same names as the Seven Butchers and plastered their enthusiastic reactions on the side of the theatre. With his hit *42nd Street*, he publicly auditioned six-year-old dancers to play in future casts of the show, confident that it would run for the next twelve years. That made the television news; as did the opening night. Merrick stood in front of the cast at the end and announced that Gower Champion, the musical's director (and lover of the leading lady), had died earlier that day. Next morning the line for tickets went round the block.

Barry Norman was a droll reporter, famous for doing his pieces to camera first take. Charles was an inspired researcher, persuading

Curtis Sliwa and his Guardian Angels to police the subway (they've now expanded into a worldwide organisation) and Father George Moore of St Malachy's (the Actors' Chapel) to say a prayer for the success of *Pirates of Penzance*. Father Moore would order the bells of the West 49th Street church to ring out fifteen minutes before curtain up (and twice a week on matinee days) to summon the faithful to the theatre.

The outstanding performance in our film (after Milton) came from Ted Hook who would literally audition young actors and actresses to be waiters in his restaurant, Backstage. 'I send back my liver and you suggest I order something else from the menu. Are you suggesting all your liver is bad?' he screamed at one. Ted had been a hoofer, in Vegas and on films (Fred Astaire liked him because he was actually shorter than the star) and would occasionally do gay pirouettes round his restaurant to the amazement of the diners. For five years he had been secretary to the notorious lesbian, Tallulah Bankhead.

Gays featured prominently on Broadway, especially in the musical theatre, and you might wonder why I didn't get Barry to make a more serious statement on the subject of AIDS, which was to devastate the cast of some shows. The answer is simple: the word hadn't been invented then; it first came into use in 1982. And from the mid-eighties the disease did its worst on Broadway and beyond.

Frequently, when you make a documentary abroad, you are so encased in the bubble of your subject that you tend to ignore the world outside. I feel I didn't truly experience India, for example, but just experienced leading a team through India. But it was not like that in New York. On the television news every night there was a reminder of the number of days the fifty-two members of the American Embassy in Tehran had been held hostage. President

Carter had authorised what turned out to be a futile helicopter mission to get them out the previous April and then recalled them, with one helicopter hitting a refuelling tanker and killing eight Americans. It cost him his re-election. On 20 January 1981 we watched Ronald Reagan being installed in the post and heard that, after 444 days the hostages were to be released. The groundwork had, of course, been done by the Carter administration but to become a famous actor you need a bit of luck and Reagan was the most powerful actor of them all.

One of the problems of being a freelance is that frequently nobody wants your 'lancing'. The word 'freelance', incidentally, was invented by Sir Walter Scott in *Ivanhoe*: it described the French and Italian mercenaries who would fight for the Scottish barons. This was where I found myself after the Broadway film was completed so Mo and I conceived a plan to go to Australia for a bit. There was no offer of work there but neither was there any in the UK and being unemployed on a Sydney beach seemed a more agreeable prospect.

There used to be advance previews of films at 6.30pm for people who might be able to do something on the movie and my name hadn't been crossed off the list – yet. Thus I agreed to meet Mo on a Monday at Fox in Soho Square for a private screening of *Shock Treatment*. Certainly it was what I needed as the lights went down. Mo arrived – in the nick of time, as usual – and whispered to me: 'I'm pregnant.' I know you're meant to burst into a rendering of 'My Boy Bill' at this point with images of him becoming President of the United States, but all I saw was a receding Bondi Beach, an empty Sydney Cricket Ground, a dissolving Opera House, followed by the cold-water flat on Campden Hill and a trip to collect the dole.

Naturally, after the screening, we celebrated. And the next day I called Marcia Lewis in LA with the good news. No prospect of any more movie stuff at the moment, I warned her. 'As a matter of fact I was about to call you,' she said. 'I have a job for you.' So for the next three years, on and off, I worked for my former Boston student.

Marcia had been working on The Oscars, produced by Jack Haley who had made his name with *That's Entertainment.* Paramount television hired him to pilot a showbiz news half-hour, *Entertainment Tonight*, and he brought the indispensable Marcia on board. They needed a European reporter so she hired me.

Cynics in Hollywood said that *Entertainment Tonight (ET)* would cover the opening of a book, so eager were they in the early days for any material. Agents and PRs were pretty sniffy about the show. So I did a lot of pieces on American soap stars who were usually making TV movies in Europe and whom I had never heard of. I didn't mind: at the daily rate *ET* paid I would have been happy to interview a bar of soap.

Later, things got a bit better. I went to Paris allegedly to talk to Roman Polanski about directing *Amadeus* on stage and playing Mozart. Unfortunately the French cameraman had shot the whole thing out of focus so I had to return. Roman was amenable but finally snapped: 'Why do you keep coming back to the rape allegations?' This was his admission that he had had unlawful sex with a thirteen-year-old girl in Jack Nicholson's Mulholland Drive home. Polanski fled the States in 1977, never to return. The truthful answer, not given by me, was that *ET* wasn't interested in anything else. Did Roman really think their viewers wanted to see a story about a play in French about a Salzburg composer?

More honourable was a piece about Ben Kingsley and *Gandhi*. What was the public's reaction to him now? 'In India, I cannot go anywhere,' Kingsley said, 'but here in England I feel the love. Wherever I go people just come up to me and say "Thank you."' We went out into a hot and crowded Lower Regent Street to do some exterior shots. I stood a hundred yards down the road and Ben, when cued, would walk towards the camera. 'Go, Ben!' I shouted and he made his way through the crowds. A couple of people stared but sadly nobody came up to him and said anything.

We covered the London premiere of *E.T. the Extra-Terrestrial* with the suggestion coming from Princess Diana herself that Steven Spielberg present her with a stuffed E.T. at the royal line-up. It was a picture that travelled the world.

Our daughter, Sophie, was born on the first day of Wimbledon. Mo and I watched the tennis on the Queen Charlotte Hospital's television as her contractions began. An American player, on Court 1, was having contractions of his own and screamed at the umpire: 'You are the pits of the world!' so Sophs decided to come out and see what this world was all about. Her cot was in my study and I christened her Space Invader, after one of the first video games. Thanks to *Superman* and *Entertainment Tonight* and the sale of Mo's flat, we were able to move to a place in Fulham, within the sound of, not Bow Bells, but the crowd at Chelsea Football Club when the home team scored.

Despite our newly acquired mortgage I wanted to keep a foothold in the Beeb. Fortunately there was a gap coming up on BBC2 for three movie-orientated programmes so I prepared my pitch. I already had Jack Nicholson in the can, all it needed was a very thorough edit and Kubrick's permission, which he readily gave. Margaret Gardner, a friend who ran Rogers & Cowan (PRs to the stars) in Europe, told me that Paul Newman was coming to London for a family holiday and that if he were to do a telly that would count as work and he could put part of the trip against tax.

Six Newmans occupied two rows in economy on the plane from JFK to Heathrow. The plan was to rent a boat on the Thames and take a leisurely cruise upriver through the many picturesque locks. (There is an annual prize for the best-kept lock and garden.)

Paul and his wife Joanne came to BBC TV Centre and we agreed that I would do the first half of the interview with him alone and the second with them both. I wasn't too comfortable with that arrangement but it turned out to be a bonus.

Paul had made his name in the early fifties on Broadway in serious plays by William Inge and Tennessee Williams. 'I had a lot of offers from Hollywood,' he told me, 'but I turned them all down. Eventually somebody said: "You know, they're going to knock for so long and then they'll stop knocking." So I signed with Warner Brothers and I was cast as Basil the Slave in a short cocktail dress. When it was shown on television in 1966 I took out a half-page ad in the *LA Times* with a funeral wreath apologising for having unleashed this thing on an unsuspecting audience. It backfired, incidentally. People thought that it was charming and they all turned it on. It had very high ratings.'

His breakthrough came in 1956 when he starred as the real-life middleweight champion, Rocky Graziano, in *Somebody Up There Likes Me*. 'I spent four weeks with Rocky to get the mannerisms and the voice – he grew up in Little Italy. But when the film came out some people accused me of imitating Marlon Brando. Several years later I was having a beer with Graziano and Marlon's name came up. "That's one of the stories I forgot to tell you," he said. "When I was training, a kid with a sketch-pad asked if he could watch me which he did, on and off, for about a year. He said he was an actor. I didn't see him for a long time. Finally he came back and said I'd like you to see me on Broadway." He was in *A Streetcar Named Desire.* Brando had taken Rocky and put him up on stage in *Streetcar* and I had put him up on screen in *Somebody Likes Me.* So maybe the critics were very astute.

'I'm not like Brando, though. I feel a lot more comfortable when I'm outside my own skin. I feel I can invent more and use a different sort of imagination to create those characters. When I simply deal with myself, I can't seem to get inside the kind of feelings that I want to put on the screen. It's sort of accidentally intentional – I've always felt more comfortable in the characters that have been farther away from me. When I hide behind the façade of another character then I can usually get away with that.'

Paul had personally bought the rights to the film that brought him to his biggest audience: *Butch Cassidy and the Sundance Kid.* 'Joanne read the script and said: "It's marvellous and the only person who can play opposite you is Bob Redford." Other people don't remember it that way, but I remember it that way. So the director, George Roy Hill, and I ran some of Redford's old films and then took him to lunch. Actually, I would rather have played Sundance – it's the easier part. He and I have had a lot of fun together. He sent me this Porsche for my birthday, except that it had hit a tree at about a hundred and thirty miles an hour and had no transmission in it. He left it in my driveway with a big bow around it. So I had it compacted. Bob was living in a rented house in the West Village and it took five guys to carry it in and leave it in the vestibule. He won, however, as he never admitted that anything was in his house. He even briefed his kids. I called up the next day and his son, Jamie, answered. I asked him: "How's it going? Anything new?" And he replied: "Nope, nothing."'

Newman told me he'd read *Dirty Harry* but turned it down. 'I'm not very comfortable with violence. I often try to get it reduced in films I'm in. There was some in *Torn Curtain*. Obviously I very much wanted to work with Hitch. But the script wasn't ready. He offered me an out but I took it on spec. I don't think he was ever comfortable with that script. It never jelled.'

Newman was happy to use his fame in good causes, especially charity. (His 'Newman's Own' food company, founded the year after we spoke, has since raised over $350 million.) He also accepted President Carter's invitation to be a Special Delegate to the UN Conference on Disarmament. 'It was the first global conference on disarmament since 1932 and it wasn't going to get very good coverage. So I thought I could help a bit. I don't have to give up my citizenship simply because I'm an actor.'

But he tried to guard his and his family's privacy. 'I stopped signing autographs when I was in a urinal and a guy came through the door with a pencil and a piece of paper in his hands. I said never again. That is the terminal insult. There was this unwritten law that anybody could stop you from doing whatever you were doing. "Smile, take off your glasses." "I'm sorry my pants'll drop off." It makes me uncomfortable. I wasn't around to vote when that rule was made. I think the only obligation I have to the audience is not to cheat them on the screen.'

He seemed a little relieved when Joanne joined us. She had beaten her husband to an Oscar, winning for *The Three Faces of Eve* in 1957.

'I was young enough for it to be really exciting and meaningful,' she recalled. 'I'd been raised on movie magazines and the idea of winning an Oscar was the most exciting thing in the world. I'd just come to Hollywood and I'd only done two pictures before *Eve*. But the excitement only lasted for about five minutes. By the time you get back to your seat you realise it's only a statue and not a competition.

'I was so angry in 1961 when Paul was nominated for *The Hustler* and Max Schell won for *Judgment at Nuremberg*. I took it as a personal affront. I was so upset I was ready to punch Max out,' she laughed.

'I would like to get an Oscar round about the age of eighty-six,' her husband observed. (He was nominated nine times – a record he shares with Spencer Tracy and Laurence Olivier – winning for *The Color of Money* when he was sixty-two.)

Joanne's loyalty to Paul – Peter Ustinov once observed 'their marriage shuts out the draughts of difference' – was evident in her support of his taking up car racing late in life.

'I think it's terrific that he decided at forty-seven to become a race driver. It's marvellous. It's what everybody should do. It's more nerve-wracking to drive on the freeway in California. At least people on the race track know what they're doing. He and Dick Barbour came second at Le Mans, you know.'

I did, indeed, know. And that when an *LA Times* gossip columnist had written he and Joanne were rumoured to be splitting up, Paul took out another of his half-page ads. 'It said something like we had no intention of splitting up until we read her column. So since we didn't want her to look inaccurate or dishonest, we thought we'd better split up right away.' Newman gave a snort of disgust. 'Too bad the people who write these things can't be dipped in boiling oil for fifteen or twenty minutes.'

To end, I asked him which film he was most proud of.

'I think the proudest moment in my life was when I was declared number nineteen on President Nixon's enemies list,' came the laconic reply.

The Newmans about to pursue a vegetarian dinner.

Strangers, usually on the Tube, only ever comment on TV programmes when they think something has gone wrong and, after transmission, several people asked me why Paul Newman didn't like me. I reviewed the tape: true there were a few pauses and grimaces when he looked as if he might be at the dentist. Maybe I should have cut them out.

But after the recording, he asked me to help find them a vegetarian restaurant. I called The Caprice where I knew they did decent veggie dishes and we went there. Can't think how we got a table at such short notice. In fact the Newmans liked it so much that they returned to the restaurant after they'd been to the theatre later that evening. The following year Newman's producer contacted me asking if I would do some TV interviews for the film Paul had directed, *Harry & Son*, including Newman himself. So the animosity cannot have been all that great.

Warren Beatty ... Presenting
Film '82 and '83

Warren Beatty won the 1982 Best Director Oscar for *Reds* – the story of John Reed, an American journalist who got caught up in the Russian Revolution and thought he might initiate something similar in America. (He didn't.) It occurred to me that few people in the UK had even heard of John Reed, so the movie might need a leg-up when the film opened over here. Paramount agreed. Not only was it a tough sell, but it was more than three hours long. So Beatty was persuaded to do an interview for the BBC to help it on its way.

Warren had displayed his green fingers in cinema with big hits like *Bonnie and Clyde* and *Shampoo*, but when Woody Allen said that if he were to come back in another life he would like to be Warren Beatty's fingertips, I think he was referring to another aspect of his life. Warren lived, for the most part, semi-reclusively in the penthouse of the Beverly Wilshire Hotel where many ladies, from Playmates to British actresses new to Hollywood, would pay him court. Naturally he denied his alleged satyriasis, insisting: 'If I tried to keep up with what was said of me sexually, I'd be speaking to you from a jar in the University of Chicago Medical Center.'

I had lunch with Warren and an attractive PR girl from Paramount at the Carlyle Hotel in New York. There I was able to witness his technique at first hand as he plied her with questions about herself and then, having admired her bracelet, began to fondle and caress it in a soft and flattering fashion, as if he were, in fact, touching her flesh.

Warren Beatty: 'speaking to you from a jar in the University of Chicago Medical Center'.

After she left for a press show, he confided in me: 'I don't think the Carlyle switchboard likes me. I asked the telephonist to monitor my calls, so that she would come on the phone in my suite first and say who it was and I could tell her whether I was there or not. But two people told me she didn't put the caller on hold so they were able to hear her asking me.' Perhaps she was just bored, I thought – or mischievous.

We duly filmed the interview, half about *Reds* and the remainder about his other work. '*Bonnie and Clyde* was a political film,' he explained. 'We had reached a period during the Depression of the thirties where the socio-economic conditions in this country simply couldn't support the way we were living. And this pair of psychotics began to exploit a certain rebelliousness among the people to become folk heroes – running around and robbing banks, and killing people.

Shampoo was also political. The more accessible sexual aspects of the film attracted most attention, but I'm rather proud of it as a working-class film, I hope an accurate reflection of the late sixties.'

He had been working for some years on a film about Howard Hughes. I suggested that maybe there was an echo of Hughes in his own life, with his preference for living in hotel rooms. 'I think that's people trying to make me a little more interesting than I am,' Warren smiled. 'I like a certain amount of privacy but I hope I haven't carried that to a pathological state.'

He was to achieve his thirst for privacy when, at the age of fifty-two, in 1992 he married Annette Bening and they began a family life and had four children. I'm not sure our interview did much to help *Reds* in the UK. I was playing tennis with Roger Wingate, who owned the Curzon Cinema, and he told me his manager had called him the previous Monday to say that nobody was coming to see the film. 'Well, run it until the end of the week,' Roger instructed him. 'When I say nobody, I mean nobody,' the man replied. 'The Curzon is absolutely empty.'

Barry Norman had been presenting the film programme for ten years and, early in 1982, he was tempted to seek pastures green and move on to *Omnibus* – a prestigious hour-long programme with huge resources that covered all the arts. On a couple of occasions, when Barry was abroad or had toothache, the producers had asked me to sit in for him. I knew the ropes and was rather available. So the thought did pass through my mind that maybe I might take over.

But it was not to be. Instead, the producers tried out a few guest presenters on the air: Tina Brown, the editor of *Tatler*; Miles Kington, an exceptionally funny *Punch* columnist; Maria Aitken, the astute, Oxford-educated actress and director; and Glyn Worsnip, one of

Esther Rantzen's chorus on *That's Life* who used to amuse her with things like potatoes that resembled genitalia.

When the programme came off the air for its summer break, the newspapers assumed the 'winner' of this competition would take Barry's job. The *Telegraph* even published odds, with Miles as front-runner. Actually, I'm not sure they all wanted the job. Tina was soon off to New York to become the doyenne of the Manhattan magazine world with *Vanity Fair*, and Miles, not that keen on the limelight anyway, was off to Bath for a change of life and wife. Anyway, I got the call.

So, after they pumped out my profiles of Newman et al in the *Film '82* slot in September, I sort of stayed on. In my heart I knew that, unlike Barry, I lacked the telegenic chromosome. But, if my scripts were good enough, I could probably just about get away with it.

Thus the BBC Press Office put out a statement saying that on 27 September 1982: 'The versatile and witty documentary film maker Iain Johnstone will present *Film '82* when it returns for its autumn run.' Witty? Well, I did have a line in my first show when I said: 'Looking at the movie listings this summer has been a bit like reading the football results:

Grease 1	*Superman* 2
Star Trek 2	*Rocky* 3

which, I was delighted to see, was plagiarised by a comedian at the Royal Variety Performance. I also wanted to show off my 'intellect', quoting Dr Johnson on the Giant's Causeway to conclude one film review: 'It's worth seeing, but not worth going to see.'

What was it like presenting *Film '82*? Wonderful: it was better than work. I've often thought that a major motivation in life is a quest for comfort. I'm excluding the few who choose to scale Everest or row across the Atlantic. But the simple majority of us just want a metaphorical blanket that we can pull over ourselves each morning and stay comfortable all day. So it was with this job. The producers, Margaret Sharpe and Jane Lush, did all the graft. I was transported to arranged film screenings, taken to lunch on the day of recording, make-up girls combed and sprayed my hair and tried to make me look almost presentable, and I was cosseted in the studio with people on hand to cater to every wish. All I had to do was write a script and read it out. Bliss.

But in late May of 1983, I was giving our small Fulham lawn its first mow of the year (not an arduous task as it was about a quarter of the size of a tennis court) when Mo shouted from the kitchen window that Andrew Neil was on the phone and had been made editor of *The Sunday Times.*

'Not editor, darling,' I shouted back, 'maybe city editor.'

Andrew was thirty-four and, in those days, the major Fleet Street editors were all over fifty. He was, at the time, deputy something on The *Economist* and he and I were far from friends since he had been Mo's boyfriend and we had battled for her affections. Not physically or even verbally – I doubt if I had met him more than twice in my life.

'No, he is going to be editor.' Mo was back at the window. 'And you'd better come and talk to him as he has a proposition to put to you.'

After I had congratulated him, he cut to the chase. 'I'm going to make it more like the *New York Sunday Times*, lots of sections, and one of them will be called 'Screen' which will deal with the television and film industries. You know a lot about that, so we should have lunch.'

I had known there was a vacancy at *The Sunday Times* as Frank Giles, the previous editor, had had to resign. He had published excerpts from Adolf Hitler's new-found diaries which had made the Führer appear a more decent chap than we thought: he had supported Rudolf Hess's peace flight to Scotland in 1941 and he only wanted the Jews to be resettled in the East. The problem, it transpired, was that they had been written by Konrad Kujau, a professional forger who, since 1967, had owned a shop in Stuttgart which sold Nazi memorabilia which he made himself. His earlier works included an introduction to *Mein Kampf* and an opera by Hitler called *Wieland the Blacksmith*. Had the eminent historian and Hitler expert, Hugh Trevor-Roper, known this when he went to the offices of *Stern* magazine and proclaimed the diaries authentic, he might have had pause for thought.

Before meeting Andrew, I had to do my final film programme of the season. Why the BBC planners take the show off the air for the summer continues to perplex me. The final *Harry Potter, Spider-Man, The Dark Knight Rises* and many other popular films all opened here in July. In the States, ever since *Jaws* in 1975, the summer holidays are the home of the blockbuster. It cannot be to save money since the programme was cheaper to put on than most repeats. Perhaps the planners, like my mother, thought there was something intrinsically wrong about going to the cinema in the summer – although, in Belfast, it had been a good place to shelter from the rain. Or maybe their job was so all-consuming that they didn't have the time to see what was happening in the real world – like moving the BBC Sports Department to Manchester shortly before the London Olympics.

Anyway, I wrapped up the series and had a drink with the directors and producers. 'See you in September,' I said cheerily. Was it my paranoia or did I catch them glancing at each other behind their somewhat wan smiles? Driving home, I recalled the RAF sketch from *Beyond the Fringe* where Squadron Leader Peter Cook orders

Flying Officer Perkins (Jonathan Miller) to get up in a crate, pop over to Bremen and take a shufti. 'Goodbye, Perkins. God, I wish I was going, too.' 'Goodbye, sir. Or is it au revoir?' 'No, Perkins. It's goodbye.'

At lunch Andrew told me Rupert Murdoch had offered the editorship to Alastair Burnet (then fifty-five), but Alastair had advised him that he should 'skip a generation'. So Andrew it was. He had discussed his plans for the paper with Rupert in New York.

Fundamentally, he wanted to make it more modern and cutting edge. Harry Evans had put the paper on the map with his campaigning journalism but there was something fusty about the back half, the arts and books and new technology. Hence 'Screen' and a radical rethink of fads and fashion which became 'Style'. *Private Eye* was later to write of Andrew: 'If he can't plug it in or fuck it, he's not interested.'

He had really liked a documentary I made on Ted Turner and that, coupled with the film stuff, made him think I was the man to edit 'Screen'. I was flattered but I knew it would be a more than a full-time job and I hadn't had one of those in a decade. Also, I wasn't sure I'd be up to it; I knew less about modern media technology than he thought. So I declined. But there has been an interregnum in the post of film critic since the departure of the legendary Dilys Powell at the age of seventy-six. The columnist, Alan Brien, had had a go but one week his copy was shortened and he went to Frank Giles to say that if his column was ever touched again he would resign. Frank told him he could leave straightaway.

Andrew rightly pointed out that I couldn't review the week's films on the telly and then write the same again on a Sunday. I said that if I had to choose, to occupy Dilys's chair would be the more prestigious post.

But I didn't have to choose. I went to see my boss at the BBC and asked him about September. He said he had been meaning to talk to me (when?). It hadn't worked out with Barry Norman on *Omnibus* – indeed he had looked a bit awkward when dealing with Seurat or Stockhausen – and had asked to come back to his old job. Where he remained for the next three or four hundred years. Actually I thought it was a fair cop although I feel constrained to quote *Time Out*: 'Johnstone is easily the better presenter. He looks the viewer in the eye, whereas Norman's merely smiling at his own reflection.' I suppose I should also quote the same magazine when I had been in *The Sunday Times* job for about a year: 'The most familiar sound on a Sunday morning is that of Iain Johnstone barking up the wrong tree' – a line first written, they didn't acknowledge, by Penelope Gilliatt in the *Observer* about the *ST*'s theatre critic, Harold Hobson, more than a decade earlier.

But, yes, I got the job. I was Andrew's first appointment. He had to send samples of my work to Rupert Murdoch who approved them by writing his initials in the margins : KRM, if you ever want to forge them.

That wasn't the best news of that summer. We had another child. I had been hoping for a son, whom we would call Olly, but, in fact, we got a Holly. Will Wyatt and his wife, Jane, came to visit Mo at Queen Charlotte's. They had two daughters and I asked Will whether he wouldn't have preferred a son and a daughter. 'Do you know,' he replied, 'I've never even thought about it.' And, from that moment, neither did I.

18

Film Critic: *The Sunday Times* ... Round the Film Festivals

Waiting in the Literary Department at *The Sunday Times* ('Screen' was still having birth pangs) was a friendly bunch of people. John Whitley was the boss and a wicked rebel. (In later years he let me have three months off on full pay to finish a novel.) Claire Tomalin was the books editor. Later she would marry my hero, Michael Frayn, and write acclaimed biographies of Pepys and Dickens. Penny Perrick, her assistant, would make her millions with a novel, *Malina*. And Nigella Lawson (whose dad was Chancellor of the Exchequer) was general dogsbody and made me a dreadful cup of instant coffee. I cannot think why they should have been so nice to me, being the first Murdoch storm trooper to land on their territory. Perhaps they had seen me on TV. There was a cracked wooden desk, heavily ink stained, where critics of yore had come to write their copy, with the names Dilys Powell and Harold Hobson prominent on the pigeon holes above, left to intimidate their successors.

My welcome at my first national press show was less warm. Or, rather, non-existent. Not that I expected one. Critics are like antiquarks in the Large Hadron Collider who spend their time avoiding each other, since you didn't want your opinion of a film to be coloured by another's or, heaven forfend, use a phrase in your column that had been voiced by another critic. I remember in my review of Hubert Selby's *Last Exit to Brooklyn*, I opined that the story was past its 'sell-by' date, and Nigel Andrews of the *Financial Times* came over to me on Monday morning and said: 'I don't know how I missed writing that; it was staring me in the face.'

The national critics got their starting orders in a letter every Thursday giving details of the following week's screenings. If you missed one, especially from Artificial Eye or the Screen cinemas, you and your section editor could expect an angry call demanding to know why. A review, after all, was the cheapest form of publicity. And if you walked out of a film there'd be a PR spying on you and demanding the same. Lavatory visits were barely tolerated. Richard Mayne of the *Sunday Telegraph* and I had similar bladder requirements and would cover the missing minutes for each other. I had to take a leak during *Dangerous Liaisons*, set in eighteenth-century Versailles, and asked Richard what had happened in my absence. 'You missed one hell of a car chase,' he informed me.

Since Andrew and I had agreed that a British television film might be worth more attention than a Bulgarian release about a man falling in love with his tractor, I led my first column with *An Englishman Abroad* – which I had seen in a BBC cutting room. This was Alan Bennett's wonderful account of actress Coral Browne meeting the spy, Guy Burgess, in Moscow and, on her return to England, sending him new shoes from Lobb's of St James's who had kept the spy's foot measurements. Directed by John Schlesinger, it was a gem. I'm not sure my review endeared me to my fellow film critics, nor to the TV critic of the *ST*.

I figured that one of my strengths was that I had seen a few films being made and could spot how the flaws might have arisen, whether in the script, on the floor, or in the cutting room. I was the critic as garage mechanic. If the vehicle was in perfect working order, I could pat it on the bonnet and send it on its way with praise. But if it just wasn't working, my job was to try and explain why. Merely throwing abuse at bad films was hardly the role of the professional critic; anybody coming out of a cinema could do that.

The Sunday Times job inevitably gave rise to ancillary opportunities: a regular slot on the Radio 2 *Arts Programme* hosted by Sheridan Morley and, on occasion, by me; a commission to write a novel for Chatto and Windus from their MD, Carmen Callil, who said she enjoyed my column; meals at the Savoy for the Evening Standard Film Awards; and an offer from Cathay Pacific to come to Hong Kong and programme the movies for their cabin entertainment in return for pretty well as many flights as I wished to take.

I got a call from Andy Ayliffe, a producer on Radio 4, to see if I would host a pilot for a quiz about the cinema called *Screenplay*. I didn't tell him I was game for anything; after the *ET* years the *ST* years had seen quite a drop in earnings. It was quite a simple concept, where two teams answered questions about, yes, movies.

The team captains were Dick Vosburgh and Robin Ray. Dick was funny in a clever way. He wrote for David Frost and he told me that if ever a joke went flat, Frostie used to add: 'As Dick Vosburgh always used to say,' whether or not Dick had written it. Robin had a hard act to follow: his comedian father, Ted, had a radio show with an audience of pretty well the entire country. Robin had a brilliant memory. He knew the K (Köchel) number of all 626 Mozart compositions – something he demonstrated on TV's *Face the Music* – and hadn't forgotten much about the movies, either. *Screenplay* started moderately well but then the head of BBC Radio told us to make it less of a quiz but more a battle of anecdotes. We began to attract a better class of guest star panellists and it lingered in the Radio 4 6.30pm slot for eight years.

19

James Stewart … Sean Connery … Robert Redford

If you think about it, the life of a film critic is a pretty peculiar one: spending your time analysing events which, for the most part, never really happened. Too much fantasy in too many dark rooms could drive a person stir-crazy – and did in some instances. Writing a novel was hardly an antidote; you cannot cure isolation with more isolation. So I seized on any opportunity to get out and about a bit.

Inevitably other gigs tended to have something to do with cinema; that was where I had stuck my flag. Channel 4 decided to broadcast a series of *Guardian Lectures* with industry players at the National Film Theatre and a perspicacious producer, Madeleine French, asked me if I'd like to be the interviewer. I would.

There was a definite buzz in working in front of a full house, many of whom knew more about the subject than I did. So, unlike my student years at Bristol, I made sure I studied hard. They say a barrister in court should always know the answer his witness will give to a question. But with the pressure on the interviewee to give the audience some entertainment, it was sometimes fun to try and lead him or her into a territory that their PR person tried to make off-limits. With James Stewart the injunction had been: 'Don't mention the war.'

I knew that Stewart was a frequent, but largely unremarked, visitor to England. His daughter, Kelly, an anthropologist, had studied at Cambridge University and married a fellow undergraduate.

She still lived in the city and Jimmy and her mother, Gloria, used to visit them every year. He liked to combine the holiday with a nostalgic visit to nearby RAF Tibenham, where he had been stationed during the war.

So when he mentioned that on stage, I was able to ask him why he (unlike Cary Grant or John Wayne or, indeed, Ronald Reagan) had experienced active service. Stewart, with a little reluctance, revealed that his family had always served their country. His father had left his hardware store in Indiana to enlist in World War I when he was forty-six. Jimmy learned to fly as a student and when he enlisted in March 1941, he had won the Best Actor Oscar for *The Philadelphia Story* just the month before. He modestly said that as a flyer he was given a commission so that he could teach other men to fly. And ended up in the Heavy Bombardment Squadron in Norfolk, part of the 8th Air Force.

What I was obliged to add was that he flew more than twenty missions over Germany, was awarded two DFCs and was promoted to Brigadier General in the USAF Reserve. It was this amalgam of bashful leading man and equally bashful war hero that earned him the epithet of 'America's most beloved man'. The chap who sat beside me on the stage at the NFT was that gentle, slightly stammering star, choosing his words thoughtfully and slowly, and endearingly modest – almost to a fault, if there can be a fault in modesty.

After the war, he said, he had doubts about returning to work as an actor but the temptation of Frank Capra's *It's a Wonderful Life* was too strong to resist. Hitchcock sent him the script of *Rope* and he accepted immediately: 'I was dying to work with him but when I drove out to the studio to see him he said "I thought you would decline and I would have to persuade you."' It was a dark story with Stewart playing a misguided professor whose 'life isn't worth much'

Brigadier General Jimmy Stewart, Distinguished Flying Cross and Oscar.

philosophy caused two of his students to commit a callous murder. He adored working with Hitch and the respect was mutual. He understood that the man who had been schooled in silent films was fundamentally a visual director, carefully casting his actors and then leaving them to their own deserts.

'When we did *Vertigo*, Kim Novak was disconcerted that Hitch wouldn't say anything to her after each take. I explained that this

CLOSE ENCOUNTERS

was his way so we developed a system whereby I would give her a little nod if I thought the take was OK.' Did Hitchcock ever give him any direction? 'Only to take it a little bit faster. In *The Man Who Knew Too Much* we were doing a scene in the Royal Albert Hall where I had to chase Doris Day up some flights of stairs while delivering a long speech at the same time. He told me "You were talking so loud I couldn't hear the London Symphony Orchestra. Let's cut it out." I said that I thought the speech cleared up a lot of things in the plot and, besides, I had taken a long time to learn it. But we did it his way and, of course, it worked.'

Looking back – he was 76 at the time of our interview – what were his favourite films? 'Do you know, I usually just see the final movie at the sneak preview and all I do is look at my performance and I think "Why on earth did I do that? Why did I scratch my nose? Why did they use that take?" But the other day, after about thirty years, I saw *Rear Window* and I rather enjoyed it.'

Sean Connery only made one film for Hitchcock: *Marnie* with Tippi Hedren. Hitch had announced that it would be with Princess Grace of Monaco but this was premature; when she found she was to play a frigid kleptomaniac, she thought not. Connery, having burst into the big time with James Bond, told me: 'Hitch phoned me and asked me to be in his next film. I thanked him and asked to see the script. He said this was nonsense. "Even Cary Grant never asked to see the script." I told him "I'm not Cary Grant and if you'd been in some of the tripe I have, you'd know why."' Connery said the only direction Hitch gave him was: 'Put in some more dog's feet?' 'Dog's feet?' the incredulous Scotsman asked him. 'Pawses,' replied the master.

My NFT evening with Connery did not start well. I encountered him in the lavatory where, after he had finished urinating, he shook my hand. No trip to the washbasin had intervened. 'We've had our arguments,' he said, 'but that's water under the bridge.' What arguments? I wondered. Apart from the retake of his interview on *A Bridge Too Far* – about which he had been most agreeable – and missing his helicopter on *Highlander* (which I had covered for *ET*) because my plane was late, I'd hardly seen the man. Perhaps he said this to all his interviewers just to unnerve them.

But he was forthright on the stage, proudly telling the audience of his humble Edinburgh upbringing working as a milkman and a coffin polisher and his route to movies through the Mr Universe contest and the chorus of *South Pacific*.

I had taken soundings from people attending in the bar beforehand and it became apparent that the thing most people wanted to hear about was Bond. I didn't want to plod through the obvious questions on this, so I threw the lecture open to the audience much earlier than usual and Sean was genially responsive to their interest. He owed the part, he said, to Terence Young who had directed him in *Action of the Tiger* and was instrumental in persuading the North American producers of *Dr No*, the first Bond, to cast him. They had thought Sean a bit too rough and ready for the part but Young assured them he knew how to act and had the right sort of body language and magnetism. Connery confessed he had stolen quite a bit of the Bond style from Young himself: the director was a stylish Cambridge graduate who had served as a tank commander at Arnhem.

Somebody suggested that Ian Fleming had not liked the casting. 'I've read the quote "I wanted a star but they got a stunt man instead,"' Sean smiled. 'I'm not quite sure it's true. I'm not sure he approved of me initially but he did have casting rights on the film so he must have come round to the idea. I found him fascinating. He had this tremendous curiosity, always wanting to know exactly how anything worked. It made the books stand out. But his Bond was a snob and Terence made him more a man of the people and added the vital ingredient that the books didn't have but the films did: humour.'

Inevitably he was asked why he decided to quit Bond. 'It was killing me as an actor. I had to find more control in films. Also, I was tired of fat slob producers living off the backs of lean actors. At the premiere of *You Only Live Twice* the Queen Mother could see I'd had enough and asked me if it was really my last Bond film and I told her it was. "Do you feel you were typecast?" she asked. Wise woman.'

'But you did come back,' I pointed out. 'After Lazenby's *Casino Royale* you did *Diamonds Are Forever*. What caused your change of heart?'

Connery shifted uneasily. 'Not the producers, certainly. David Picker, the President of United Artists, made me an offer I couldn't refuse. A lot of money upfront which went to my Scottish International Educational Trust. A large percentage of the gross which helped me settle my finances after my divorce and, most persuasive of all, the promise to back two more films – not Bonds – which I could produce.'

Connery is a litigious man and, fuelled by his hatred of Cubby Broccoli – his comment 'I wouldn't piss on him if he was on fire' was cut from the TV broadcast – sued him and United Artists for not paying him what he thought was due under their profit-sharing deals. It was a lengthy and bitter case but was eventually settled out of court. A lawyer whom I knew from university had been working on the case and he told me that one of the clauses in the final settlement was that no-one should mention that there had been a settlement, although Sean evidently did rather well out of the merchandising rights.

'How come Broccoli didn't have the rights to the *Thunderball* remake *Never Say Never Again?*' asked a girl in the audience. 'He thought he did,' Connery replied, 'and he spent two years and more than two million dollars trying to prevent Kevin McClory making it. But McClory had written the original story with Ian Fleming and the court ruled that he had the right to do so, although Broccoli got eighteen per cent of the profits, so I don't know what he was complaining about. I was offered control over the script and the casting and the final cut, plus a good fee ($5m) and my wife, Micheline, urged me to do it. So I did. And it broke records in several European countries.'

'I understand there were some production difficulties,' I prodded.

'There were,' the star agreed. 'Jack Schwartzman, the producer, solved them by moving to the Bahamas with an unlisted telephone number in the middle of production. I hate parasites. I hate incompetence. When you get into a situation where somebody who is totally incompetent is in charge, a real ass, then everything is a struggle. There was so much incompetence, ineptitude and dissension during the making of *Never Say Never Again* that the film could have disintegrated. What I could have done is just to have let it bury itself. I could have walked away with an enormous amount of money and the film would never have been finished. But, once I was in there, I ended up getting in the middle of every decision. The assistant producer and myself really produced the picture.

'I wouldn't touch Schwartzman with the proverbial bargepole. Micheline even came up with the title and Schwartzman said he would buy her a mink coat if it was used. She's still waiting for it.'

And with that, the Connery Bond saga came to an end. (Incidentally, the researcher on the TV series was a twenty-two year old called Jonathan Ross. Later he went on to present some television programmes himself. I'm not sure that I was his inspiration, though.)

The *Guardian Lectures* were always full but for Robert Redford we could have filled the Albert Hall. Following the success of *Butch Cassidy and the Sundance Kid* in 1969, he remained the world's most popular film star for more than a decade. He was fifty-five when I interviewed him but had lost little of his allure, the epitome of cool in his T-shirt and jeans and his trademark auburn hair, lush and lustrous, every strand carefully lacquered into place.

His glamour aside, I knew he was a serious man and asked him if he had ever thought of going into politics. 'Never,' he assured me. 'I'm political but I have a cynical relationship with the system which can be better expressed outside it than being part of it. *The Candidate* was my idea: a man who runs for the Senate to draw attention to the environmental principles he believes in, but when he finds he might win if he abandons his principles, he sells out. We're naive. We elect people for cosmetic reasons. The studio had the idea of putting me on a train to Miami where there was a Democratic Convention and seeing how many people I attracted at the same stops as the real-life candidate had. He got about five hundred people and I got about three thousand. I told them: "I have absolutely nothing to say" but they seemed happy with that.'

He had proved his point. But, by chance, the political reporters on his train were talking about the break-in at the Watergate building. None of them wanted to pursue it as it might alienate them from the Nixon administration. Redford soon discovered that the two men who were following the story were Bob Woodward and Carl Bernstein. He left messages for them but got no reply. So he went off to make *The Sting*, reuniting him with Paul Newman. 'Neither of us knew what was going on. We were rarely in the same scene together. It was the director, George Roy Hill, who carried it in his mind.

'By now Woodward and Bernstein had exposed a trail of breadcrumbs that led to the cottage [Hansel and Gretel], the Committee to Re-elect the President. It was denied and they were taken to court, but one of the burglars wrote to the judge and said it was true. I got in touch with them again. They apologised, saying they thought my earlier calls had been part of a set-up. But they agreed to meet me in my New York apartment where it was safe to speak – which we did for six hours. I thought their story would make a terrific film: one Jewish liberal guy and one Republican WASP. So we bought the book and tried to make *All the President's Men* as faithful to it as we could. I was only too aware that this might be the record of this event that future generations would see.'

With the money from his movies, Redford set up The Sundance Institute on land he had bought in Utah. 'I wanted to put something back. Film needs new blood and new ideas. This was a place where writers and actors could come and fail. Some succeeded, like Quentin Tarantino and *Reservoir Dogs*. As independents we were somewhat feared by the studios, as if we were insurgents who could come down from the hills and make a run on Hollywood. But when I started the Sundance Film Festival, Hollywood started coming to us.'

Since he came to prominence Redford had vigorously fought for local initiatives to address climate change and preserve the wilderness. He made two movies to remind people of the purity of the time when man was closer to nature: *Jeremiah Johnson* and *A River Runs Through It*.

I asked him if he was still Chairman of the Provo Canyon Sewer District Committee.

'Yes,' smiled Bob. 'The number one guy in a number twos job.'

20

The Making of *A Fish Called Wanda*

One evening in 1987 John Cleese dropped by. Sophie was especially pleased to see him: she, John and his daughter, Camilla, and I would go swimming every Sunday morning in Kensington New Pools (although the pools were a bit old by then). We all would have to change into our costumes in the men's dressing room as the girls were too young to be let out of our sight. Mo, John and I had a drink and as he left, he pressed a brown envelope he had been holding into my hand. 'Have a read. I'd really welcome your comments.'

I eagerly tore it open. It contained the script he had been writing with the English film director and editor, Charles Crichton: *A Goldfish Called Wanda*. This was John at his best: crisp, clever and very, very funny. Not only did it have a compulsive 'what's at stake?' plot and deft double-crosses and triple-crosses but also, in the grand tradition of Footlights Smokers, two risqué running fillers: Otto shooting the tails off passing cats (which he keeps, neatly arranged in a bowl in his room – scenes never shown in the final cut) and animal lover Ken's attempts to murder an old lady witness but killing her pet dogs instead.

Cleese was on the phone the next morning. 'Now, I want the truth.' I said it was damn well perfect. 'But there must be something?' 'Maybe I wasn't too sure what Wanda really wanted,' I replied. 'Control,' John asserted. 'She wants to wrap all the men round her little finger. Like any woman who can get away with it. Now, any obvious mistakes?' 'Well,' I ventured, 'when George says "We won't have to look for work and it won't have to look for us – Oscar Wilde,"

I'm not sure Wilde ever wrote that.' 'He didn't,' John came back triumphantly. 'George is just saying that to impress Wanda.' Duh!

As with *Fawlty Towers*, John's ancillary art was in the casting. While he was in Australia making a coffee commercial, the American producer, Michael Shamberg, suggested he meet Kevin Kline who was promoting a film there. As Kevin later told me: 'We found we were both interested in the same thing: ourselves.' In his first film, *Sophie's Choice*, as the fantasist Nathan, Kline was the perfect match for his friend, Meryl Streep. John and he had acted together on the Western *Silverado* and as a result of this connection Cleese custom-wrote the part of Otto for Kevin.

John was utterly beguiled by Jamie Lee Curtis as the tart with a heart in *Trading Places*. He told me he had never seen an actress who was so sexy and, at the same time, had such first-rate comic timing. There was a crossover at a certain level in transatlantic comedy. For instance, Tony Hendra had been in Footlights with John and then in *This Is Spinal Tap* with Christopher Guest, Jamie's husband. Having made contact with her, John studied her and created the part of Wanda. 'I've never met anybody like Wanda,' Jamie was to tell John at the end of filming. John was pretty obsessed with her by then so he omitted to say that Wanda was based on the flirting/control facets of her own character.

Michael Palin was a shoo-in. He was the best Python actor and, although he didn't write with John, in another age they could have been a musical hall duo, taking their 'Dead Parrot' and 'Cheese Shop' on tour. (Michael's father had a disabling stutter.)

The final piece of the jigsaw was the director. John had been an admirer of the Ealing Comedies. If he had been born earlier, quite possibly that might have been where he fitted in. Charles Crichton had directed *The Lavender Hill Mob* and *The Titfield Thunderbolt*. In

1961 he went to the States and began directing *Birdman of Alcatraz*, but he fell out with its star and owner of the production company, Burt Lancaster, and was fired. Charlie didn't return to LA for more than a quarter of a century. He ended up teaching at a film school. But John had unwavering faith in his talent and used him to direct many of the half-hour comedic training films for his company, Video Arts. And to work on the script and direct *Wanda*, although he was by then seventy-seven years old.

This proved a stumbling block when Cleese went to Hollywood to raise money for his film. The most obvious port of call was Columbia Pictures, known as 'British Columbia' since David Puttnam had become the boss in 1986. But Puttnam did not want to back the film with Crichton as director. The message came in Hollywood-speak. 'Mr Puttnam is not prepared to take a pitch meeting with Mr Cleese but would be happy to have dinner with him,' presumably to persuade John to drop Charlie. But John was not prepared to drop Charlie, so no dinner. (It might have been better for Puttnam if he had taken the pitch. Cleese was only looking for $7.3m; Puttnam instead backed Bill Cosby's *Leonard Part 6* which cost $25m and took $5m. Puttnam's tenure at Columbia lasted fifteen months.)

John had spent more than $150,000 of his own money in pre-production, much of it in going through the script with his leading characters, individually and together, to get as much input as possible. So it was something of a shock to get this rebuff from Puttnam, as he also did from Universal Studios and from Dino De Laurentiis.

Michael Shamberg had come on board as one of the producers. Hollywood can be quite a small club in the higher echelons. Michael's *The Big Chill* had been directed by Lawrence Kasdan who had written *The Empire Strikes Back* and was a great friend of George

Lucas. George would never have got the *Star War* series off the ground if it had not been for the persistence of Alan Ladd Jr in the face of opposition from the other Twentieth-Century-Fox senior executives. Shamberg knew that Laddie, as he was universally known, son of the star of *Shane*, had recently taken over the reins at the ailing MGM Studios and was looking for new product.

Fearing a final turn down, Michael and John didn't send him the script but he was prepared to take a meeting. John did the talking. 'After fifteen years of making management training films which frequently dealt with salesmanship, I think I knew instinctively how to pitch. And that is no different in Hollywood than anywhere else. You describe the benefits, not the features. If I were selling you a mixer, I wouldn't say this is a revised version of the Gordonsplatz rotator valve. That is a feature. You say it can grind coffee in six seconds. That is a benefit. I told the MGM execs the story and they laughed. And that for $7.3m we had put together a package that could be of real value to the studio.'

The bosses conferred in private, then Laddie said he was prepared to put up part of the money for the film. Satisfied, Cleese and Shamberg got into their car to return to Santa Monica. With MGM in place, especially as distributor, the rest of the budget should be easier to raise. The car phone rang. It was Laddie. 'I've been thinking,' he said. 'I'll back the whole thing.' It was the same calculated hunch that had made him back *Star Wars* for $11m; within two years Fox had recouped eight times that sum.

John thought it might be fun if I did a documentary during the filming. He already had a title: *John Cleese's First Farewell Performance*. I knew this prevented me from reviewing the film in the *ST* but it might be even better if the second string did it. Second strings always use words like 'I urge you to see this film' to try to get their name on posters. I've never quite understood how you can urge strangers to see a film – Tarantino, for instance, is hardly for grannies.

Charlie Crichton had always wanted to direct a scene where a man was run over by a steamroller and this was to be Otto's fate in *Wanda*. Kevin was caught in some fast-drying cement (made largely from porridge) at the end of the film and an angry Ken drove the steamroller at him in revenge for the death of his fish. 'I want you to give a blood-curdling yell as the blood is squeezed out of your body,' Crichton instructed the Juilliard-trained Kline.

Charlie was exceptionally young at heart and relished the killing of the terriers and when the last one went under a ten-ton block of concrete, he ordered entrails from a local butcher to spill out on all four sides. Prudently, Shamberg suggested an alternative take without them. At the American preview, the audience was horrified by the bloody scene and it was replaced. John observed that Americans, generally, were far more worried about the doggies dying than the fact that Ken was attempting to murder an old lady.

Charlie had a walking stick which, Robert Lindsay once told me, he hit him with when he failed to get a scene right in a Video Arts film. But, on *Wanda*, he was the soul of concern for his actors, a father figure to them all. Kevin asked him what was really wrong with Otto. Unhesitatingly Charlie replied: 'When you were a soldier in Vietnam, a mosquito buried its way through your forehead and it's still flying around inside your brain.'

It was a workshop to observe Kevin Kline at work. 'What time of day is this scene, Charlie?' he would ask. 'After lunch, Kevin,' came the improvised reply. Kevin walked away, satisfied, saying to himself: 'I wonder what Otto would have had for lunch? Sushi, probably.' He is the consummate actor, knowing that if you invest comedy with a strong degree of verisimilitude, it is all the funnier. When he found

Sophie – shocked child in *A Fish Called Wanda*.

the stolen jewels were not, as expected, in a safe in a garage, he executed a balletic leap and ad-libbed: 'I'm disappointed,' – a phrase later shouted at him by fans on the streets of New York. His recitation of an Italian menu when turning Wanda on: '*un ossobuco Milanese con piselli, un melanza parmigiana con spinaci*' plus '*dov'è la farmacia*' was sublime.

John, of course, used the same language trick to seduce Wanda, but he had taken the trouble to learn a Russian poem by Mikhail Lermontov. She indicates his seduction is successful and he undresses, his underpants over his head when the Johnstone family returns to the flat from Hong Kong. I had written a letter to my six-year-old daughter's headmistress asking if Sophie could be granted a couple of days off to appear in a major MGM film, not mentioning it was to stare at a naked Cleese, something familiar to her from the Sunday-morning changing room. When Jamie was later asked on chat shows about this poor little child, she would retort: 'Oh, it was all right. He went round to her house the night before and showed it to her.'

There was something intriguing, even intimidating, about Jamie Lee Curtis. To well-behaved public-school middle-class boys like Cleese and Palin, she was a sliver of pure Hollywood. Both her parents, Tony Curtis and Janet Leigh, had been major stars, she had been schooled at Beverly Hills High (the model for TV's *Beverly Hills, 90210*, although the school board wouldn't let them film it there), dabbled in drugs, hit the heights with her first feature, *Halloween*, which earned her the epithet 'Scream Queen', and then transformed herself into an exceptionally nubile queen of the gym in *Perfect*.

Jamie Lee Curtis re-enacts her finest hour in *Halloween*.

But Jamie was a major Python fan and, perhaps, a little intimidated herself by such illustrious company. Not that it prevented her from adding input. Her insult to 'Don't call me stupid, Otto – I've worn dresses with higher IQs' was pure Jamie. She was schooled on script analysis, pointing out to me how halfway through most episodes of *Charlie's Angels*, Kate Jackson would sum up the plot for the inattentive viewer: 'The drugs are going to land at 2am, but they've still got Jill and we have to free her before that or else they'll use her as a bargaining tool.'

Although she was very much one of the boys, she still did film-starish things like hiring Battersea Go Karting track on a Sunday morning for our families and dispensing Bollinger Mimosas to the somewhat nervous parents. She came to our kitchen for supper and when she was asked to reunite with her father on *The David Letterman Show* in London, she persuaded Mo to accompany her. (Ever the professional, she stuck socks in her bra before the programme to give herself a fuller figure.) Afterwards Tony Curtis took them back for a drink at Dodi Fayed's apartment where he was staying. He ransacked the cupboards in vain. 'Fucking Arabs,' he expostulated, 'they never have any booze.'

Michael Palin has such English reserve that, in all probability, the need to perform was his best escape from it. Few knew that, shortly before *Wanda* rehearsals began, his elder sister Angela committed suicide. One Tuesday he buried Angela's ashes accompanied by their eighty-five-year-old mother and Angela's family and by the next Tuesday he was back in action, his usual self. It was as if God had given him an extra battery.

There was a spirit of exuberance in all the cast by the time they filmed at Heathrow; they sensed they had a hit on their hands. Michael was obliged to tumble down a luggage slide amid all the heavy bags. It didn't prevent him from going off on one of his delicious pieces of extemporising for my documentary. When John suggested: 'I wouldn't be wrong in suggesting Stanislavski, would I?' 'I'm glad you noticed, John,' the battered Palin came back. 'That last take had more baggageyness. It's only there for those who want to see it. I said to myself: "Michael, you're not an international superstar, you're just a bag." But I couldn't do it. My greatness couldn't help coming out. I have this amazing film library of famous people coming down luggage shoots: Boris Becker, Bismarck, Kierkegaard, even Eleanor Roosevelt. Somehow, she retained her dignity. Eleanor could come down a luggage shoot with her skirt tucked in at the bottom as if she was going to a dinner party.'

What informed John's writing, to an extent, was his apartness from the conventional English middle classes. He spells it out in his seduction speech. 'Wanda, do you have any idea of what it's like being English? Being so correct the whole time, being stifled by doing the wrong thing. Of saying to someone: "Are you married?" and hearing: "My wife left me this morning." We're all terrified of embarrassment. Most of my friends are dead, you know. We have these piles of corpses to dinner.' I had known that it had long been a contention of John's that the ambition of every middle-class Englishman is to get into his grave without ever having made a mistake.

A video of the rough-cut was sent to Laddie who liked it but felt the Wanda character was too hard, the audience should feel she really does want to escape with Archie at the end of the film. John invited me to do the rewrites with him. And, generously, gave me a quarter of a per cent of his profit share. I suggested, among other ideas, that maybe Wanda's body language in the car on their way to Heathrow could indicate her new feelings. John, inevitably, added some humorous dialogue. When he accuses Jamie of lying from the moment they met, she comes back: 'Oh right, so nobody lies in England. Like, Margaret Thatcher never lies.' This gets a good laugh in the cinema. *Wanda* was to take $63m at the US box office, $71m internationally and was the biggest American video release of 1989 – $77m, all gravy, as they say in the movies.

The film was feted with awards. Kevin won the Best Supporting Actor Oscar, unusual for a comedy performance. John was nominated for a couple of BAFTAs but, as he was at the time living in LA (not least to keep in contact with Jamie), he asked me if I could find out if he had won one as he couldn't be bothered to write a funny acceptance speech if he hadn't. I contacted a man at BAFTA, called, I think, Reg, explained the problem and was told it was completely out of order to release such information. But later in the week I got an embarrassed message that it might be worth Cleese's time to put pen to paper.

Inevitably, he wrote one of his lists, beginning by thanking real names on the film and then going into the realm of the absurd, thanking a long list of random people ending with Ann Haydon-Jones and her husband, Pip (this had been a running gag on *Python* ever since the Wimbledon champion married a man five years older than her father), and the Olympic diver, Brian Phelps (who was the subject of indecent assault allegations at various swimming pools and eventually did nine years bird).

It would have been out of character for John to celebrate his triumphant moment with an outbreak of good taste.

21

Covering The Oscars ...
Tom Hanks ... Mel Gibson

Nothing can quite prepare you for The Oscars; they could only take place in Tinseltown. The PR company where the press pick up their credentials was just along from the Roosevelt Hotel where the first Oscar ceremony was held in 1929. Douglas Fairbanks was President of the Academy and 270 people gathered for a lobster dinner. There were few surprises that night as Emil Jannings, winner of the first ever Oscar, had to be presented with his some time before the ceremony as he had to nip back to Germany where he went on to make some Nazi propaganda films.

My first awards ceremony was at The Al Malaikah Temple, headquarters of The Ancient Arabic Order of the Nobles of the Mystic Shrine. The Shriners were out of town that day (probably sporting their conical red hats as they did their good deeds) and handed over their 6,000-seat temple to the worship of showbiz. The temple is located in a pretty rough area of south LA where, on a bad day, bullets whine overhead as the Bloods and Crips indulge in gang warfare. Why would the Shriners wish to build their temple in such a location? I suppose the answer is best given by the American who asked: 'If the Queen doesn't like aircraft noise, why did she build Windsor Castle so close to Heathrow?'

I was early and drove past the Shrine where a crowd had already assembled on the hustings. They were watching a man in a green boiler suit with the words 'Termite Control' on the back vacuuming the red carpet. Presumably he was getting rid of the remains of any Bloods or Crips. I had been allocated a slot in the University of Southern California car park, a seat of learning where students are reputedly advised not to go off campus without bullet-proof clothing. In the sweltering heat of the April afternoon, the air was rich with the odour of goat stew and sizzling squid and, most challengingly, cow foot soup being sold at every street corner from Belizean stalls. I resisted the temptation. Although there were still a couple of hours to go (the ceremony started at 5.30pm to hit prime time on the East Coast) a limo traffic jam had formed on West Jefferson Boulevard and many arriving guests had decided to get out and walk. It was an incongruous sight to observe the rich and coiffured from Beverly Hills threading their way past their less privileged fellow citizens. I sensed no animosity; I suppose we need the glitterati to provide us with our circuses.

I watched the later arrivals from the comfort of the ample press room where every beverage was provided, save alcohol. On the large screens, the arriving actresses were grilled not about their films but their frocks. It slightly amazed me, then as now, why serious actresses should twirl around and praise dress designers at a ceremony about cinema. But that's part of the unique flavour of the event, a piece of Americana. They didn't take much cajoling from the compère but, there again, Halle Berry and Michelle Pfeiffer were once beauty queens and Meryl Streep and Sandra Bullock cheerleaders. Americans love a parade. One day an enterprising reality-TV producer will devise a programme where stars just twirl their way up a red carpet with no prize-giving at the end – it would probably get the same ratings.

Winners were escorted from the stage to a press interview, most in a state of dazed delight, and several lingered. I was impressed by

Marlee Matlin, winner for *Children of a Lesser God*, who is deaf but able to lip-read with 100 per cent accuracy. Dianne Wiest, who won Best Supporting Actress for *Hannah and Her Sisters*, politely asked me to move up on the sofa so she could sit and sip her coffee. I congratulated her and, on hearing my accent, she said that her mother came from Auchtermuchty in Scotland. She told me she used to sing to her: 'You can go to Auchtermuchty and to Drumnadrochit too, but you'll never find a Nessie in the zoo.' I agreed and added you probably wouldn't find a Nessie in Loch Ness either, which seemed to disappoint her as one day she intended to make the trip. Just what the Inverness Tourist Board wanted, I suggested. Woody Allen had won Best Screenplay for *Hannah* but, on principle, wasn't there. 'Woody says he doesn't want to live on in the hearts of the people,' Dianne smiled. 'He says he would rather live on in his own apartment. But I do feel a little alone tonight. My boyfriend couldn't make it, either.'

I later learned that Miss Wiest's boyfriend was theatrical agency ICM's New York boss, Sam Cohn, and he was at home with his wife. Dianne went on to have a good career in Woody's repertory company and copped another Oscar for *Bullets Over Broadway*. Woody was eventually lured to The Oscars in 2002. 'When I got the call I was afraid they wanted my Oscars back but the pawn shop has closed down,' he joked to the audience. He was there to introduce Nora Ephron's montage of New York movies in the light of the tragedy of 9/11.

On the basis, I think, of my columns, Sky TV invited me to anchor The Oscars, unfortunately from a draughty studio in a Hounslow business park. I put on a dinner jacket and they put a palm tree behind me. The object was to fill in the hour or so during the ceremony when NBC ran profitable commercials. Sky, at the time,

SB

TOGETHER : DISCOVER

For more on our authors and titles, visit our website
spellbindingmedia.co.uk

Follow us on Twitter
@SBMediaUK

Join the conversation
facebook.com/spellbindingmedia

Subscribe to our free newsletter
spellbindingmedia.co.uk/subscribe

For interviews and audio excerpts
youtube/spellbindingmedia

was not similarly deluged with advertisers, especially at 3am, so I invited the pretty, witty columnist, Victoria Mather, to dress up and sit beside me. She fluently conversed on movies, frocks, royalty, railway timetables, anything, until dawn broke over London.

A budget increase in 1992 meant we could actually do the programme from LA. It was fun to sit through the Sunday rehearsal in the Dorothy Chandler Pavilion where all the presenters were obliged to show up. They duly came on stage and actually tore open the envelopes but preceded their announcement by saying: 'And the winner, *for the purposes of this rehearsal only*, is Paul Newman', or whoever. (No Reg of BAFTA to let the cat out of the bag here.) Actually, the nominees were already placed in their seats, or rather large photographs of them were, so that the hand-held cameramen could provide the director with close-ups for the five-way split-screen. Meanwhile, elsewhere in town, the real nominees were practising that throw back of the head, fixed smile and forced applause in case they were one of the four remaining in their seats. Now that's real acting.

The budget, sadly, didn't extend to Victoria so I suggested to the producer that my friend, Marcia Lewis, would be brilliant in the job as she knew The Oscars inside out.

Marcia's *Entertainment Tonight* experience was invaluable as she won the 'most celebs' competition in the roped-in TV-reporter compound. She later explained she used the *ET* 'grab and bag' technique. You grab the star with your left hand, shove the mike in their face with your right and then, trump card, tell them: 'You're speaking live to London.' They weren't, actually, as it was recorded for a quick edit and turnaround or, even, dropped. But they didn't know that, so they were blackmailed into singing for their supper. Tom and Rita Hanks sent a prolonged message to friends they stayed with in England and Anthony Hopkins addressed his relations in his home town of Port Talbot. Tony had, in fact, relocated to Malibu where, to paraphrase Alan Bennett, 'the blue of the sea reminded him of the miners' eyes'.

I had predicted that Tony would win for his 'I ate his liver with some fava beans and a nice Chianti' performance as Hannibal the Cannibal in *The Silence of the Lambs*. I'd also predicted that the film would win the five top awards – it is there in black and white in the previous day's *Sunday Times* – but it didn't take the powers of Tiresias, the blind prophet of Thebes, to do this as that was the Beverly Hills buzz, backed up by bookmaker, Jimmy the Greek, in Las Vegas. I also told the Sky viewers before the ceremony but such hubris inevitably invites a tumble and mine was not long in coming.

Marcia had told our director that there was a thirty-second tape delay in the ABC transmission. The Oscars had not been shown 'live' since 1974 when a naked streaker interrupted David Niven who, with English aplomb, calmly went on: 'Isn't it fascinating that the only laugh that man will ever get in his life is by stripping off and showing his shortcomings.' But our producer, John Rowe, insisted it was definitely live this year and thus I proudly told UK viewers: 'And now, Sky's exclusive coverage of the sixty-fourth Academy Awards' only for ABC to continue with a long commercial. Rowe quickly cut back to Marcia and me as we hoped our make-up was thick enough to cover our reddening cheeks.

Apart from *The Silence of the Lambs*, the other highlights of the ceremony were George Lucas getting his Irving G. Thalberg Award, appropriately, from outer space: the crew of the space shuttle, *Atlantis*, had taken an Oscar on board, although George remained firmly rooted in the Dorothy Chandler Pavilion. And Volodymyr Jack Palahniuk, better known as Jack Palance, getting Best Supporting

Actor for *City Slickers*. The Oscar host, Billy Crystal, had been in the film with him and knew that the seventy-three year old's party trick was to do one-arm press-ups which Jack proceeded to perform for the audience. Crystal made a succession of clever ad-libs about Palance's powers throughout the rest of the evening. When a children's choir left the stage, Crystal quipped: 'Jack Palance fathered all those children.' His jokes culminated in how Palance was last seen bungee jumping off the Hollywood Sign. Well, not quite ad-libs; they were scripted for him by the writer of the ceremony, Bruce Vilanch. Not everything in Hollywood is for real.

The highlight of the 1994 ceremony was Tom Hanks winning the Best Actor Oscar for his gay lawyer dying of AIDS in *Philadelphia*. (He was to win again the next year for *Forrest Gump* – making him the only actor since Spencer Tracy to win back-to-back Oscars.) I spoke to Tom after the ceremony.

Johnstone: You were in tears as you ended your acceptance speech: 'I know that my work is magnified by the fact that the streets of heaven are too crowded with angels. They number a thousand for each one of the red ribbons that we wear tonight.' Had you prepared that deliberately?

Hanks: No. Part of it was spontaneous. The one thing I wanted to communicate was that the reason I was standing there was because so many gay men were dead of AIDS. We had made this movie to say: 'If you think you have made your decision, you have to think again, because there is more to it than just gay men get AIDS and then they die.' I knew if I won I was going to have to say something to three billion people [sic] so I wanted to try and say the right thing. Now my syntax was a little busted up and some stuff didn't come out quite the way I wanted it to come out but, by and large, I felt pretty good about what I said.

Johnstone: Some people were surprised that you 'outed' your high-school teacher, Rawley Farnsworth, in the speech.

Hanks: That came from one of the more idiotic tabloids. Nothing was said that wasn't agreed. But the idea of 'outing' somebody wasn't such a bad idea. Frank Oz made it into a film with Kevin Kline, *In & Out*, and I keep thinking they should pay me something for it.

Johnstone: What was Rawley's influence on your career?

Hanks: Total. Usually in American schools the drama teacher gets the seniors together and they do a bad production of some horrible show that was specifically written for high schoolers to do. But at Oakland's Skyline High School, we had the chance to do plays like Tennessee Williams's *The Night of the Iguana*, *Twelfth Night* and *South Pacific*. It was the best acting school I've ever been to and it changed my life. There were times in my high school when I got up on the stage and felt as excited and special there as I even still do in movies.

Johnstone: But movies didn't immediately attract you?

Hanks: They were way beyond my reach. Movies and television were another world and I didn't, at the time, have the slightest idea how to get into it. My scholarship to Cal State was as a stage carpenter. But as a kid I did pretend an awful lot. I could entertain myself in a room for hours on end doing sort of bizarre stuff. Not just one-man theatre but one-man audience as well.

Johnstone: You usually associate that sort of self-entertainment with being an only child, but you were far from that.

Hanks: That, Iain, is a very British understatement. First I had a sister and two brothers, then I was the youngest in a family of eight which included four stepsisters whom I would not recognise if they walked into the room right now. Then there were another

244

three more and finally another two when my father moved on again. It was an odd sixties dysfunctional version of the extended family. It seemed there was always someone new coming or going. But within all that, I was able to entertain myself. I never had a problem being by myself – it was a comfortable place to be.

Johnstone: You played bit parts in TV sitcoms but your big break appeared to be in *Bosom Buddies* which I have to confess I have never seen.

Hanks: You haven't seen *Bosom Buddies?* I'm amazed it didn't take England and Europe by storm. I was under the impression that the world was gripped in *Bosom Buddies* mania and now you're telling me you've never even seen it. I'm so horribly disappointed. Peter Scolari and I played two advertising executives who arrived in New York to find the apartment they had rented was going to be knocked down. So they found refuge in an all-woman residence hotel. It was a bit of a one-joke series. Peter and I would linger in the doorways of each other's dressing room pondering life's great questions while we were wearing pantyhose and women's undergarments. I always thought the show would be cancelled and my creative life would be over and I would have to get a job at the Post Office or in a bank. We were just another failed sitcom.

Johnstone: So what happened when it was cancelled?

Hanks: I was unemployed for a year. It wasn't like *Bosom Buddies* has been cancelled so now this guy is available. Nothing.

Johnstone: But within two years you were a film star. How did that come about?

Hanks: Being in the right place at the right time. Since I wasn't working, I occasionally played on a charity softball team with the people from *Happy Days* whom I knew just slightly. Ron Howard had left the show and I never saw him. But the writers of *Happy Days*, Lowell Ganz and Babaloo Mandel, had stayed on as supervising producers. And, casually, at softball one day Lowell asked if I would like to drop by and do a couple of days on an episode. I didn't let him know how desperate I was. And, unknown to me, they had already written a feature film called *Splash*.

Johnstone: To be directed by Ron Howard, who called you in.

Hanks: The truth is they couldn't get anyone to do a movie Ronnie Howard was directing for Disney about a mermaid. Everybody on the A-list of Hollywood actors at the time turned them down, God bless them. So it just kept slipping further and further down the casting food chain. So Ronnie brought me in. By then the film was so under the radar, so far below the profile of mainstream Hollywood that it was just this inconsequential thing that was going to be made. It only cost about eight million but took more than a hundred.

Johnstone: It turned your career and your life around. Why do you really think they cast you?

Hanks: You know, I had some chops that I had developed, something of a technique they wanted. I had been able to handle stuff that required me to be funny. I was young enough and just barely good-looking enough. And they were looking for a particular type of character, the sort that permeated movies in the 1980s. Relatively unthreatening. Not classically handsome. The guy who is having problems with relationships and doesn't quite know why he's having trouble with commitment. He's harried at work, he can't get his life together and then he meets a girl or a dog or finds a kid or something like that, which helps him to grow up at last.

Johnstone: And you found Daryl Hannah, a mermaid.

Hanks: Yes. Who would have thought that I would find the most beautiful woman in the world and she would love me and who would have imagined that she would be a fish? I owe it all to her.

Back in London, there is a willow that grows aslant a table in the Osteria San Lorenzo in Knightsbridge. Actually, it's no longer there and I'm not sure if it was a willow. But, anyway, it was a tree and gave a measure of seclusion to the celebrities who were placed there by the effervescent owner, Mara. They'd been coming since the sixties: Peter Sellers, Princess Margaret, Mick Jagger, Princess Diana. You name them and that's where they sat. I'd been invited to have dinner there with Mel Gibson and it wasn't hard to find him. The glances of the other diners led to the table by the tree. With three *Mad Max*s and two *Lethal Weapon*s behind him, Gibson, at thirty-four, was at the apogee of his career and I think people were intrigued to see him sitting in a London restaurant. He had formed an independent company to make *Hamlet* and, because of Franco Zeffirelli's *Romeo and Juliet* and *The Taming of the Shrew* with the Burtons, Mel had invited him to direct it.

Gibson was an engagingly modest man. He had wanted to keep a video diary of his experience on the film. Ruth Jackson, a top BBC director, had covered much of his work but there was a problem with the script. 'I like writing,' Mel confessed, 'but I just don't like writing things down.' Hence me. He was concerned when I tried to order beef since Britain was at the height of its BSE scare and the USA would no longer import our meat. So I settled for chicken.

We fell into conversation about his career. When he was at NIDA (Australia's National Institute of Dramatic Art), the school's director had asked each of the new entrants why they wanted to become an actor. His turn came and he stuttered: 'I don't know.' 'Well, do you enjoy it?' 'Yes, I enjoy it,' Mel replied. 'That's enough,' his teacher reassured him.

'My five year old wants to be an actor,' Mel told me. 'So, rather unfairly, I asked him why. He came back: "So that I can take your place when you die."'

Mel had played in Shakespeare on the stage in his early days in Melbourne but he felt intimidated by the fact that there were three eminent former Hamlets – Paul Scofield, Ian Holm and Alan Bates – in his own film. I could see from Ruth's footage they thought he was doing OK. 'He cannot emotionally tell a lie,' Bates observed. But Gibson had growing misgivings: 'It's more than a part. It's an assault on your personality. Every day Hamlet's doubts become your doubts. You can go so many different ways with the character. It's a minefield. It's just so personal. Nobody else can give you an interpretation. You're on your own.'

He had wisely engaged Julia Wilson-Dickson, Britain's leading dialogue coach, to go through every line with him before he went on camera. 'Franco says she's Shakespeare's widow,' Mel laughed.

At the time, the press had him happily married to Robyn Moore, with five children. The family-man image was a little tempered by the approbation he whispered to me as every pretty woman went past our table. The conversation moved into areas we were unlikely to put into the diary. Glenn Close had accepted the part of Gertrude, Hamlet's mother, but, perhaps wanting to emphasise that she was only nine years older than her son, arrived in England for the shoot with her face considerably 'improved'. And Franco, although operatic in his staging and vision, was adding to his inspiration with a couple of bottles of whisky each day. Mel had ultimately had to give the director an ultimatum: either they go or you go.

We were to meet a few more times and the 'Diary' fell into place. On the film's release, his performance was acclaimed. 'Mel Gibson's Hamlet is strong, intelligent and visceral, tortured by his own thoughts and passions, confused by his recognition of evil, a Hamlet whose emotions are raw yet who retains the desperate wit to act mad' wrote *The New York Times*. Five years later, Mel won an Oscar, not for Best Actor but for directing *Braveheart*. The next film he directed, *The Passion of the Christ*, an extremely violent portrayal of the days leading up to the Crucifixion, filmed in Aramaic, Latin and Hebrew (Mel had to be prevailed upon to add subtitles), grossed $600 million worldwide.

Nothing in my meetings with this gentle, self-effacing star could hint at the turbulence that lay ahead. In 2006, he was arrested for drunk-driving, with the police officer accusing him of a tirade of anti-Semitic remarks, including: 'The Jews are responsible for all the wars in the world.' His wife, Robyn, left him, at a reported cost of $400 million. He subsequently had a baby with a Russian pianist with whom he later fell out, both sides applying for restraining orders regarding the child.

But that night, in San Lorenzo, a father came up with his young daughter and said he had met Mel before. The star asked for the girl's name and wrote her a friendly message on her menu. At a nearby table, a girl was having a twenty-first birthday party and Mel willingly signed all the eleven cards she had been given. It seemed that nobody in our section of the restaurant left without a greeting and a signature. And they all probably went out into Beauchamp Place with a glow on their cheeks, eager to tell their friends and families about this lovely man.

By coincidence, John Cleese asked me to have dinner with him the following night. He had also booked San Lorenzo. We were given the same table, same tree. He had decided to write a sequel to *Wanda*.

All the studios had made offers but Tom Pollock of Universal's was the best. John's Python writing partner, Graham Chapman, had since died (enabling Cleese to tell the congregation that Gra would have wanted him to be the first person to say 'fuck' at his memorial service) and he wondered, after our collaboration on the *Wanda* rewrites, if I would write it with him. I was overjoyed; I knew I had stayed at *The Sunday Times* for too long but had been fearful of taking a step into the unknown.

The restaurant was crowded, as ever. But nobody dared come up to John. Some celebrities are more approachable than others.

I cannot recall any loud lamentations or beating of breasts when I informed 'The Culture' at the *ST* that I was leaving to write a film. Morale in the place was a bit low since a woman boss had arrived from a tabloid newspaper and attempted to liven up interviews by inserting quotes that the interviewees hadn't actually said. She eagerly seized on my vacancy to make her friend, Julie Burchill, film critic. When she arrived, Miss Burchill pronounced it to be the best job in journalism and when she left, after a year or so, she said it was the worst. She later divulged that she often 'skived' the screenings and just made up her reviews. I doubt if this did much to maintain the integrity that Dilys Powell had established.

It's usually best not to pay too much attention to your successor in any job; there's always the danger they may be better than you. I am just grateful that I was able to write a co-ordinated essay, good or bad, for my film reviews and not have to mark the movies out of five stars at the top of the column, as most editors insist critics do today. There's always the danger that the public will only count the stars and not bother to read the review. Not just a danger, a likelihood.

22

Up the Nile with Cook and Fry …
Oz with Dame Edna

Cleese is not a man who likes deadlines. He and Connie wrote the first six episodes of *Fawlty Towers* in their own time and it was another four years before the next six were broadcast. He had completed writing and casting *Wanda* before any studio came on board. Equally with *Wanda 2*, he had the clout to tell Universal that it would be delivered when it was ready. So he decided to treat forty friends to a trip up the Nile. He had been on his own a couple of years before, enjoying the company of Rabbi Julia Neuberger and her husband, and found it an exhilarating experience. *Wanda* had been the most successful video in the United States and John had just sold his training company, Video Arts. He doubted he would ever have another year when so much money came his way so he decided to allocate part of it (maybe as much as £250,000) as this generous gift to his friends.

What was a bit bizarre was that, although all of us knew John and his third wife, Alyce Faye, most of us didn't know each other. As students, that might have been fine, but in your fifties and sixties you're that much less comfortable. There was a sprinkling of television faces but most of us were anonymous, hard-working civilians – well, not that hard-working as we would be away for three weeks.

We flew from Heathrow to Cairo on EgyptAir, a Muslim airline which did not serve alcoholic drinks. We were given three seats in

Business Class and it was agreed that these would be allocated to those with the longest legs: Cleese himself (6 foot 5), Stephen Fry (6 foot 4) and Peter Cook (6 foot 2). The latter two had taken the precaution of purchasing a couple of litres of vodka at Heathrow; not all of it reached Cairo unimbibed. There was an apprehensive silence as the coach threaded its way through the city to our boat on the Nile, broken only by Stephen Fry who announced to all and sundry: 'I'm gay. A gay Jew.'

It was a tone that was to be continued throughout the trip, with Cook and Fry matching each other wit for wit. Fry had brought a Perudo set – 'the *second* most addictive thing to come out of South America' – and he and fashion designer Tomasz Starzewski indulged in endless games. Peter, quick to learn, couldn't resist a new pastime and was soon addicted. Some months after the trip ended, Starzewski brought out his 'Egyptian Collection'. I remarked to Alyce Faye how it was amazing he had achieved this since he had barely looked out of the boat's window. She replied: 'That's exactly what John said.'

But Peter Cook was different. He never missed a trip to the pyramids and graves and mind-boggling temple at Karnak, rising at dawn with most of the rest of us so we could avoid the fierce heat in the middle of the day. To see him striding from the Pyramids to the Sphinx in his pith helmet and baggy shorts, he looked every inch the colonial administrator he might have been.

The guides crammed us with more information about the graves, the Valley of the Kings and Karnak than any human mind could accommodate, but the endless outpouring of immediately-to-be-forgotten names and dates added an otherworldly enchantment to this heady journey back into the wonders of the past.

Eric Idle had brought a copy of *Billy Bunter on the Nile* as a gift for John, and Cook persuaded Stephen to read it on deck after lunch

Stephen Fry reads *Billy Bunter on the Nile* to Peter Cook and Lady Rachel Billington.

each day, which he did, seamlessly interpolating naughty, largely gay, obscenities into Frank Richards's prim text. On the coach taking us from the boat through the Egyptian desert, Cook and Fry formed a pair of commentators from the back seats with immeasurably entertaining *obiter dicta*. Crossing the desert, Peter observed: 'I spy with my little eye something beginning with S.' They also coerced the rest of us into a game of 'Up Christopher Biggins's Asshole' wherein each passenger was obliged to repeat all the previous entrants and then add another even more improbable name. Both Lady Rachel Billington and Lady Carla Powell joined in with relish.

John took a vaguely amused attitude to this, but in the evenings he would engage William Goldman, the screenwriter, in an insoluble argument about the respective merits of basketball and cricket.

'Cricket can go on for five days with no goddam result at the end,' exploded Goldman. 'That's the whole point, Bill,' John explained.

Peter Cook was a rejuvenated man with a warmth that made him very popular in the party. His devotion to his wife, Lin, was undoubted, but his devotion to drink went unabated. Having a post-breakfast coffee with Stephen and Mo on deck one morning, Peter saw Lin approaching across the deck and whispered to Fry: 'Hide the evidence, Poirot,' as the two men tipped their hidden brandies into their coffee cups.

Towards the end of the trip, a certain amount of brain fade set in. There are only so many temples, tombs, Pharoahs and ruins you can absorb. (By the way, if you are asked for the name of a specific Pharaoh in a pub quiz it is best to answer Ramesses II – he reigned for sixty-six years, much longer than any other.) Besides, people were keen to get home to their families and their various projects. The mood as we sat around the pool of the Nefertari Hotel in Abu Simbel reminded me of those British prisoner-of-war movies where the inmates laze around in the sun waiting, I suppose, for the war to end. The plan was to have an early night as we had to be up at 3am to catch the rare sight of the rising sun penetrating the recesses of Ramesses's Great Temple and illuminating the sculpture of the Pharaoh making offerings to the goddess Hathor, in the guise of a cow.

Peter sensed the lethargic atmosphere and, being the senior officer on parade, decided to do something about it. Seizing a beach ball he rolled it along the side of the pool and through the hoops at the top of the metal swimming-pool ladder. He then announced that there was going to be a competition of 'No Pin Bowling' between Egypt and The Rest of the World. The hotel waiters were eager enough to form a team. This galvanised the forty pilgrims: everyone wanted to play and Eric Idle struck up his guitar and gave us an early foretaste of *Spamalot*. Spirits were revived.

Martin, Alyce Faye's son, videoed the event and Peter transformed himself into an American sports commentator. 'Welcome to WNPQKLZ and the Lyndon Baines Johnson Memorial Pool for this exciting tournament. The object is to get the balls – or "los cojones" as we experts say – through the specially crafted aluminium hoop ...' To the amazement of not just the Egyptians but the Brits as well, Peter then extemporised the rules of his new game. An 'Abu Simbel' was getting the ball clean through the hoop – five points. If it touched the side it was a 'Rufford' – only two. If it stopped between the hoops it was said to be 'Strottled' – one point. And if it fell into the pool, that was a 'Trote' – minus two. How did Cook come up with these terms so spontaneously? The answer was that he was just about the funniest man any of us had ever met.

Unfortunately, although we all rose at dawn, the sun forgot to or, at least, was blanketed by thick cloud. So, no illuminated Hathor. There are some occasions on any sightseeing trip when you just have to rely on the postcards. We flew to Cairo and mothers of small children and those who had not been cured of the invasive national tummy bug by Chris Beetles (a doctor turned comedian turned art dealer and misguided Spurs supporter) flew on to London.

John and Alyce, generous and considerate hosts to the end, had booked us a slot in the Cairo Museum so that we could examine the contents of Tutankhamun's tomb undisturbed. From a close examination of the boy king's golden face mask, I was sure that he had been reincarnated as Tiger Woods.

It seemed appropriate to end the trip at the Great Pyramid of Giza, the only one of the Seven Wonders of the World to remain intact – and probably the greatest wonder the world has ever seen. Nobody knows exactly how it was built. But not by slave labour. The benevolent Pharaoh, Khufu, realised that during the three-month Nile flood each year his people had no work and were starving. So he employed 100,000 of them for over twenty years to build this 480-foot-high Pyramid and it remained the highest man-made structure in the world for 3,800 years.

John had arranged for the Pyramid to open an hour early just for us, but only about ten Nilers crawled 130 feet up through a narrow passage to the King's Chamber where Khufu's imposing red-granite sarcophagus remains. We had agreed to meditate there for half an hour and lay on the stone floor. I didn't really know how to meditate, but it was impossible for the mind not to go on a journey into the past. Then John's daughter, Cynthia, burst out in a fit of giggles after about fifteen minutes. It was contagious. Soon we were all laughing. I'm sure the spirit of Khufu wasn't offended. It was the laughter of joy, relief, friendship and the knowledge that we would probably never again, in this lifetime, have such an experience.

My last job for *The Sunday Times* was to cover the 1994 Australian Tennis Open. The assignment came my way: (a) because I could pay my own fare using Cathay Pacific tickets and (b) because I could stay with Don Bennetts in Melbourne from whose apartment in Beverly Hills, Toorak, you could see Flinders Park (where the tournament took place). I also agreed with my producer at BBC Radio that I would make a two-hour *Arts Programme* Australian special and was loaned a precious Uher tape recorder which took up much of my suitcase.

So most days I would make my way along the path by the murky Yarra River to the tennis. I was able to file on Saturday's Ladies' Final for the *ST* but, unfortunately, it was a blink-and-you-might-miss-it match. Corporate guests, after a wine-fuelled three-course lunch, made a leisurely arrival at the Rod Laver Arena in time to see Steffi Graf holding up the trophy. She had beaten Aránzazu Arantxa Isabel Maria Sánchez Vicario, 6–0, 6–2, in about the time it takes to say the Spaniard's name. (Steffi's only serious challenger, Monica Seles, had been stabbed in the back in Germany the previous year.)

At the press conference, John Parsons of the *Daily Telegraph*, the doyen of tennis correspondents, congratulated Steffi on being the first woman to do the 'Grand Slam', i.e. win all four major tournaments in the same year. Steffi said she hadn't as the other three had been in 1993. But Parsons insisted that the Australian Open was technically a December event and had only been moved to January in 1987 as an experiment. The debate still rages.

Pete Sampras won the men's singles (his volleying achieved perfection) and I came pretty well bottom of the journos and umpires tournament which was played on the fast indoor Reebok Ace court. No other British correspondent entered; did they know something about those dozens of Aussie scribes that I didn't? Perhaps they were all Davis Cup veterans: it certainly felt like it.

The tennis was attended by 333,000 people and bang next door was the Melbourne Cricket Ground which can accommodate 100,000 spectators. Don managed to sneak us into the ground's members' area but we didn't last long as we had no ties. You are allowed to wear shorts, but shorts and ties – a slightly incongruous combination. However, I did see my hero, Dean Jones of Victoria, who smacked a hundred with his immaculate cover drives. Nobody had stroked the ball away so elegantly since Denis Compton and P.B.H. May (another hero since we had, fleetingly, attended the same prep school).

Back in London in the seventies Don's girlfriend, Althea, had a substantial house in Chelsea which actually had a 'priest's hole', a hidden room where Catholics could hide from Queen Elizabeth's predatory soldiers. It was occupied for part of each year by the Australian writer, Thomas Keneally – an appropriate lair since Tom was about to become a priest until he met and married Judy, who belonged to a devout Catholic nursing order. In the pub in the evenings, Tom was an amusing raconteur and quite an influence on me spiritually. He felt it was easier to believe in a God if you did not see him as an *interventionist* God. I argued that this made the power of prayer redundant, but he said the actual fact of praying might do almost as much good for one's soul as any answered prayer.

I had little idea how gifted he was as a novelist until he started being nominated for the Booker Prize. He won it with *Schindler's Ark*, which went on to win Oscars for Steven Spielberg as *Schindler's List*.

On my trip to Australia, Tom invited me to his home in Sydney where he lived with his wife and two daughters. He showed me his workroom: 'I have to sit with my back to the Pacific or else I wouldn't write a word.' He took me to see the World Rugby Sevens at the Sydney Cricket Ground. 'The reason we, as formative crustaceous creatures crawled out of the Pacific, Iain,' he said, 'was to go to the SCG.' Tom's celebrity was not in doubt: people pointed him out and the TV interviewed him. (*Schindler* had already opened to acclaim in the States and was soon to do so in the UK and Australia.) He was knowledgeable about the game but passionate about his local team, Manly-Warringah Sea Eagles, whom he urged on with expletives he might not have employed had he become a priest.

After I did a radio interview with Keneally, he signed his book: 'Shalom to Iain, my old cobber, love, Tom,' and then took out a piece of card and wrote down two names and a telephone number, saying: 'They'll be happy to talk to your programme. They live not far from Don.'

'They' were Leopold and Helen Rosner and they were expecting me: the living-room table was blanketed with butter cookies and honey cakes and chocolate *babkas*. In 1939, Helen had met her future husband in a coffee house in the Krakow ghetto. He was entertaining the customers with his accordion. On their wedding night in 1943, Leo was sent to Plaszow labour camp. The brutal commandant, Amon Goeth, ordered him to play his accordion to accompany Goeth's drunken orgies. Helen was sent there two months later. One day Goeth caught her smoking a cigarette: she told him she had exchanged it for a piece of bread. He pulled out his revolver to commit another of his summary executions, but she pleaded with him, saying she was the wife of Leo, the accordionist. Amazingly, he spared her, but sent her to an almost certain death at Auschwitz. Leo remained and Oskar Schindler recruited him to work in his factory. When told of Helen's plight, the sainted Schindler miraculously managed to get her out of Auschwitz and reunited her with her husband.

In 1949, the Rosners were resettled in Australia, the most generous country outside Israel to house Holocaust survivors. And there they sat with me that day, forty-five years later, generous with their horrendous memories and their lavish tea. Leo made a good living with a musical group, Dayan Receptions (named after the Israeli general). It was almost impossible to believe their nightmare. In my copy of Tom's book, they wrote their names. 'Love, love, love – Helen' and 'With very best wishes – Leo' and beneath it, most poignantly, a sketch of his life-saving accordion.

I love Australia: its welcoming beaches, its sometimes intimidating Outback but, above all, its 'no problems, mate' attitude to life. Yes, Britain shamefully transported 165,000, usually petty, criminals there in the nineteenth century but they were outnumbered by double that number of immigrants who arrived in the gold rush of 1852. Had I not had the good fortune to have had a few lucky breaks in my twenties, I would undoubtedly have tried to find my fortune there: not in gold, but in the media. But in the sixties the luminaries of the Australian media were moving in the opposite direction, most notably Germaine Greer, Clive James and Barry Humphries. While a student at Melbourne University, Barry had been something of a Modernist, exhibiting 'Dadaist' sculptures including a pair of wellington boots filled with custard which he entitled 'Pus in Boots'. As Dame Edna, Barry had hosted a very funny edition of *Friday Night ... Saturday Morning* which may have contributed to his popular series on ITV *The Dame Edna Experience*. Don Bennetts would help Barry in various escapades, not least when he was staying at the Mayfair Hotel in London and thought he had a genuine Richard Parkes Bonington painting of the Venice lagoon on his bedroom wall. It was distinctive because Bonington had developed a technique of mixing watercolour with body colour and gum to achieve an effect close to oil painting. So Don smuggled in the necessary art materials and Barry, a talented painter, spent two days making a copy which he then inserted in the frame in place of the original. Barry subsequently took that one to Christie's, expecting a valuation of several thousand pounds only to discover that it, too, was a forgery.

He was in town with his one man/woman comedy *Look at Me When I'm Talking to You*. He agreed to an interview with me, after the show. The politically incorrect humour was there from the moment people entered the theatre foyer. A notice read: 'Paraplegics' lavatory. Fourth floor. Please walk up.' Les Patterson was on top form: 'Please forgive me, I've had a drink tonight. I'm as full as a Pommie complaint box, as full as a seaside shithouse on a bank holiday.'

Nevertheless he was able to introduce Dame Edna: 'Put your hands together warmly across her opening and give her the clap she so richly deserves.'

I waited for him in his dressing room afterwards. 'How's Lord Snowdon?' he inquired, knowing I had been filming with him. 'As far as I know, his usual self,' I replied. 'Why?'

'Well, in my drinking days in the sixties, I was having dinner in a French restaurant, Mon Plaisir. It was a small place and Snowdon and Princess Margaret were across the room. I got up to go to the loo, as pissed as a wombat's fart, and when I came out my trousers accidentally fell down pretty well in front of Margaret's face. Snowdon got hold of the manager and had me thrown out of the restaurant. So I went to a phone box on the corner and dialled Mon Plaisir. "I want to speak to Lord Snowdon," I demanded. "Who is it?" asked the receptionist. "It's about his mother," I said – if you ever want to get through to somebody famous say it's about their mother. Snowdon came to the phone and I told him: "Don't you ever treat that nice Barry Humphries like that again" and put down the phone. About twenty years later, when I had acquired a modicum of fame, I was being profiled for *The Sunday Times* and the chap they sent along to take my portrait was Snowdon. All through the session I kept wondering: "Does he remember? Does he remember?" But he never mentioned the incident. However, when he was leaving he thanked me for my patience and said: "It's been a long time since we had the Plaisir."'

Barry suggested he did the interview as Edna. I happily agreed; we had done this on radio before and it gave greater scope for humour. He put on a wide-brimmed velvet hat and, unlike the title of his show, did not look at me again until we finished.

'Did I tell you, Iain, I had the most spooky experience back in drab, rain-lashed England?' she began. 'I'm not a superstitious woman but I do believe in reincarnation now it has been scientifically proved. I've been Boadicea, Mary, Queen of Scots, Ethel Merman and Cinderella. Isn't it exciting? As a matter of fact I was also Anne Hathaway who wrote most of Shakespeare's material. And here's the really spooky thing. When I went to Anne Hathaway's little cottage in Stratford for the first time, I walked through the front door and went instinctively to the kitchen and made myself a cup of tea. I knew exactly where the power point was. Now that definitely proves something.'

I agreed that this must be the case and then enquired about the health of her bedbound husband, Norm. 'I'll let you into a guilty secret. You know I have a wicked sense of humour. Well, last April Fool's Day we pretended he was going to be discharged from hospital. Matron was in on the joke and she packed his suitcase where he could see her doing so in the mirror above his page-turning machine. He's had *The Thorn Birds* open at the same page for the past seven years but, then, who hasn't? We put on his dressing gown and took him to the front door of the hospital where there was an ambulance waiting. Norm stepped through the automatic glass doors and the ambulance just whizzed away down the drive. It was so funny: he fell flat on his face. You know, I was born with a priceless gift: the ability to laugh at the misfortunes of others.'

I agreed it was hilarious and asked about the rest of her family. 'My beloved son Kenny is still a dressmaker and has relocated to San Francisco. I did a show there and I'm afraid to say there were a lot of same-sex couples in the audience. It's sad to look out at those disorientated people. Who knows, they may get better one day. Kenny's brother, Bruce, is a feng shui specialist and my daughter, Valmai, from whom I am still unfortunately estranged, lives with a former East European tennis player in, I am told, a run-down part of Poland where she breeds pit bulls.

And so Dame Edna merrily rolled along. 'Sex is the most beautiful thing that can happen between a happily married man and his secretary.' 'New Zealand is a country of thirty thousand sheep, three million of whom think they're human.' I could have laughed all night but I knew we had only a final segment of the radio programme to fill and Barry had generously filled it.

Before I left for home, I had a call from a slightly subdued Mo in London. 'What's the matter?' I asked. 'My head,' she replied. I had been a judge on The Evening Standard Film Awards before Christmas but had missed the prize-giving dinner at the Savoy Hotel. Not wishing to go on her own, Mo teamed up with Stephen Fry as his date. At the end of the dinner, Robbie Coltrane had said to them: 'Follow me.' They took the lift to the top of the Savoy and Robbie knocked on the door of a sort of Presidential Suite. Emma Thompson opened it and embraced them all. There was a vast picture window with all of the South Bank lit up beneath them. 'You certainly have an incredible room, Emma,' Mo said. 'It's not her room,' growled a familiar American voice, 'it's my room.' It was Robert De Niro, in town to star in her husband's, Kenneth Branagh's film of *Frankenstein.* Assorted celebrities arrived, bottles of brandy were produced and a hardened corps remained to watch the dawn reflected in the Thames.

'The telephone woke me the next afternoon,' Mo said. 'It was Stephen. He merely said: "Mo, tell me I didn't sit on Robert De Niro's knee last night and kiss him." I had to tell him the truth. "I'm afraid you did." "Oh, God!" said Fry.' And my wife went back to her record hangover.

23

The Road to Hollywood
with John Cleese

I suppose John and I worked on the script of *Death Fish II*, as it was first known, for four years. Not all the time. He had commitments to do advertisements and business ventures and movies (not least Ken Branagh's *Frankenstein*). And I took advantage of these numerous breaks to do some work of my own, not least for Steven Spielberg, a gainful employer.

People would ask me what John was really like. Well, he's very tall. Cooks a mean steak. Likes goldfish: he had about twenty aquaria in his secretary's office in a converted shop, just round the corner from his house. A high point of each week was when the fish man came to clean them up, bring new specimens and remove the dead and infirm. And cats – all over the place. Football supporter, although fluctuating from Fulham to Chelsea and coming to rest at West Ham. Loves maths and statistics. And cricket. Mike Brearley was a frequent visitor and, one evening, the entire Somerset squad came for a barbecue. And shrinks. John liked to say he was the most psychoanalysed man in Britain, although I never discovered which medical directory confirmed this. His favourite was a mittel-European psychiatrist in his eighties called George who had worked with Freud.

He entertained regally. Most of the new wave of comedy performers would be invited to his parties. I first met a young Rowan Atkinson sipping his drink shyly in the kitchen as he was nervous of engaging with the great J.C. Mo once arrived late at a dinner and slipped in beside a man in a brocade waistcoat. She made conversation in the way you do when you're trying to find out who you're talking to, without coming out and asking them. It was only when John referred to him as 'Little Kev' that she got the hint. On *Silverado*, Kevin Kline had been 'Big Kev' and Kevin Costner 'Little Kev'. Mike Nichols was there one evening, eager to find the name of the Paris shrink who specialised in the problems of children with famous parents. Virginia Wade, a friend of Alyce, would give us the gossip during Wimbledon. Paddy Ashdown suggested to John he become a working peer for the Lib-Dems but Cleese liked to go to the sun in the winter and knew he couldn't fulfil the brief.

And children. He doted on Cynthia (by Connie) and gave her a treadmill with a TV, quite an unusual combination at the time, and provided her with videos of *The World at War* so that she could become fit and educated. And Camilla, his daughter by his second wife, Barbara, got a basement swimming pool to entertain her friends.

He was good to my children, too. He knew how to talk to them. When John was writing with Graham, Gra liked to go to an Indian restaurant where the owner revered him as 'The Doctor'. When anything was wrong, like a wonky table or a dirty fork, the owner would turn on an unfortunate small waiter and scream: 'Rasheed, why has the Doctor been given this table? Why did you not inspect his fork?' John did a perfect impression of the angry Indian. When Sophie, my eldest, came to John's, she begged for 'Rasheed' and was never disappointed. He even sent her birthday cards signed 'Rasheed'. Holly (Johnstone 2) became a friend of Camilla and we piled into his stately Bentley for trips to the countryside. The favourite destination for all the daughters was Walthamstow Greyhound

John Cleese does his superannuated Silly Walk in Venice.

Stadium in north London. We sat in a row at dinner, the waitresses collected the bets (money that their fathers would seldom see again) and dispensed the fish and chips. Despite an arthritic knee, John entertained my son, Oliver, (and the others) with his Silly Walk in the back garden.

We didn't laugh a lot when writing: comedy with John was a serious business. In the summer, the TV in the outer room was usually on teletext to get the latest Somerset cricket score. On occasion, after a minor character had been introduced into our script, John would click his fingers and say: 'I think I know someone who could play this.' He would find a VHS of an episode of *Fawlty Towers*. There was a doctor in the one inspired by Andrew Leeman's dead guest at the Savoy. Inevitably, we would watch to the end, including Basil's rant about the breakfast news to the corpse sitting up in bed: 'Another car strike. Marvellous, isn't it? The taxpayers pay them millions each year so they can go on strike. It's called socialism. If they don't like making cars, why don't they get themselves another bloody job – designing cathedrals or composing violin concertos. That's it! The British Leyland Concerto in four movements, all of them slow, with a four-hour tea-break in between.' He would convulse himself with laughter ... and so would I.

Cleese had already mapped out the basic concept for the movie. He had a not wholly irrational hatred of Rupert Murdoch whom he maintained would halve the quality of anything he bought if he could double its earnings. This was not strictly true: for instance, both Sky News and *The Times* ran at a loss. John was often given to impetuous judgements. When loss-making Granada TV made Gerry Robinson, who previously ran their catering division, their CEO, John faxed him: 'Why don't you fuck off out of it, you upstart caterer?' Robinson drily faxed back: 'Reading between the lines of your message, I detect that I am a greater fan of yours than you are of mine.' Later they had a placatory lunch and Robinson turned out to be a pretty worthwhile citizen, chairing the Arts Council for six years and helping small businesses in the BBC's *Troubleshooter.*

From his Bristol schooldays, John had formed a love of zoos and became a friend of Gerald Durrell who had founded a conservationist zoo on Jersey where he bred endangered species. It was quite easy to find. There were large brown signs with elephants on them all over the island – the elephant being the official European Union symbol for a zoo. It must have been disappointing for some visitors to discover that Durrell's zoo didn't actually have any elephants, but you knew when you got there by the ominous statues of two dodos standing sentinel on the gates. Sadly, Gerald didn't look after himself as well as he did his animals and died in 1994.

So there it was: Murdoch-type buys zoo and uses various marketing stratagems to make it profitable. The plot never greatly varied from that. As we wrote in his small back study, I told John he must be the senior partner as my comedy record was virtually non-existent or, to be precise, non-existent. But, generously, he said that what we needed were ideas, the jokes would follow naturally, and an idea was not something owned by either of us but arose in a middle ground after it had been batted to and fro between us. When we had finished a writing session, we took the pages down to his assistant, Amanda Masefield, and she unfailingly laughed as she typed them up, whether they were funny or not.

In the winter, the whole team moved to California where John and Alyce had bought a beach house in Santa Barbara. The landmark for finding it was not an elephant sign but the famous Montecito Inn, built in 1928 by Fatty Arbuckle. He mentored Charlie Chaplin, who frequently holidayed there. It was later immortalised by Rodgers and Hart in the song 'There's a Small Hotel' (their wishing-well had been replaced by a floral fountain in the fifties). The tranquil beauty of watching the sun slip into the Pacific at the end of the day was spoilt by the presence of a series of vast and ugly oil-rigs on the near horizon. John placated Camilla by telling her that they were, in fact, pirate ships.

I answered a small ad in the local paper and became part of a tennis four (a professor, a former ambassador and a gardener) who met twice a week in the vast, but empty, municipal stadium. We had iced tea afterwards and I learned about the town. It had been Spanish, then Mexican, then American after the 1847 war but was destroyed by the 1925 earthquake. The authorities decided to rebuild it in a Spanish Colonial style so, in a sort of way, the town became Spanish again. What it isn't is very African-American; African-

Americans made up about one per cent of the population. I went for a drink one evening with the Cleeses' estate agent, Tammy, and, in the street, she introduced me to a black chap, Josh. I said hello and he pulled out a stool and began to clean my shoes.

Camilla was keen on riding and Tammy discovered that there was a nearby ranch going reasonably cheap because of a divorce. Further investigation revealed that it belonged to Diandra Douglas, then divorcing the film star Michael. John knew from experience that if his name was in the frame prices tended to go up. So he got someone else as named buyer. After the sale was finalised, Diandra discovered the true purchaser and, piqued, drove away a $25,000 tractor which was on the premises.

On occasion, John had to make the ninety-mile trip to Hollywood to discuss film details with Universal. So as not to disrupt our daily writing routine, I would come too. We would be given a room on the Universal lot so that we could get on with our work and, thus, I almost fulfilled what had always been a youthful fantasy of working in a Writers' Building on a Hollywood lot, like Scott Fitzgerald or Dorothy Parker, with Jack Warner shouting through the door: 'I don't want it good. I want it Tuesday.' At one point, MGM had ninety writers in harness and they used to come to work in suits and ties. What was common to a lot of them was the need for a fortifying Scotch, which was why most studio commissaries became alcohol-free. Universal only introduced booze into their restaurants when they were taken over by the Canadian drinks company, Seagram's.

John and I fortified ourselves at the Chaya Brasserie in Beverly Hills. It was friendly rather than trendy. One evening a waiter plonked a bottle of red wine on our table, saying it was a gift from somebody 'in back'. We had to accept – it was a sort of Hollywood thing – but Cleese, guessing it was someone trying to slip him a script, said emphatically: 'Do thank whoever it was and ask them to say goodbye *on their way out.*' I took a sip of the stuff. It was a Cabernet Sauvignon Opus One and had a taste that was smooth as it was pricey. Somebody had parted with a few hundred dollars.

The 'somebody' turned out to be Keanu Reeves. He was with a couple of chums and had come, not with a script, but to worship at the shrine of Monty Python. 'You'd better sit down and help us finish the wine,' John suggested. Young Americans tend to know Python not from the TV series but from the films and Keanu knew *Monty Python and the Holy Grail* off by heart. 'We are no longer the knights who say Ni, we are the knights who say, Ecky-ecky-ecky-ecky-ptang-zoom-boing-mumble-mumble,' he and his friends merrily chimed. John, less abstemious than usual, sat amazed as Keanu perfectly mimicked his French soldier. 'I don't want to talk to you no more, you empty-headed animal food-trough wiper. I fart in your general direction. Your mother was a hamster and your father smelled of elderberries.' Cleese was only too happy to indulge in Python reminiscences and another bottle of Opus One made its expensive way down our throats.

Our most exotic place for writing was under the shade of a laurel tree in Fall Creek Falls Park, Tennessee. John was there to finish his part in *The Jungle Book*. He'd already filmed in Rajasthan in India and this was a more convenient location to conclude the story. There was a tulip poplar forest that ran down to a gushing gorge with a specially constructed old-fashioned wooden bridge. I asked the director, Steven Sommers, if it would match and he invited me to come to his cutting room at the Holiday Inn after the wrap for the day. But it wasn't a cutting room; it was a computer room. He and his editor were at the forefront of the new technology and, thirty years ago, had already made a digital assembly of the Indian footage. (Until nearly the turn of the century, it would still be scissors and paste at Pinewood.) I could see how, deftly worked, the babul and banyan and mango trees of India could lead to the tulip poplar and hemlock forest that lay beyond the moist summer gorge of Fall Creek.

We ate dinner in the Apple Barrel Restaurant, Pikeville – John and Alyce, Sam Neill and his wife, Noriko Watanabe, Cary Elwes (whose mother, Tessa, I knew – an heiress who had famously eloped with his father, Dominick, who later committed suicide after the Lord Lucan scandal) and a very droll American producer, Mort. When they were in India, Mort said a boy had come up to him in a field offering his sister for a dollar. Being a producer, he negotiated him down to fifty cents – and then, certainly not availing himself of the deal, gave both sufficient money to try to stop the practice.

We went for a walk after the meal and Mort said: 'Do you know you can buy a gun in this town at any time?' Cleese was intrigued: 'I don't believe you.'

Pikeville was a run-down town of less than two thousand inhabitants. Most local shops had been cluster-bombed out of existence by the arrival of a large Walmart store. Mort led us to the gun counter which was manned by a 250-pound young man with 'Dave' pinned to his sweater. 'I'd like to buy a gun,' said Cleese. 'Yes, sir,' Dave replied, indicating a range of weapons around him. He didn't appear to have any notion of who Cleese was. 'How about that one?' John chose a revolver in a glass case. 'Mighty fine weapon, sir,' said Dave. 'Crosman Air Mag C11 Soft Air Pistol Powered by CO_2.' 'Can I take it now?' asked John. ''Fraid not, sir. You'll have to go up to the Sheriff's office in the morning, fill in some forms and bring them right back here to me.'

John pointed to Alyce Faye. 'But what if I wanted to kill my wife tonight?' 'No problem, sir,' said Dave, removing a rifle from the wall.

'This is a Mossberg 930 Tactical 12 GA Shotgun with Stand-Off Barrel. Take out a deer at fifty yards. You can walk away with this little beauty right now.' As they used to say in the *News of the World*, we made our excuses and left.

John kept Kevin and Michael Palin appraised of the progress of the script and I met up with Jamie Lee Curtis in Orlando, Florida, where she was finishing *My Girl 2*. 'We're only here because of the child labour laws,' she told me. 'Anna Chlumsky is fourteen and they can work her eight hours a day, unlike in California.' Jamie thought our script needed more work. I'm not sure she was too keen on playing second fiddle to Kevin, having been the lynchpin of *Wanda*.

We ate dinner at the Peabody Hotel where I was staying. It was renowned for its 'Duck Walk' through the lobby at 11am each morning. Jamie was on a diet (which actress isn't?) and ordered just a Shirley Temple, a non-alcoholic drink made of ginger ale and lime soda. 'Put it in a proper cocktail glass,' she told the waiter, 'I don't want to look like a child.' As I munched my way through my burger, her appetite returned. 'What's that?' she asked the waiter, pointing to a dish that was warming on a hotplate. 'Miso rolled Atlantic salmon,' he replied. 'I'll have it,' she said.

As she left, she assured me that the film would be fine and we would have a great deal of fun working together again. I repaired to bed but was awoken by a phone call at about 4am. It was Jamie. 'That salmon, it was off,' she groaned. 'I've got the most lethal stomach ache.' I offered to drive her to the hospital but she said there was a unit nurse in her hotel and she would try her first. Fearing I had killed our leading lady, I didn't get back to sleep and called the *My Girl* set the next morning to inquire if Miss Curtis had come to work. She came to the phone. 'I'm fine now,' she assured me. 'It's all gone, probably swimming back to the Atlantic.' 'Should I complain to the hotel?' I asked. 'Naw, It will only get in the papers. I've had enough of that stuff. Love to John and see you in London.'

The main cast was due to assemble in Cleese's back garden on the first of May 1995. I can hardly forget the date: it was the day of Peter Cook's memorial service at St John's Church in Hampstead. John and I had been writing in the LA Four Seasons Hotel in January when Lin had telephoned him during the night to say that Peter had died. John told me at breakfast. 'The liver?' I asked. 'Lin said it was a gastrointestinal haemorrhage,' John replied. 'But yes, the liver – and the will to live. He never really recovered from his mother's death in June.' We didn't write that day. But now he had to write something about his great friend. I arrived early at his house in Holland Park. Alyce was waiting. 'You'd better go up. Somebody's got to get him out of bed,'

There were open books littered across John's bedspread. I had never seen him quite so distressed. 'Listen to this.' It was a piece from Elisabeth Kübler-Ross: 'There was no need to be afraid of death, but, when alive, not to be a captive of other people's expectations.' 'Peter,' I said. 'Peter never allowed himself to become a captive.' 'No,' said John. 'More than anyone else I ever knew.'

In the church, we were shown to seats in the second-row pew where Mo was waiting, talking to David Frost and Dudley Moore. We sang John Bunyan's hymn, 'He who would valiant be'. Alan Bennett spoke first and recounted how, when the *Beyond the Fringe* cast had been staying in Connecticut, Frost had visited them and had somehow fallen into the swimming pool. He couldn't swim so Peter dived in and pulled him out. 'Peter used to say that the only thing he really regretted in his life was saving David Frost's life,' Alan added. I looked at David in front of me; he was laughing as heartily as everybody else.

It set the tone for the service: moving and amusing. The tears came when Dud went to the piano and sang: 'Now Is the Time to Say Goodbye'. But, as ever, Peter had the last laugh. Lin had arranged for a recording of E.L. Wisty, Peter's park-bench philosopher, to be broadcast to the congregation. 'I must do something with my life, something to be remembered for,' said Wisty, and then read from a day in his diary. 'Got up. Went out. Came home again. Went to sleep. Didn't even go to the lavatory.'

Later, back in John's Holland Park house, there was a read-through of the script. I felt sad, not just for Peter but for me. My writing job was over, for better or for worse. Now it was up to the others to make a movie.

24

The World of Steven Spielberg

In June 1984, Paramount had asked me to chair a European Press Conference for *Indiana Jones and the Temple of Doom*. It was in the ballroom of a West End hotel. I sat in the middle between Steven Spielberg and Kate Capshaw. Beside her were George Lucas, Kathy Kennedy, associate producer, and Ke Huy Quan, a ten year old who played the character Short Round in the film. Ranged opposite was a firing squad of at least thirty cameras.

It had been ten years since I had met Steven at Martha's Vineyard but he greeted me warmly: no other TV crew had visited *Jaws* so he had added my documentary to the DVD release. He told me that *Temple of Doom* had a couple of strong swear words and at the Royal Premiere he had been instructed to cough loudly in Princess Diana's ear when they were said.

He kept scribbling notes which he gave me to pass to Kate. I couldn't resist reading the last two. 'Will you star in my next film?' he wrote. 'I might,' she wrote back. In fact, she didn't, but she did become his second wife in 1991.

'I think we should do some more things,' he said as he thanked me at the end of the conference. I thought nothing more about it but, true to his word, Steven's man in London got in touch with me eight years later. Things move slowly in Spielbergland. 'Steven's doing a thing about dinosaurs,' he said. 'He thinks you might be right to do a BBC-ish documentary about their history.'

It was great to work for Steven. He was so passionate about anything he was interested in, so interesting himself, and as stimulating a person as you could meet. No wonder universities in the States and across the world invited him to speak on degree day. As they set out on life's journey, students wanted to learn the secret of his alchemy. He has to employ two people to write polite letters declining the hundreds of annual invitations.

Every documentary is an education, for the maker at least. I knew more about Polish than I did about palaeontology. Steven was fascinated by the fact that, although ancient man had dug up parts of animals which he must have realised didn't belong to any known species, it wasn't until 150 years ago that a skeleton was discovered in Haddonfield, New Jersey which was clearly a bipedal creature. They called it a Hadrosaurus after the area. An English scientist, Richard Owen coined the word 'dinosaur' from the Greek meaning 'terrible lizard'. Spielberg was fascinated by the subject but had no desire to make a 'Godzilla-type movie'. It wasn't until he read a proof of Michael Crichton's novel, *Jurassic Park*, that he immediately saw what he lucidly termed the perfect combination: 'Dinosaurs and DNA'.

Crichton had used his Harvard medical education to good effect: not to practise as a doctor but to continue studying scientific journals as research for his writing. He told me the seed of his fiction usually lay in the last paragraph. After an academic had outlined his findings, he would end by saying: 'It's interesting to speculate where this might go.' Michael would turn the speculation into a story. He had been struggling with a dinosaur script for many years until he read the palaeontologist Bob Bakker's theory that dinosaurs were not the cumbersome, cold-blooded, lizard-like creatures that they were always portrayed as, but warm-blooded animals that walked upright on two feet and were agile, fast and as dangerous as tigers to those below them in the food chain.

This cracked the code in Crichton's mind. With recent discoveries of the possible creation of life from DNA, he blended two established facts to come up with a tantalising factoid. When we filmed Dr George Poisner at California Tech, he said that it was likely that insects of the time had dinosaur blood in them and, if preserved, his laboratory could sequence their DNA. But recreate them? Crichton laughed: 'No. The conditions for fertilisation, even with frogspawn, are impossible. It was a completely fanciful notion. The strange thing is that when I mentioned my idea to academics at MIT some would say: "It can be done." But it can't.'

Crichton had already written and directed a film, *Westworld*, set in a Western amusement park, and rather hoped to direct *Jurassic* himself. 'I thought you wrote this movie for me,' Steven said to him. The two men were already involved in the incubation of television's *ER*. When Michael confessed he had written it for himself, Steven told me: 'I fell over myself to make this movie. I would have gone down on my knees and begged.' His instinct, possibly the greatest of his gifts, was for the most part unerring and Michael bowed to the inevitable and agreed to write the script instead.

At the time, Steven didn't know how he was going to direct it. He assumed the dinosaurs would be done with animatronics (filmed puppets) which he had used in his previous films, but agreed to let George Lucas's Industrial Light & Magic create a computer-generated herd of Gallimimus dinosaurs which would be in the distance so it wouldn't be a disaster if they fell short of perfect. But George's wily technicians put in a full-size T. rex chasing them. Steven was bowled over and, later, so were the rest of us. CGI was inordinately expensive but, artfully, there are only six minutes of it in the film, with animatronics for the closer shots of dinosaur limbs and heads.

In the book, the owner of Jurassic Park, John Hammond, is a somewhat dark character. 'I wanted him to be gentler,' Spielberg told me. 'A showman. A cross between Walt Disney and Ross Perot. It had to be Dickie Attenborough and I persuaded him to return to acting after fifteen years. We even waited for him to finish *Chaplin*.' Nobody who saw Attenborough as the circus owner in *Dr Doolittle* could doubt that ebullient but slightly seedy entrepreneurship. (The fact that Attenborough's *Gandhi* had beaten *E.T.* to the Best Director Oscar a decade earlier was a source of amusement rather than rancour between the two men.)

Paradoxically, Spielberg dressed Attenborough, the misguided entrepreneur, in white, and Jeff Goldblum as Dr Ian Malcolm, the good-guy chaos mathematician, in black. Malcolm dismisses the argument that, since all the dinosaurs are female, they cannot reproduce themselves outside the controlled laboratory. 'If there is one thing the history of evolution has taught us, it's that life will not be contained ... life finds a way.' I wonder if his contention that: 'A butterfly can flap its wings in Peking and in Central Park you get rain instead of sunshine' has ever been scientifically proved. It was certainly greatly quoted after the film came out.

Clever casting is more than the icing on a compelling plot. In order to involve us, the audience, in the story Steven said he needed a certain anonymity in the characters in peril. 'Without taking away from the charisma of Sam Neill and Laura Dern, they didn't come to the project with iconic movies behind them. I made the mistake of having Kate scream for ninety minutes of the two hours of *The Temple of Doom*. Laura hardly screams at all in this film.' This lack of screaming actually increases the tension for the audience.

That Spielberg can build tension with the finesse of Hitchcock can hardly be doubted since *Duel* and *Jaws*. Two water glasses shaking on the dashboard of a jeep can announce the arrival of a T. rex in the most terrifying way. Richard Attenborough, his fellow director, observed that, although Steven arrived at each set-up with storyboards, 'He will suddenly see an angle that will create an atmosphere with his camera and shoot the scene again.'

I find Steven at his most relaxed in the cutting room with his editor, Michael Kahn, who has edited all his movies since *Close Encounters* in 1977. 'I relish post-production,' Spielberg admitted. 'On the set, I like to move really fast. But now it slows down. Coming to work every day gives me a chance to be more thoughtful. Directing demands a lot of intuition but now I have the time to mull things over. The whole process of slicing the film together gives me the time to consider my options. I also like the smell of celluloid all over the place. The scent of experience hangs in the air.'

Until very recently, Spielberg and Kahn chose not to use digital technology – 'Most other directors use electronic editing bays and when you walk into those rooms they smell like a typical office' – but, of late, he has bowed to the inevitable and, although he will shoot on 35mm film, he has it digitised to make his first assembly.

So those are the main ingredients of his professional alchemy: the plot, the choice of cast, the scene-by-scene tension of 'what's at stake', a more thoughtful reappraisal of his material in the cutting room, the art of immersing his audience in the experience and, above all, his passion. Spielberg aspires to perfection and, frequently, he gets pretty close.

I got to know him quite well over the years. I wouldn't presume to call myself a friend, merely a professional acquaintance. But there was always a warm welcome at Amblin', that adobe compound on the Universal lot, given to him by the grateful studio after the success of *E.T.* Outside the offices, meeting rooms and cinema, there is a

Steven Spielberg at Amblin'.

comfortable courtyard, dotted with wooden tables and chairs and serving hot and cold running food for free to those lucky enough to be allowed in. It seemed to me that the sun was always shining there which, in a way, it was.

I'm also in debt to Steven in an unexpected way. My daughter Sophie was due to go for an interview at Oxford. Since she had been cramming for exams, she had not had much time for a wider culture outside her set courses. I tried to help a little by giving her short books to read, like Ian McEwan's Booker Prize-winning novel, *Amsterdam*, and taking in a few plays, most notably Michael Frayn's brilliant *Copenhagen* which dealt with whether Werner Heisenberg had the capacity to make a nuclear bomb for the Nazis. 'Try and get the admissions tutors on to that,' I suggested naively.

To help her relax on the week of the interview, I asked her to come as my PA to Hatfield in Hertfordshire where I was hired to film an interview/profile of Tom Hanks to help Paramount promote *Saving Private Ryan*. But when we arrived at the location, Tom was stuck in a dug-out pool (with a breathing apparatus) lining up an underwater shot of the Normandy landings. The camera was having problems and Steven beckoned us over to take a seat by the monitors beside him. He explained that he was filming a 'murder hole', caused by shelling. If a soldier stepped off a landing craft into one of these, the weight of his equipment could drown him; that or the next man off standing on his head.

It was nearly the end of the shoot and Steven was in an expansive mood, drawing on a Havana cigar. He told Sophie about the need for this suicidal mission to save Ryan. The camera was still giving problems, so the conversation broadened into World War II as a whole, and the Allied failure to bomb the railway transportation feeding the concentration camps.

At her Oxford interview, the chairman opened with a slow ball, asking her what she had done that week. As she told them the panel straightened up in their chairs. 'Spielberg? What's he like? We offered him an honorary degree but he can't find time to come and accept it.' The questioning then expanded into the morality of war. No *Amsterdam*, no *Copenhagen*. But, yes, the offer of a place at Trinity College. I told Steven about this and he was gently amused. Apparently, he had always intended to go to Oxford. His plan had been to stop off at the home of the philanthropist, John Paul Getty, who lived near the university and ask for a donation for his Shoah Foundation, but Getty was suffering from a prolonged depression and could not agree a date before he died.

Spielberg had set up the Foundation after *Schindler's List* to create an oral history of the concentration camps. It was the cause – family apart – that was dearest to his heart: the idea was to have a first-hand memorial of this terrible time, so future generations would never forget. About 125,000 people survived the ordeal and half of them agreed to talk to the cameras of his volunteers.

One morning I was chatting to Steven in his room at Amblin' when his assistant, Kirstie, burst through the door. 'Oprah Winfrey's being shown round,' she exclaimed. 'I saw her at the Beverly Hilton last night,' said Steven. 'I told her to come by before she went back to Chicago. Didn't think she would.' He got up and with a glance at me and the words 'Stay there' went in pursuit of the TV host. She had acted in his film *The Color Purple*.

Within ten minutes he was back. He patted the breast pocket of his jacket. 'A quarter of a million bucks for the Foundation. I wasn't sure it was the sort of thing she would support.'

At the time, the Foundation was housed in temporary buildings on the Universal backlot. I spent some time there. Students were working to log and index all the interviews. What I had never witnessed before was an audio word-recognition computer system. An operator typed in the words 'train' and 'thirst' and 'die' and was able to call up the testimonies of survivors who had witnessed fellow Jews die of thirst, usually on the train to Auschwitz. It made for sickening viewing, the barbarity of the way they were treated like cattle severely tested your faith in the human race.

Steven's idea was to use these witness stories to make *Broken Silence*, a series of individual documentaries for different countries – Hungary, Russia, the Czech Republic. Andrzej Wajda had already made one, *I Remember*, for Poland. I was flattered to be asked to make the film for Britain but the money ran out – Andrzej had spent most of it. Besides, when I began work on it, I realised there were relatively few British in the concentration camps and my story would have to be about the soldiers liberating them, which was slightly off message.

The Chicago-born science-fiction writer, Philip K. Dick, had his plots mined for the movies; *Blade Runner* and *Total Recall* were early successes. But nobody could see the film potential in his 1956 short story, 'The Minority Report', until a script found its way to Spielberg who took the premise of Dick's 'precogs' – mutants who could predict murders that were about to take place – and used it as a springboard to create a future fifty years away.

Spielberg assembled a think tank of academics and futurologists for a weekend at the Shutters on the Beach Hotel in Santa Monica in 1999 and invited them to help him with this vision. (To prevent any Hollywood espionage, they pretended to be a conference of dental technicians.) 'I'm not sure that things will be that wildly different,' Steven warned them. 'Remember, we had phones and television in 1950, but I think the quantum leap has been and will be in computers and the dissemination of information.'

I recreated the event for my documentary on police investigations in the future. Some of the ideas were logical enough but not suitable for a movie. People would sleep for one hour a night, they would live to be 180 and smoke freely once more, as a cure for cancer would have been found. One designer had sketched a car without controls. 'Where are they?' asked Steven. 'Not necessary,' the man replied, 'the driver will control it with his mind.' 'But what's the actor going to do?' responded the despairing director.

Automobiles did, however, play a major part in the debate. 'No flying cars,' Spielberg insisted. It was agreed that fossil fuel would be a thing of the past so the city of the future would have freeways that powered vehicles with magnetic levitation – 'Maglev'. Roads would go up the sides of skyscrapers and there would be no accidents thanks to computer control.

'We will still be watching television,' Steven told me, 'but it will be watching us and we will agree to collaborate. So video billboards will call you by name and customise their advertisements to you. It's beginning to happen with cookies on our home computers.'

But computers in *Minority Report* are very different animals. After three decades of research at the MIT Media Lab, science and technology advisor John Underkoffler and his team had developed an entirely new way of operating computers which Tom Cruise, as Chief Anderton, uses in the movie. He is more like an orchestra conductor than a keyboard tapper. John showed it to me. 'We've called it "g-speak". Tom is able to move video and other data across a screen using a gestural user interface, his commands are communicated via gloved hands.'

For my documentary, I flew up to Orion Scientific Systems in Sacramento. It has, reputedly, the most sophisticated crime-solving computer program in the States. Eric Zeidenberg, the vice-president, said they had trained more than 35,000 frontline police officers and showed me one program which tracked criminal gangs and, if a gang leader were killed, they could identify who would take over from him. Between the end of filming *Minority Report* and its release, the tragedy of 9/11 took place. Zeidenberg was certain that Orion could have pinpointed Khalid al-Mihdhar and Nawaf al-Hazmi who had masterminded the attack. They were trained in San Diego, they were known to the National Security Agency (NSA) but the bad blood between the NSA and the CIA meant that they were never put on a combined 'watch list'.

Minority Report's plot revolves round Anderton learning that a 'precog' has fingered him for a murder he will commit and his desperate quest is to prove the creature wrong. It takes him to a house on an island just off the coast of Virginia. We stayed at a resort hotel near there where Steven was already using state-of-the-art technology to give a live press conference from the hotel lounge via satellite to Japan to promote his previous film *A.I.* Tom Cruise and a slightly drunk Colin Farrell ran round the place like kids and burst into the lounge to say hello to the crowded Tokyo theatre. They were greeted with wild applause.

The island shoot was a haven for everyone – no press, no public. Tom's mother and sister arrived with his adopted children. (He had divorced Nicole Kidman earlier in the year and his body language expressed a new-found freedom.) Kate Capshaw sat in Steven's canvas chair, knitting, while keeping an eye on the six young Spielbergs. (Her daughter, Jessica, had a part in the movie.) All the children had been provided with earphones so they could, if they wished, listen to the dialogue and direction as they played in the sun. Spielberg had arranged for stalls to be set up all around the garden, serving hot dogs and ice cream, candies and cookies. Inside the house, serious film making was taking place. Steven had told me his one direction to Tom had been not to smile: 'Well, maybe he would be allowed a maximum of three throughout the film.' Outside, it was party time.

I had by then begun to know Steven's family a little. His sister, Anne, had invited me to Thanksgiving at her house. She worked occasionally for her younger brother and had been nominated for an Oscar for co-writing *Big*. Their mother, Leah, was there. A tiny woman with short white hair, she had left their father, Arnold, for his best friend who had since died. Now she ran a restaurant on West

Pico Boulevard, The Milky Way, which was said to serve the best kosher food in LA. They were a grounded, very non-show-business family. Spielberg had been estranged from his father for a bit but it was he who had given the young Steven his first movie camera and had been a jeep driver chasing Rommel's troops in his son's schoolboy movie *Escape to Nowhere*. But father and son now seemed very close when Steven introduced me to his eighty-four-year-old dad at the premiere of *Minority Report*.

Although Steven makes daredevil adventure movies, he freely admits he is still a bit of a wimp himself when it comes to physical challenges. At the opening of the Jurassic Park Water Ride at Universal, he made a point of getting out of the tourist raft before it made its near-vertical 85-foot drop into the tropical lagoon. In *Temple of Doom* there is a scene where Harrison Ford and Kate Capshaw try to get away across a swinging rope bridge high above a vertiginous gorge. Although the Steadycam operator followed them, the director confessed to me he had no intention of leaving the stable pathway on the rocky cliff. He was apprehensive of accompanying Tom in his helicopter to the island during *Minority Report*, preferring to be driven the long way round, until a studio executive assured him: 'Helicopters with Tom Cruise in them don't crash.'

Spielberg has good reason to be fearful in everyday life. In June 1998, a stalker, Jonathan Norman, was arrested in the grounds of his California home. He was carrying a 'rape kit' and was found guilty of a plot to invade the house, hold Steven and his family hostage and rape the director. Under the state's 'three strikes' law he was jailed for twenty-five years. I once interviewed Steven in the Hamptons and there were armed guards on the roof of his home there. Wherever he goes, an anonymous pair of bodyguards are not far away.

If a novelist had created the story of Frank Abagnale, Jr and sent it round the publishers, it would have been universally rejected as being preposterously unbelievable. Yet Frank does exist and in his autobiography, *Catch Me If You Can*, chronicles how he forged cheques as a teenager, pretended to be a pilot, a doctor, an assistant state attorney, was imprisoned in France and Sweden but escaped from the FBI agents accompanying him back to the States by jumping on to the airport runway from the hydraulic landing gear of a British Airways VC 10. The moment I met him it was immediately apparent that he could charm the birds from the trees. Indeed he did charm the birds from the lecture hall at Arizona State University and decked them out as Pan Am air stewardesses so that he could bank their overseas expenses cheques.

How he actually kitted them out and got them on the same rota as him is not a matter that he explains in detail. Like any liar and con man, Frank's own story does not always stand up to detailed examination. But, as the newspaper editor said in *The Man Who Shot Liberty Valance*: 'When the legend becomes fact, print the legend.' Which is what Spielberg did in his film.

Frank today is an open-faced, cheerful individual, a sinner turned saint who makes his millions from advising firms on how to detect fraud. He had been sentenced to twelve years' jail in the US for his crimes but, he claims, the FBI let him out after five, when he was still only twenty-six, provided he would advise them for free.

He was a gift to any documentary maker, an engrossing raconteur, a man who will, and does, tell you anything about his life and who still sends me cards at Christmas. But sadly, in this life, virtue does not provide its own rewards. I travelled to a run-down neighbourhood in Cobb County to meet the FBI officer who had tracked down Frank. Eighty-three-year-old Joe Shea was living on his own in reduced circumstances. Twice a day he visited his wife in a nearby hospital where she had advanced Alzheimer's and didn't recognise him. But he had great admiration for Frank and the two had managed to stay in touch. Joe died in 2006.

Steven, too, had admiration for the hero of his film because of his penitent redemption. He loved the story: 'It has a Robin Hood element to it. As Mark Twain wrote: "The reason truth is stranger than fiction is that fiction has to make sense."' Steven chose not to give the role of Frank to Tom Cruise, preferring Leonardo DiCaprio instead. Having got to know Frank Abagnale, I can see why. Tom certainly has the ability to turn on the charm, but Leo can just radiate it. There is a stillness in the way Leo acts that runs deep. They're very different men. Tom tends to dominate any gathering he attends. Leo has the capacity to make himself almost invisible.

I had been asked to introduce Steven, Frank and the stars at the London premiere of the film. There was a gathering beforehand where I caught up with Leo. I told him I had just been skiing in France where the Celine Dion *Titanic* song, 'My Heart Will Go On', was constantly played in French on the resort buses. Towards the end of it she was accompanied by shouts of people in the water but they were in French: '*Au secours!*' '*Aidez moi!*' Only there were no French people on the *Titanic*. He laughed and said he and a friend had escaped to France to avoid *Titanic* fever. But when they climbed the steps of the Sacré Coeur de Montmartre, it was only to find a drawing of himself on the side of the church. And every time they went into a bar for a drink, the pianist would strike up the *Titanic* song. It was a short holiday. I asked him if he knew who the woman with the video camera circulating the hospitality room interviewing people was. Leo raised his eyebrows. 'That's Irmelin. My mother.'

I thought it appropriate to introduce Steven to the audience that night as Sir Steven Spielberg. He had been knighted in 2001 and, although being American he was not permitted to use the title, it had a certain alliteration. He appreciated it.

For the *War of the Worlds* TV documentary it seemed to me that the best tack was to concentrate on H.G. Wells's vision and the earlier interpretations of it. Wells had written the work as an attack on British colonialism, inviting us to consider how we would feel if superior Martians took over our country. Sucking the blood from Earthlings, they created Red Weed – Red being the symbol of the spreading British Empire – to 'terraform' England's green and pleasant land into their own environment.

A radio play by Orson Welles had panicked New York in 1938. I had been involved in a Frost programme with Orson who recalled that many people rushed out of their homes with towels over their heads. 'Why towels?' David enquired. 'I have absolutely no idea,' Orson laughed. We managed to unearth an extract from a radio discussion between H.G. and Orson but it largely consisted of the author asking the actor why he had an 'e' in his surname.

Wells situated the initial Martian landings on Horsell Common near the author's home in Woking, Surrey. Today, in the centre of the town, there stands a chrome-plated, stainless-steel Martian Tripod, 23-foot-tall, made by Michael Condron. It was an ideal image for the documentary.

Tom Cruise was back on board. (My colleague, Laurent Bouzereau, would later cover the action on the Universal backlot where Tom, after some opposition, had a Scientology tent erected to spread the faith.) The script was so secret that I had to be locked in Tom's office at Paramount to read it. The adaptation was by David Koepp, one of the best action writers in Hollywood. 'We couldn't make them Martians since we now know there is no life on Mars,' he said. 'Steven didn't want to see the Aliens landing so we have them under the ground, waiting maybe for hundreds of years. And he didn't want a big disaster film with things like the Taj Mahal blowing up. So we see everything through the eyes of Tom. I thought it needed to be the biggest small story ever told, and the smallest big story ever told. We wanted some emotion as well as fear in the film. So Tom is a loser, an unemployed dockworker, estranged from his wife and despised by his son. But his main quest is to get back to them through all the mayhem, at the same time protecting his little daughter from the terror.'

More secret even than the script was what the alien Tripod would look like. Sworn to the utmost secrecy, I was given permission to go and see the full-size one that had been designed and constructed at vast expense by George Lucas's Industrial Light & Magic. Steven's assistant gave me the address: 3155 Kerner Boulevard, San Rafael. I flew up to San Francisco, hired a car and bought a map.

I drove north over the Golden Gate Bridge, glorious in the setting sun. But as I progressed through the suburbs of San Rafael, domestic housing petered out into an industrial wasteland. There was a Burger King at the corner of Kerner Boulevard but, apart from that, a barber's shop, a bank, a real-estate office, some run-down shops – and no people. I pulled up at 3155. It had a sign saying Kerner Optical and below it a warning: 'Beware of Toxic Waste', but it, too, seemed closed down. This wasn't the Lucas film empire; clearly I had the wrong address.

I had no mobile phone and no idea of what to do. I got back in my car to head for my hotel to see if somebody there could help me. Just as I set off, I caught sight of a figure on the sidewalk who had come out for a smoke. I quickly turned round but, before I could reach him, he disappeared. He may have gone into Kerner Optical so I went back to the door. There was a window to the left with shutters that didn't quite close. I peered through the crack and there, in an empty reception area, stood a full-size figure of Darth Vader. I hammered on the door and, after about twenty seconds, a man opened it. 'You're a bit late,' he said. 'I'm Garry, George's one-man publicity team.' I said I thought I had come to the wrong place. 'You were meant to,' he explained. 'All these buildings are just a front. George left them there when he built ILM. They keep the *Star Wars* fans away.'

As we walked through workshop after workshop, computer room after computer room, he said that when they were in full production 900 people could be working in this secret factory. 'I guess you want to see the Tripod tonight,' Garry surmised, correctly.

And there it was. The full-size, no-expense-spared, man-eating Tripod. I didn't like to say it was exactly the same as the one that proudly stood in the centre of Woking.

25

Failing in Hollywood …
Saved by James Bond

The first version of *Fierce Creatures* unfortunately didn't come up to expectations. While Universal had liked the script they didn't like the way it turned out and asked for a change of ending and a change of director. So instead of Kevin Kline being killed by a charging rhino he was accidentally shot by Michael Palin dressed as a giant bumblebee. I'm not sure that either change made a great deal of difference except to the escalating cost which meant that those of us who had worked for a percentage of the profits would get a percentage of nothing. I had gone to LA for the opening and early on Saturday morning got a call from Michael Shamberg to say the movie wasn't going to make money. Evidently, from the box-office take on the first Friday, the studio can make a fairly accurate estimate of future earnings. What can I say? 'Tough' would be the shortest word.

Nevertheless, thanks to Bruce Feirstein (my Boston student), I got a Hollywood agent: David Saunders of the Agency for the Performing Arts. I said that *Fierce Creatures* wasn't going to break the box office. 'Never mind,' said David, 'It got good reviews in the *LA Times* ("Gets the year off to a good laugh") and *The New York Times* ("It's head and shoulders above most of what passes for comedy on the American movie screen"). Don't be negative. You've been working with class acts – Cleese, Kline and Curtis. I can sell you on that.'

He tried. I had written an action adventure called *Minx* about rival CIA agents vying to uncover an antiquities scam in Egypt. 'The art,' said David, 'is not to get "coverage" from some junior studio reader, but to pitch it in person to people with power.' His secretary later gave me a list of appointments all over Hollywood, lasting for more than six weeks on and off. I knew my way round the town so I booked into a hotel and set out in my hire car on three or four days a week to 'take' meetings.

I found I was about as good at pitching a script as I would be at pitching a baseball. I wasn't an actor; just a self-effacing Englishman. My spirits sunk lower with each successive session. After a couple of weeks I asked Raffaella De Laurentiis, then running her father's production company, if she couldn't just read the two-page synopsis. She said, nicely, it wasn't the Hollywood way. If it made it to the screen, it would be played out by actors and it was up to the writer to give a flavour of the twists and tensions in the story. The tradition stretched back to Louis B. Mayer who, it was suspected, couldn't read.

One person who actually read *Minx* and quite liked it was Stanley Tong, director of the Jackie Chan action movies. He sat in an imposing office in the Brill Building, made all the more imposing by the fact that sitting with him was Albert S. Ruddy who had produced *The Godfather*. Stanley thought that the right person for the lead was Salma Hayek, then an up-and-coming Mexican actress. He would get the script to her people. My spirits rose only to come crashing down again when Tong said the story would have to be set in India as Egypt was such a visually boring country. He would get back to me.

He hasn't. Well, not yet. I returned to London with my confidence in small pieces. Those hundred-thousand-dollar deals rewriting scripts that would never be made into movies were not to be.

Salvation came in the delightful shape of Barbara Broccoli, producer of the Bond films. I had hosted a tribute at the National

Film Theatre for Maurice Binder, who had designed the titles for fourteen Bond films. Maurice had created the memorable opening of *The Grass Is Greener* in 1960, with the star names – Cary Grant, Deborah Kerr and Robert Mitchum – at the top of the screen but, beneath them, babies in nappies on the lawn at Pinewood. They gambolled on the grass ending with a near-impossible shot (that no Norland Nanny could have orchestrated) of eight one year olds sitting up straight with their backs to camera. Cubby Broccoli snapped him up for *Dr No* and Maurice rewarded him with the classic 'Bond through the barrel' opening followed in subsequent films by various beauties dancing, writhing and jumping, usually in naked silhouette.

At the reception afterwards, Cubby Broccoli sat in state, like a benign pontiff. He beckoned me over, thanked me for playing my part and said that he was worried about the future of the franchise. A shady Italian, Giancarlo Parretti, had attempted to take over MGM/United Artists, Cubby's partner in the Bonds, and sell the back catalogue off cheap to pay for it. Against the advice of his lawyers, Cubby was prepared to fight this to the bitter end.

He did, and won. But his health did not permit him to oversee the resumption of play, after more than five years, with *GoldenEye* and a new Bond, Pierce Brosnan. He handed over producing to his daughter, Barbara, and son-in-law, Michael Wilson. When Cubby died, in June 1996, they asked me to host a celebration of his life, as I had with Maurice, but on a slightly larger scale.

When the limo dropped me off at the Odeon Leicester Square on the morning of Sunday 17 November, it was as if it were a film premiere. Crowds had assembled to witness the arrival of Q, Miss Moneypenny, various familiar villains and three James Bonds.

Over coffee and croissants, I was conferring with them – Roger Moore, Timothy Dalton and Pierce Brosnan – to ensure that their speeches did not overlap, when Mo and my daughter Holly arrived. I introduced them and I would like to say that my younger daughter was surprised to meet the three action heroes, familiar to her from the films and television, face to face. But thirteen year olds tend to take things in their stride and she chatted to them as if this were an everyday occurrence.

The Odeon was full and the portrait of the man who had created the world's most successful film franchise was painted with love and laughter. Cubby may have been a tough negotiator but once a film was under way he became the paterfamilias, cooking spaghetti for the crew and making sure, if any of his workers fell ill or on hard times, they would be looked after.

He had grown up on a farm in New Jersey which, among other vegetables, had grown broccoli, and after selling Christmas trees in LA, became an agent and then a producer. He had asked Cary Grant, the best man at his wedding to Dana, to play Bond but the star declined. I think he would have been wonderful. Ian Fleming wanted Noël Coward to play the title part in the first film, *Dr No*, but got a cable back from The Master which simply said: 'No, no, no, no, no.' Cubby took that as a 'no'.

Sean Connery, still bitter over his dispute with Cubby, did not deign to attend. Some people can forgive and pretend to forget. Not Sean. Roger Moore said his producer would call him a 'bag of old farts' but declined to collect the £2 million Cubby had won from him during ten years of backgammon games. Tim Dalton emotionally stated it was hard to be great, but harder still to be good. Pierce revealed that when he had arrived in Putney from Ireland at the age of eleven, it was seeing *Goldfinger* that made him determined to be an actor. Bryan Forbes regretted turning down the chance to script *Dr No* but had endeared himself to Cubby on an earlier film, *The Dark Knight,* when Alan Ladd was due to jump from a battlement and ride off on a Saracen's horse. Mrs Ladd, protective of her husband's reputation, stated: 'Alan Ladd does not steal horses.' So Bryan resolved the stalemate by writing a new line for the man holding the animal: 'Here is the horse you ordered, sir.'

Dana, Michael and Barbara had taken over the whole of La Famiglia restaurant in Chelsea for Sunday lunch afterwards. Inevitably Alvaro, the owner, served Cubby's favourite spaghetti. Mo and I were put on a table with Roger Moore and Kiki Tholstrup, Bryan Forbes and Nanette Newman, and Shirley Eaton. Roger and Bryan had known each other for a long time; they had been together in the British Army on the Rhine in Germany in 1947. Roger had recently parted from Luisa, his wife of thirty years, the last few of which, he told me, had been somewhat turbulent. He sipped alcohol-free lager to celebrate his new relationship. Inevitably the talk turned to Bond. Mo asked him how he had managed to run across the backs of the crocodiles in *Live and Let Die*. Roger laughed. 'It wasn't me. Do you think I'm crazy? It was the owner of the alligator farm in Jamaica. His father had actually been eaten by an alligator. Guy Hamilton wouldn't even film me running along a sidewalk. He didn't like the way I ran so he always used a double.'

Shirley, who had retired many years ago and was recently widowed, said that the shot of her painted gold lying dead on the bed in *Goldfinger* had made her. She was always in demand at Bond conventions and was even writing an autobiography called *Golden Girl*. It had certainly been a seminal moment in movies. Bryan and Nanette were still furiously writing books, she for children. He died in 2013. They had had a bookshop in Virginia Water but the pressure of the big book chains had forced them to close. Bryan had done the screenplay for *Chaplin* for his closest friend, Dickie Attenborough, whom he still referred to as 'Bunter'. Nobody else would dare address the noble lord as that.

Some time later Michael and Barbara took me out for dinner. I mentioned that John Cleese had always wanted to play the villain in a Bond film. Michael thought throughout the main course and then said: 'It wouldn't work. He is too associated in the public mind as a comedy actor. But I have an idea. Desmond Llewelyn is in his eighties now and can't go on playing Q forever. Perhaps Cleese could be his assistant and then take over the part.' When I reported this back to John, he leapt at the idea. His part in *The World Is Not Enough* was short and snappy, with Desmond silencing him by pulling the tag on an inflatable jacket which swallowed him up.

Barbara had been having different thoughts. Each Bond film had a book about it, telling the inside story of its creation. Maybe I would like to think about writing one. I certainly would.

One of the first people to greet me on the set was Desmond. We went to the lunch tent together and talked about his schooldays at Radley, Peter Cook's old school. He had started work as an actor but, when he was twenty-five, World War II began and, having been born in Newport, he was commissioned into the Royal Welsh Fusiliers. This was a piece of bad luck. The regiment was part of the British Expeditionary Force that was sent to France early in 1940. They came up against a division of German tanks who outnumbered and outfought them. Desmond dived into a river, hoping to join up with British troops on the other side (and eventually, with luck, be evacuated at Dunkirk). Unfortunately he was met by Germans and spent the entire war as a POW, primarily in Colditz. His luck didn't get any better during an escape attempt: he was caught in the tunnel.

But every actor needs a break. Peter Burton, who had played Major Boothroyd, otherwise known as Q, in *Dr No* wasn't free to do *From Russia With Love*, so Desmond got the part and kept it for sixteen further Bonds, to date the longest-serving actor in the series. Although the role was small, Llewelyn made his mark. Tragically, he was driving back from a book signing of his autobiography when he died in a car crash shortly after the premiere of *The World Is Not Enough*.

Bond films had long since run out of stories based on Ian Fleming's books – not that they ever ran with them that closely. But the plots remain immutable: a Bad Man is intending to take over the world and Bond stops him. Barbara got the idea for the new film when she watched a Ted Koppel *Nightline* whose subject was that, after the fall of the USSR, the independent Muslim state of Azerbaijan was now the owner of the world's largest oil fields. Drilling for the oil in the Caspian Sea was relatively uncomplicated. Distributing it presented the problem: the projected pipelines had to go through politically turbulent states. What if someone were intent on destroying all opposition and ensuring his pipeline was the only conduit of the 'black gold' to the West? Add to that a maniac called Renard, a KGB agent turned terrorist, who steals plutonium from the pipeline and intends to blow up Europe, and you have a plot.

At least, I think that was the plot. The producers with their writers, Neal Purvis and Robert Wade, and new director, Michael Apted, wove these ingredients into an adventure with glamorous locations and girls. Apted had been at Cambridge with Cleese, learned his craft, where many British directors began, on *Coronation Street*, had a quality list of Hollywood credits including *Gorky Park* and *Gorillas in the Mist*, and on television has chronicled the lives of fourteen people who were seven in 1964 by filming them every seven years.

A Bond film without girls would be like a martini that has been stirred. Gone are the days when Roger Moore would be surrounded by a bevy of vacant beauties in bikinis. The girls are just as pretty today but their minds have to be pretty good, as well. In the screening room of the Bond HQ on Piccadilly, I watched William Nicholson's *Firelight* with Barbara and Michael. They wanted to take a look at Sophie Marceau, playing a nineteenth-century governess, cerebral and sensual. She got the part of Elektra, the oil heiress who is not the honest innocent she first appears.

The relish with which she garrottes 007 nearly to death, eager to take advantage of the erection that is caused by pressure on the cerebellum, seems more an exercise in lust than a purely scientific interest. Elektra tells him with regret: 'I could have given you the world.' Bond, resilient to the last, gives her the film's title: 'The world is not enough.' (As it happens, the Bond family motto.) Off set, Sophie revealed a schoolgirl naughtiness. She told me she had pinched the sign from the Avenue Marceau in Paris to decorate her flat. So, if the gendarmes are still looking for it, they know where to go.

Pierce Brosnan is a relaxed, friendly Irish chap although as one watched him walking from his dressing room, where he was frequently watching Wimbledon, to the set, you could see his shoulders straighten as he imperceptibly became 007. He developed the annoying habit of always addressing me as 'Mr Johnstone', although he is less than ten years younger than me.

Denise Richards, former cheerleader and Starship Trooper, whose home life was later chronicled in the cable channel E!'s series *It's Complicated*, was not necessarily a natural to play a nuclear scientist, but in her vest and short shorts she brought some sexy decoration to her scenes. She was called Dr Christmas Jones for the benefit of two gags. On their first encounter, Bond asks her what she is called

Pierce Brosnan for whom the world is not enough.

and the reply comes: 'Dr Jones. Dr Christmas Jones. And don't tell me any jokes. I've heard them all.' Bond: 'I don't know any doctor jokes.' At the film's climax they inevitably end up in bed. Bond: 'I was wrong about you.' Dr Jones: 'Yeah, how so?' James Bond: 'I thought Christmas only came once a year.'

Robert Carlyle, the Scot who came to fame in *Trainspotting*, was the villain Renard, who had a bullet lodged in his brain (cerebella play an unusually large part in this film). The good news was that it made him impervious to pain; the bad news was that it was gradually destroying his senses. Robert was the only actor to get a percentage of the money-spinning *The Full Monty*. A down-to-earth nice guy, he modestly told me that the best thing about having money was the ability to help out friends and family.

Certainly with *The World Is Not Enough*, I was to learn that Bond films are something of a sleight of hand. One of the soundmen told me the main camera crew was essentially 'the close-up dialogue unit'. The stars perform the interior dramatics in Pinewood, while other units get to see the world. First off was John Richardson, who took his twelve-man crew and miniature submarine to the Bahamas to film its exploding demise. Second unit director, Vic Armstrong, took his 170-strong crew to Chamonix in the Alps (playing the Caucasus Mountains) for four weeks to film Bond and Elektra being chased by lethal black Parahawks. The two stars were doubled by 'extreme skiers' but came out for a day of close-ups. Both could ski, but the film's insurers wouldn't let them. I asked Pierce's 'extreme' double if many of his colleagues had been killed. He said they hadn't; the most frequent cause of fatalities on Mont Blanc was vacation skiers stopping for a rest and being wiped out by snowboarders.

The climax of the film was set in Istanbul. A Foreign Office advisory warned that the separatist Kurdish group, the PKK, were out to get publicity by attacking tourists and Bond would be a prize scalp. Michael Apted took a brave twelve-man crew to the city where their clapperboard said they were making a documentary called *Danny*. Judi Dench was especially miffed. When she read in her script that M would be held hostage in Istanbul, she had already planned some sightseeing.

They hired a plane so that they could film Pierce making a day's whistle-stop drive around the pipelines in Azerbaijan, but the pipeline the audience mainly saw was a model built in Black Park which backs on to Pinewood Studios. (Adrian Biddle, the gifted Director of

Photography whom I had got to know on *Fierce Creatures*, confided that he would have been happy to shoot the entire movie in Black Park.) 'There are lots of gloomy, cloudy locations like Azerbaijan,' wrote Peter Bradshaw in his *Guardian* review. He was nearly right. Black Park is gloomy and cloudy.

The main unit did travel to Spain to film the opening sequence in Bilbao, including Frank Gehry's magnificent Guggenheim Museum. Outside it is a giant puppy by the American artist, Jeff Koons. It is impossible to film the museum without including it and Koons wanted a lot of money for his dog. So they just CGI'd it out in post-production.

To the south-east, we were quartered in Zaragoza so that they could film Pierce and Denise escaping from a flash fire and huge explosion in the pipeline. The arid Bardenas Reales desert would play Kazakhastan. Michael Wilson remarked: 'They used to say that once you got out into the desert, a rock is a rock and a tree is a tree.' The lady who initially leased out her land to the film changed her mind when she heard there was going to be an explosion as it would upset the baby eagles nearby, so the unit moved to the east.

It was a big bang: a combination of petrol and isopropanol exploded in an 80-foot pillar of flame. Of course, the stars couldn't be risked so the stunt team of Mark Mottram and Jo McCaren stood in for them. Mark was wearing Nomex underwear beneath his suit, the kind that racing drivers used, but Jo was in Denise's vest and shorts so her body was smeared in Zel gel. When Mark realised just how furious the fire would be, he intuitively interposed his body between Jo and the fierce heat. Apted picked up the sequence later with Pierce and Denise rolling down a small hill. When 007 rose to his feet for their close-up, make-up girls carefully reset and sprayed his hair. This Bond always remained immaculate, whatever rough and tumble he had been through.

Michael Wilson had seen a Canadian documentary of helicopters with giant chainsaws suspended beneath them to lop branches from inaccessible trees and had always wanted to incorporate them in a terrifying Bond sequence. Such a scene had been written into *GoldenEye* but was never shot. However, Michael persisted and it went into *The World Is Not Enough* with Bond and Christmas Jones dodging the giant blades as they cut up the wooden walkways in Zukovsky's (Robbie Coltrane's) caviar factory. Zukovsky, incidentally, was hoist with his own expensive taste, as he nearly drowned in a deep pit of Beluga caviar.

It was the nearest action to reality in the film with the chainsaw slicing Bond's (specially prepared) BMW in half. 'You'll answer to Q for that,' Bond observes as he escapes in the nick of time.

It also led to a dispute between friends. Bruce Feirstein had been polishing dialogue on the film (when showing Bond round the lethally prepared BMW, Bruce had Cleese say: 'and it has eight cup holders') but not enough to earn him a credit. The Writers Guild collects 'residuals' from studios when a movie is sold to video or abroad. But they only go to the writers who are on the credits. Bruce argued furiously that since he had written the helicopter sequence for *GoldenEye*, he had done enough work on the film for him to deserve a credit. It went to arbitration and he won his case.

But Michael and Barbara have the capacity to separate the professional from the personal. Bruce went on to write several video games for the Bonds. Barbara even came to his mother's funeral.

It was a rule laid down by Cubby that Bond films took place 'ten minutes into the future'. Michael further elaborated: 'They should not be so fantastical as to be impossible. The idea is that if you had all the time and all the money in the world, whatever inventions we come up with should be possible.' This was transgressed in *Die*

Another Day where Bond drives an invisible car and the thrill of the chase is all the weaker because of this.

I suppose Bond films, like his girls, have to change with the times but I do have a weakness for the earlier, snappier wit, such as 'He disagreed with something that ate him', when a villain is swallowed by a shark. Or when another is ballooned to death by a shark-gun pellet, 'He always did have an inflated opinion of himself.' These are now few and far between. *Skyfall*, a film without flippancy, was the first Bond to make a billion. So the public appetite would seem to prefer a more sober, *Mission: Impossible*-type thriller to one that winks at the audience from time to time.

Why has Bond run for fifty years with increasing popularity? As my old jurisprudence professor used to say: 'Familiarity breeds compatibility.' We know that Bond will survive the movie; he's got to live for another adventure. We know the mad, bad guy will fail. We look forward to Bond's adversarial relationship with M, his flirtatious one with Miss Moneypenny and being put in his place by Q. We expect a few spectacular chases, a glamorous night at the gaming tables where he doesn't really care if he wins or loses since money simply doesn't matter to him and at least a couple of the most beautiful girls in the world to fall into his bed without any nervous courtship or promise of a continuing relationship.

If only life were like that. Sadly, it isn't. But, for a couple of hours, we can live it vicariously.

26

An Encounter with J.K. Rowling …
the Life of Whiteley

Except where relevant, I haven't written very much about my family. This is deliberate; it has been a story about professional encounters, not personal revelations. But, so far, Mo and I have been fortunate: the children grew up straight and tall. I mentioned that Sophie went to Oxford with a little help from Steven Spielberg; Holly, after Edinburgh, is in hotel PR; and Oliver, after RADA, is an actor.

Both girls found jobs they liked and husbands they liked: Ed and Olly. Scott Fitzgerald wrote that 'there are no second acts in American lives', but there are in Fulham lives as I play by the side of the Thames in Bishop's Park with my grandson, Ralph, as I did with his mother.

Iain Duncan Smith who was, unexpectedly, made Leader of the Conservative Party in 2001, lived at the end of our road and, although I had never actually spoken to him, I had noticed him walking briskly past our house, sporting that brown trilby that ex-army officers tend to wear. I wrote him a letter congratulating him, gently enquiring if my vast experience in television and film might be of use to his shadow government. Surprisingly, he replied that there could be, perhaps, some sort of expert industry advisory committee for the Shadow Culture Secretary, Tim Yeo.

A few months later I got a letter from Anne McIntosh, MP, who worked with Yeo, asking me to tea in the Commons. Julian Fellowes, who had agreed to be on the committee, kindly came with me and, as we were escorted through the Central Lobby, I fantasised about the peerage that would finally reward my work and a gilded retirement sleeping in the Lords. We bombarded Anne with ideas, Julian with expertise and eloquence, and she seemed taken with the notion and said I would be hearing from her.

Unfortunately, I didn't so much hear from her as read about her. She and Yeo were sent to a new department in a reshuffle and the new guy wasn't interested. Not only that, but it was Julian who got the peerage, deservedly so: *Gosford Park* and *Downton Abbey* did more to promote British film and television than any crummy committee.

When Warners released the first *Harry Potter* movie, as is customary with such events, a junket was held before the premiere with journalists and TV reporters flown in to see the film and have an opportunity to interview the stars, the biggest of whom, in this instance, was J.K. Rowling herself. She had already published three further books and she was rich and famous. But, for reasons unknown, she declined to join in the junket.

But Warners prevailed upon her to film a televised interview which could be shown to the assembled press and she agreed. And they hired me to do it. There was a slight problem in that when I tried to read *Harry Potter and The Philosopher's Stone* to my son, I made the mistake of putting on a Somerset accent when it came to the school gamekeeper, Hagrid: 'Don' expect you've had a lotta presents from them Dursleys, Harry.' I couldn't keep it up and developed a sort of Potter-block. I found reading the next three books for research daunting: after all, they weren't aimed at middle-aged men. But a friend of my daughter had had a nervous breakdown in his first term at university and returned to his parents' home. There he had immersed himself in the first four *Potters* and they had had the therapeutic effect of bringing him out of his despair. (Maybe there is a restorative quality in the subtext of the stories – Rowling herself had had such a breakdown.) So he tutored me in the subject, almost up to *Mastermind* standard.

We set up the cameras in a suite in The Scotsman Hotel in Edinburgh. I knew that Rowling had little love for the press, always suing when there was any intrusion into her daughter's life. She arrived with a small entourage and a greeting which, though not as frosty as the weather outside, was a little less than cordial. I suppose I was a representative of the enemy and I wondered how readily she had acceded to Warners' request. Fortunately, I had brought along my niece, Charlie, as my PA. She was engaged to an Edinburgh doctor and so, it transpired, was Jo. The two chatted about long hospital working hours as coffee was delivered and the lighting adjusted. So when we were ready to roll, she was more relaxed – and candid. Here's a bit of our chat:

IJ: I understand you were reluctant to sell the film rights.

JKR: Yes, I was reticent. There was a flood of film and television offers. And I said no to all of them, including Warner Brothers. But, after a year, I had an assurance from them that they would do it in a certain way. The absolute crux of the matter was that they did not take my characters off to do something that I didn't want them to do because I obviously am in the middle of a seven-book series, so I didn't ever want anyone to make *Harry Goes to Las Vegas*.

IJ: You can be quite controlling, I've heard. I remember when the BBC wanted to put the first *Harry Potter* on the radio you either suggested or insisted that they had the lot or none. Is that true?

JKR: Controlling is one word. I just wanted to keep the thing pure. So that is how we ended up with eight hours of poor Stephen

Fry ... I don't know why I say poor Stephen Fry, I mean he does a magnificent job ... but that is how we ended up with eight hours of Stephen on the radio on Boxing Day. When I'm cooking I like to listen to books on tape. You know there is nothing more irritating to me than producers cutting and shortening them. So yes, call me controlling if you like!

IJ: What was your reaction when you saw Harry on film?

JKR: I was enormously relieved. The first time I met Chris Columbus, the director, he promised me two things: he would remain as faithful to the book as he possibly could, within the constraints of film, and he would have an all-British cast. He kept both promises, so I was a happy woman. Warners have been very generous in letting me have my say. They said to me at one point, 'Have you ever had any thoughts on casting?' I had sat at home with a friend and drawn up my dream cast list! And I said casually, 'Oh, I've had one or two thoughts,' and then produced this list that I had done a good month before. I think I got everyone on that list bar two.

IJ: I know Robbie Coltrane was important to you.

JKR: He was top of the list in my dream cast. Robbie Coltrane for Hagrid and Maggie Smith for McGonagall. Hagrid's obviously a very loveable character, quite comic. But there is a certain toughness underneath Hagrid for him to work and I think Robbie does that perfectly.

IJ: Is it true that you advised him a little bit on the history of his character?

JKR: He phoned me one night and we talked for two hours. I told him nearly everything I know about Hagrid. Actually, I've never asked him if that was helpful. Maybe it impeded him.

IJ: There's one moment when they are entering platform nine and three-quarters and Ron lets out a shout of 'Wicked!' in the film. I don't think I remember that from the book.

JKR: No, I don't use 'Wicked!' I use 'Brilliant!' all the time, which is very British although I think they do use 'Brilliant!' in the film as well. No, 'wicked!' would have been Steve Kloves, the scriptwriter. Mind you, I think Ron *would* say 'wicked'. My editor would never let me swear in the books. They've got away with it a bit in the film and I actually said a quiet 'Yes!' when I heard a 'bloody'.

IJ: When you were fourteen, I heard you were very much a Hermione.

JKR: Yes, my American editor took me to task after he'd read *Goblet of Fire.* He said 'You keep saying she's shrill,' and I said, 'Well she is,' and he said, 'You're being very hard on her.' And he then said, 'I think it's because she's so like you.' I love Hermione as a character, but I can see Hermione for what she is because, yes, there is a huge amount of me in Hermione and at fourteen I was shrill. But that's OK – Hermione has got a political conscience, she is a feisty little thing. Those kind of fourteen year olds can be quite annoying and Hermione is sometimes.

IJ: Regarding Quidditch, you hated hockey at school, I believe.

JKR: I absolutely loathed hockey, yes.

IJ: So this is your revenge, is it?

JKR: I'm not a sportsman. I am not a sporty person at all; I'm a very lazy person. I managed to break my arm playing netball, which is not easy to do. Quidditch is my idea of a good spectator sport – watching the athletic people get mangled. I invented Quidditch when I was living in Manchester one evening after a row with my then boyfriend, which may explain some of the violence.

IJ: So what's your next book, *The Order of the Phoenix* about?

JKR: I'm not telling you!

IJ: I had a feeling you were going to say that.

JKR: Yes! Are you mad?

IJ: And will the Hogwarts saga come to an end with the seventh book?

JKR: Definitely. There is absolutely no question whatsoever that the novels will end on book seven.

IJ: What are you going to do then?

JKR: Take a break from publishing. I won't be taking a break from writing because I actually don't have a choice in the matter. Writing for me is a compulsion, it's not a choice. I was writing long before I was published and I will continue to do so until I literally can't write any more.

Jo wrote me a nice note after the interview; there was no need to do that. I didn't manage to discover where her voluminous imagination comes from but I suspect not even she knows that. These people just happen.

Thanks to my agent, I ghosted a couple of autobiographies: one strictly secret and the other about Johnny Gold, the jovial owner of Tramp, the Jermyn Street nightclub which was the only place to be for four or more decades. Of course, we wrote about the royals, film stars, pop stars, sports stars, bestselling writers, kings of industry, a few master criminals, all those fortunate enough to be admitted to the court of King John. But, of greater interest to me, was Gold's life in wartime Brighton as the son of a bookmaker.

'Why are there so many crooks in Brighton?' the question used to run. Answer: 'Because the train doesn't go any further.' The audacity of the post-war wheeler-dealers who sold anything from copper to ships and, in some instances, second-hand tanks and submarines to foreign countries beggared belief.

The one biography I never wanted to write was that of Richard Whiteley, my closest friend along with Alan Riding. When we were younger men, Richard's home in Yorkshire was my second home and mine, in London, his. We experienced a mutual thrill in our passion for making television. We holidayed together, we were best man at each other's weddings, godfathers to each other's children. (Richard had an unexpected son whom he provided for.)

He was a bright man, as politically informed as any I have known, but his persona on *Countdown* was that of a bit of a buffoon. This initially arose because he recorded five shows in a day and his puns were written by other people, so he frequently laughed at them because he was reading them for the first time. He embellished the image with loud jackets and louder ties. He was endlessly self-deprecating and this, along with his warmth and wit, endeared him to millions.

He died of bad luck. Whiteley luck. His younger sister, Helen, died of cancer aged forty-eight. Her daughter, Alex, died of cystic fibrosis at twenty-eight. We were due to have lunch in London the day he fell ill, but he returned to Yorkshire and to hospital where a series of ill-fated, domino-like disasters hit his system, ending in endocarditis. He died on Sunday, 26 June 2005. He was sixty-one.

Christine Stewart, Richard's sister-in-law, who had been helping to look after him, asked me to come and stay with Kathy Apanowicz, his partner. The shock and grief which led the national news bulletins on TV and radio on Sunday night spread out into nearly every other live programme that following Monday.

Carol Vorderman came round in the evening; they had worked together for twenty-three years. She and Kathy and I sat and reminisced and cried. The next day both *The Times* and the *Guardian* led their second sections with long appreciations of Richard.

Kathy, Christine and I drove across the Yorkshire moors to say a final goodbye to Richard in the mortuary and Kathy pinned his OBE to his lapel. There was a private service in his local church and he was buried in its graveyard, a soft rain sweeping his beloved Dales. Two thousand people came to his memorial service at York Minster and more than 200,000 sent condolences to Yorkshire Television or to Kathy or Vorders. For nearly a quarter of a century, children had come home from school or students had gathered in their common rooms to spend half an hour with Richard Whiteley. I count myself fortunate to have spent more than half an hour.

At a Bristol University reunion I encountered David Hunt and he asked me to lunch at the House of Lords. David had been in Thatcher's and Major's Cabinets and went on to chair the Press Complaints Commission. When I said that I would like to put my law to some use, he suggested that I become a Commercial Mediator. He knew the man who ran the Alternative Dispute Resolution group and said he would try and get me on a course.

Thus I ended up back in Bristol having gatecrashed my way into a class of chartered surveyors who were being trained as mediators. I loved it. Litigants go to mediation to try to avoid the cost of lawyers and a court case. The art of the mediator lies in the Caucus Room (smaller than the Watergate one) where you take each side separately, if necessary several times, to try to find an acceptable compromise to their dispute.

I passed and found myself going fairly regularly to the Central London County Court to apply my recently learned skills. After a couple of wobbly cases, I discovered that the opposing parties were rarely arguing about the same thing. Whether it was a builder's bill or a right of way, there was usually a personal misunderstanding from which neither side wanted to back down. If you could earmark this and clear the air, you had the satisfaction of watching the opposing sides walking out into the fresh air of Regent's Park with a burden off their backs. The only cases where I regularly failed were over wills: the bitterness of sibling disputes required a more almighty power than mine to resolve.

To write a book about writing books would be a perverse, indeed tedious, undertaking. But I had signed a very decent contract with Hodder and Stoughton for a biography of Tom Cruise and work was under way when, the following year, Kathy called. Various publishers had asked her for a book on Richard's life and, since she didn't write books, would I do it? When I asked if she was sure she wanted a biography so soon, she said she was, and so was Carol, whose publishers, Virgin Books, had told her it was important to publish while Richard's memory was still fresh in the public mind.

I asked for time to think about it. I didn't take too long to come to the screamingly obvious conclusion: Hang Tom Cruise, do it for Dick. If there was going to be such a book, I didn't want anyone else to do it. So all involved had a meeting at Virgin and sealed the deal over lunch at the pricey River Café behind their offices.

Fortunately, my main interviews with Cruise had already been done on *Minority Report* and *War of the Worlds* so I could concentrate for a while on Richard. Unfortunately, Hodder had discovered that

Andrew Morton, who had written the book on Diana, was now doing one on Cruise, so my editor suggested I had better dig up some revelations about his private life and Scientology. I pointed out that Morton had not been able to interview Cruise and, anyway, I was coming to the subject from the view of a film critic. The thought did pass through my mind of the London theatre critic who, when asked by his editor why his review had not mentioned the fact that the theatre had burned down during the play, replied: 'I'm a critic; not a reporter.' As it turned out, Morton's book was not published in the UK due to the risk of a libel law suit.

Following in Richard's footsteps proved to be unexpectedly uplifting. Christ's College, Cambridge, was a distinguished place to have been educated. It included among its famous alumni Charles Darwin, Earl Mountbatten, John Milton and, now, Richard Whiteley – not that the last, although he read English, was able to quote the poet. Richard had spent most of his last year editing *Varsity*, the student newspaper, which led to ITN and his TV career. Shortly before his finals, his English tutor summoned him to her rooms. 'I just wanted to see what you looked like, Mr Whiteley,' she said. He got a third.

I already knew many of his friends from London and Yorkshire but there was something cathartic for them to talk about him on tape. Vorders came round some evenings with reminiscences about *Countdown*. I never knew that at Christmas he entertained every single person who worked on the programme to lunch and would go round the table, not only giving them presents but making a short speech about each one of them.

Kathy was his partner in so much of this. In the end, I insisted we put the biography solely in her name. Perversely, but happily, it remains the only book I have ever written to have got into *The Sunday Times* Top Ten.

Life wasn't all writing. I still had the H.G. Wells documentary to complete and I made a couple of films in Israel about the Weizmann Institute, an eye-opening place where scientists are going into the unknown. Most have no idea where their research will lead, if anywhere. It was humbling to interview such a dedicated collection of pioneers. One of them, Ada Yonath, won the 2009 Nobel Prize for Chemistry for her work on the way antibiotic drugs could conquer hitherto resistant strains of illness.

No longer having any children to rear, Mo stepped up her work as a script supervisor on commercials. Budgets had slimmed somewhat since the days when she and John Lloyd and Rowan Atkinson had spent two weeks in Bali to film a pair of binoculars falling into the water. Caroline Aherne always asked her to work on *The Royle Family* and this spread to TV dramas such as *Pierrepoint* and Jamie Oliver documentaries.

For me, the pen proved mightier than the lens: I wrote another novel, *Pirates of the Mediterranean*, and a biography of Meryl Streep.

Encroaching old age is something we try to pretend happens to other people. I remember Chris Brasher writing that, after the 1980 Olympic Downhill, journalists were allowed to attempt the course. The pros did it in 1 minute 30 seconds. The fastest journo took just under 8 minutes. This was like golf correspondents, who are invited to play the course at Atlanta the day after the Masters, going round in about 350. To show off to my children, I attempted the Olympic Downhill at Val d'Isère on my sixtieth birthday. It took about an hour. But recently I was playing doubles against a pair of weaker opponents with Piers, Barry Norman's former son-in-law, and I noticed he was following his serve in with a volley. I decided to emulate him and we won the two games on my serve, the second almost posthumously.

Obviously, you don't make your way through life, professionally or personally, alone. I have had the good fortune to be supported by more buttresses than Chartres Cathedral. My parents, my sister and her husband, David, and their family. Mo, her mother, Isabel, and, latterly, our family. And friends. Richard, obviously. Sheridan Morley, throughout his life. Donald MacCormick, a friend and mentor until his dying day. Gordon Arnell organised things and I did them. We actually made five pilots for a lunchtime TV series called *Tabletalk from Covent Garden*. We had guests like Cameron Mackintosh (the theatrical producer), Ian Hislop and Julian Fellowes who still insists 'it was before its time' (there wasn't any lunchtime television then), but no TV company was interested in trying to find out if there was an appetite for it. Most important of all was Alan Riding, my friend from university and a formidable foreign correspondent who wrote the definitive book on Mexico, *Distant Neighbors.* Whenever I have hit problems he has always been there for me.

Michael Frayn has said we write in order to try to make sense of life. Has this Memoir made sense of mine? To begin with, I think it may have. A combination of purpose and optimism and energy might have helped pave the path. But also, most importantly, luck – bearing in mind that, as the French chemist, Louis Pasteur, observed: 'Luck favours the prepared mind.'

I count myself fortunate to have worked in television at a time when a producer, like an author, could get his or her own ideas published ... if they were good enough. Today, there is a perception that the public wants reality television – cooking, talent shows, quizzes etc – and this is satisfied by TV managers giving it to them. More democratic, I suppose, but I wouldn't be much use producing Sharon Osbourne.

Thereafter, I'm not so sure. I recall getting nearly the same marks in all nine O-level results. And, without daring to compare myself to a man of genius, I also recall what Kenneth Tynan said of Orson Welles: 'He grew fat and spread himself thin.' My career spread through news reading, Watergate, studio shows, disparate documentaries, film criticism, radio programmes, telly programmes, screen writing, novels, biographies.

Maybe if I had stuck to one trade and truly mastered it, I would have made a more memorable mark. As Pliny wrote: 'A cobbler should stick to his last.' But at least it passed the time, although, to quote Beckett's Estragon: 'It would have passed in any case.' But, hey, it's not over yet: maybe some producer will buy *Glenn Gould* or *Elsinore: The Day Before* or even some as yet unwritten idea.

A writer rarely does a full day's work. He may do more, he often does less. The last honest day's work I did was as a volunteer London Ambassador at the 2012 Olympics. They sent me an engraved relay baton for doing this. I have skipped the next generation and passed it on to Ed and Sophie's son, Ralph. I hope he runs with it, fast and far into a peaceful future.

Acknowledgements

My thanks to Jane Butcher for her assiduous editing, Vicky Holtham for her original cover design, Richard Blanshard for his flattering photo and Spellbinding Media, the most attentive publisher I have ever written for.

Andrew, who co-owned some London restaurants, had been trained in the hotel business. John asked him what was his worst experience and Andrew unhesitatingly told of the morning in the Savoy when it was discovered that a guest had died during the night and it fell to him to get the body down to the morgue without upsetting the other guests. This he successfully did, unlike the time when the film star Richard Harris was carried through the dining room en route to hospital (where he died) and managed to shout to the diners: 'It was the food!'

A character called Andrew Leeman duly appeared in episode nine of *Fawlty Towers*, 'The Kipper and the Corpse', as a guest who dies. Basil thinks the cause of death was serving him out-of-date kippers and he and Manuel make maladroit attempts to dispose of the stiff in a laundry basket. I, too, 'appeared' in the next series as Mr Johnson, played by Nicky Henson, whom Basil is convinced is a Lothario with a woman in his room. (He does have one, only it's his mother.)

'Mr Johnson' was a gentle reprimand for some slightly naughty behaviour of mine during the holiday. In the evenings we would descend to the waterfront for supper. The taverna did have a menu but one nearly always ended up with red mullet. I think it was a spam, spam, spam situation. After a few days John decided he was falling behind with the book adaptation of the first series of *Fawlty Towers* scripts and elected to stay in the villa and babysit Cynthia.

Fuelled by industrial quantities of retsina and the heady romantic spell of the island with the sweet aroma of jasmine and hyacinths and cyclamen, Georgie and I took to walking arm in arm back to the villa, and then snogging a bit and then ... fortunately it was time for me to return to England. I don't think I ever saw her again but, on the rare occasions I have tasted retsina since then, the antidote to its foul taste is that it is a pleasing reminder of Georgie's lips.

John and Connie went on to write the next six *Fawlty Towers* and I would usually go along to the recordings on Sunday evenings. They were nothing like the riotous Sundays at the Playhouse where the Cambridge Circus crew recorded *I'm Sorry I'll Read That Again* which had a huge cult following baying for familiar routines. My favourite was The Tillingbourne Folk and Madrigal Society who would render a cappella versions of football chants. With *Fawlty Towers*, on the other hand – especially in the first series – the studio audience would sometimes sit in stunned silence as Basil bashed Manuel over the head with a frying pan, shouting gems like: 'God knows how you people ever got together an Armada.'

The people who recruited studio audiences for the BBC quite liked groups who could be easily shipped from some institution in coaches. And these institutions were not infrequently old folks' homes. Frank Muir once told me he was getting an especially poor reaction to his routine hosting *Golden Silents* one afternoon which was partially explained by the fact that when the audience got up to leave at the end, one of them – er – didn't. (Python delighted in poking fun at the BBC Ticket Unit by frequently showing a cutaway of applauding ladies in their eighties, one of them with her knickers on display.)

John maintained that much of the audience for one of the first *Fawlty* recordings were non-English-speaking sailors from a Norwegian warship which had docked in the Port of London and, indeed, there are two episodes of *Fawlty Towers* with hardly any laughter – but thirty years later nobody appears to notice. After the show the cast and chums and girlfriends would take off for a Chinese restaurant where highlights of the episode would be recalled rather more raucously.

One day Connie rang me asking if we could meet for lunch. She was clearly worried. Melvyn Bragg was making a *South Bank Show*